Alexander Robey Shepherd

Alexander Robey Shepherd

The Man Who Built the Nation's Capital

John P. Richardson
Foreword by Tony Williams

PUBLISHED FOR THE
UNITED STATES CAPITOL HISTORICAL SOCIETY

BY OHIO UNIVERSITY PRESS • ATHENS

Ohio University Press, Athens, Ohio 45701
ohioswallow.com
© 2016 by John P. Richardson
All rights reserved

Frontispiece: Henry Ulke 1871 oil portrait depicts Alexander Shepherd as head of the Board of Public Works. (Courtesy of Krystal Branton, Office of D. C. City Council Member Jim Graham)

Printed in the United States of America
Ohio University Press books are printed on acid-free paper ♾™

25 24 23 22 21 20 19 18 17 16   5 4 3 2 1

Library of Congress Cataloging-in-Publication Data
Names: Richardson, John P., author.
Title: Alexander Robey Shepherd : the man who built the nation's capital /
    John P. Richardson ; foreword by Tony Williams.
Description: Athens, OH : Ohio University Press, [2016] | Includes bibliographical
    references and index.
Identifiers: LCCN 2016024887| ISBN 9780821422496 (hc : alk. paper) |
    ISBN 9780821422502 (pb : alk. paper) | ISBN 9780821445891 (pdf)
Subjects: LCSH: Shepherd, Alexander Robey, 1835–1902. | Washington (D.C.)—Politics and
    government—19th century. | Mayors—Washington (D.C.)—Biography. | Territorial
    governors—United States—District of Columbia—Biography. | District of Columbia.
    Board of Public Works—Biography. | Public works—Washington (D.C.)—History—19th
    century. | Washington (D.C.)—History—19th century.
Classification: LCC F198 .R525 2016 | DDC 975.3/02092 [B] —dc23
LC record available at https://lccn.loc.gov/2016024887

Contents

Foreword

I FIRST CAME close to Alexander Shepherd many years ago when I re-searched a presentation on city maps I was to give at the Library of Con-gress. I was amazed at the painstaking detail, captured in various maps, in converting Washington from a Civil War casualty into a modern city. As an inveterate walker of Washington's streets and boulevards, I get another view of Shepherd. I delight in my own "reaction shots" of a visitor's embrace of the National Capital, the awe of a tourist looking skyward to the Wash-ington Monument, the reverence of the school child at the steps of the Lin-coln Memorial, and the enchantment of the convention attendee taking in the Mall for the first time.

And then there's the quizzical look of the sightseer viewing the bronze statue of Alexander Shepherd in front of the Wilson Building in downtown Washington, D.C. The look tells you everything you need to know about what the average American doesn't know about the establishment of the Washington, D.C. of today.

I'm often asked about the statue. Who was Shepherd? Why was he impor-tant? What impact did he have? He only served a relatively short time, and yet was of enough consequence to earn a statue on Pennsylvania Avenue! Fortunately, I can now confidently refer inquirers to this wonderful biog-raphy of Shepherd by my friend John Richardson.

Shepherd's story, told in this book with skill and confidence, is at once the story of a great American character, with all his great achievements— bold, visionary, pragmatic, entrepreneurial; and notable flaws—racially insensitive, ethically myopic, and not infrequently, completely unrealistic. After all, how many political figures retire to Mexico to single-handedly establish a silver mining operation, using state of the art technology?

And it's also the story of a great and complex American city's recovery from the Civil War, growth in the Industrial age, and implementation of one of the world's greatest urban plans. In short, it's how Washington became a city.

A larger than life figure in an impossibly difficult situation, Shepherd made things happen, and Richardson tells us how. In a way, Shepherd was the ultimate homebuilder, building the Washington that today is the home for the world's largest diplomatic corps, the home of the federal government, and the home to District citizens and residents.

At a time when Washington struggles to get the basics done, at a point where risk avoidance is all too prevalent, and in an era when confidence in government is at an historic low point, it's good to know that there's another story. We can turn challenge into opportunity, economic despair into hope. Shepherd did all this, and John Richardson shows us how.

Tony Williams
Mayor of Washington, D.C., 1999–2007

Preface

ALEXANDER ROBEY SHEPHERD built the infrastructure of the nation's capital after the Civil War, which had torn the country apart and left Washington, D.C., a muddy, treeless place. The stresses of the Civil War exposed the physical inadequacies of the city in the face of postwar demands for a national capital able to represent the aspirations of the reunited nation. Shepherd's actions made it possible to realize the grand design for Washington, D.C., of Peter Charles L'Enfant,[1] the French-born engineer appointed by President George Washington in 1791 to plan the new "Federal City" as it was then known. The lack of congressional financial support had kept the city's infrastructure largely undeveloped and had prevented the realization of L'Enfant's vision. Much of Shepherd's work, carried out hastily, had to be redone, but he initiated critical changes that would not be reversed.

Shepherd's methods, motivation, competence, and integrity are still debated, but he did succeed in making the capital a handsome, workable city and, in the process, overcame threats to remove the seat of government to a location closer to the center of the nation. In a brief but remarkably active period as chairman of the Board of Public Works and a short nine months as territorial governor (1873–74), he put flesh on the bones of L'Enfant's design for an elegant, European-style capital. In doing so, Shepherd succeeded in his most important goal of making Washington a workable city. He also achieved his second objective, (although the result was subject to reversal): forcing Congress to accept responsibility for maintaining and improving the city where it met. This narrative follows the events of Shepherd's life as closely as available records permit, and much of the story is told in the words of major participants and close observers.

---

[1]Scott Berg, *Grand Avenues: The Story of the French Visionary Who Designed Washington, D.C.* (New York, 2007), p. xi. L'Enfant Anglicized his first name shortly after arriving in the United States in 1777.

While much is known about the whirlwind years during which Shepherd brought change to Washington, less is known about his final twenty-two years, lived in a remote mining town deep in the Sierra Madre Mountains of Mexico. Even less well known is that Shepherd's Mexican silver-mining operation—intended to restore his fortune and permit a triumphal return to Washington—proved a disappointment that hyperbolic press reports about his lucrative "Eldorado" in the wilderness could not overcome. While the setting for his labors shifted dramatically, Shepherd lived by the same set of principles in Mexico as he had in Washington. The nature of the challenges was different, but Shepherd, once having identified an objective, brought intensity and energy to the task. The same intensity and energy that made it possible for him to overcome obstacles that would have defeated a lesser man proved to be weaknesses, because he was constitutionally incapable or unwilling to question the choices he made.

Shepherd's intensity helped him to rise rapidly to the top of Washington business and society after the Civil War, turning his plumbing and gas fitting company into the engine for a complex real estate and construction empire. His rise reflected the social and political changes brought about by the Civil War, which disrupted the old, "southern" social patterns of Washington and allowed and encouraged ambitious men like Shepherd to rise. However, Shepherd's elevation to czar of the capital's road, sewer, gas lighting, and tree planting whirlwind during the years of territorial government left him unable to manage his own affairs, with disastrous personal consequences.

Although relatively little survives of Shepherd's thought process in the form of letters or diaries, his life before voluntary exile to Mexico in 1880 was lived largely in the public eye and intersected with major controversies gripping the nation in the wake of the Civil War. These included challenges no less significant than the ongoing sectional controversies, the issues of political and social equality for African Americans, competition between the Republican and Democratic parties, as well as factionalism within the Republican Party. The role of Congress in District of Columbia affairs was central because the Constitution gave it authority over all legislative matters within the District, and yet, prior to Shepherd, Congress had approached its responsibility for the welfare of the nation's capital only sporadically and, at worst, abdicated it altogether. Because of the constitutional dominance of Congress, most analysis of the District's development has focused on Congress and assigned Shepherd a supporting role. But it can be argued that this man—with a clear vision for the future—was better equipped than Congress to bring about the city's transformation, since most members of Congress were not full-time residents of the capital city, had little personal involvement in the city's development or self-governance, and focused their energies on representing the interests of their constituents.

Race posed a persistent issue for D.C. governance in the post–Civil War era, and for Shepherd personally. Shepherd's racial views were a product of his upbringing, and he was therefore no supporter of social equality for blacks. He was a staunch Unionist during the war and a mainstream Republican, thereafter accepting emancipation for blacks but resisting full political and social equality of the races. During Shepherd's years in D.C. politics, Radical Republicans in control of Congress were determined to impose socially progressive measures on the nation's capital. Shepherd came down strongly on the side of physical improvement over social justice for blacks. As Reconstruction ideals receded in the years after the Civil War, the social justice agenda also receded, leaving a permanent social imbalance in the nation's capital.

Public corruption often dominated public discourse after the Civil War, heightening during the second term of President Ulysses Grant (1869–77), who was an avowed supporter of Shepherd's program to build the District infrastructure. The scale and pace of public improvements under Shepherd and the methods he employed, particularly after expenses mounted and funding ran short, led to persistent criticism and allegations of corruption, echoing attacks upon perceived corruption within the Grant Administration. Means became subordinated to ends, and the management measures Shepherd instituted at the outset crumbled.

Shepherd's twenty-two-year sojourn in Mexico, managing a modern silver-mining operation, was intended to restore his fortune lost following the Panic of 1873 and allow a triumphant return to Washington, which would permit Shepherd once again to prove his critics wrong. Older and more experienced, Shepherd exhibited a relentless determination to succeed and an unwillingness or inability to acknowledge—let alone accept—defeat, regardless of the impact on those around him. Shepherd's life in Washington and in Mexico brings to mind Shakespeare's Othello, whose final words urged others to "speak of me as I am; nothing extenuate, not set down in malice. Then must you speak of one that lov'd not wisely but too well."[2] Shepherd's action-filled life left a similarly ambiguous trail for later generations to trace.

---

[2]William Shakespeare, *Othello*, Act V, Scene 2.

Chapter One

"An Apollo in Form"

Coming of Age in the Nation's Capital, 1835–1861

ALEXANDER ROBEY SHEPHERD was one of the most influential local figures in the nation's capital in the nineteenth century. He was also a product of his time and place. He came to manhood in a Chesapeake slave society in which his family prospered, and while he later accepted, if not embraced, emancipation as a Union war measure, he never progressed beyond the paternalistic racial views of his upbringing to accept the political or social equality of the races. The wealth and social standing built up by his grandfathers as Maryland tobacco planters and by his father as an enterprising businessman in early Washington, D.C., formed Shepherd's frame of reference as he strove to make his own place in the capital's economic, social, and political life. His father's early death forced Shepherd to become the male head of the family in his early teens. Thrust prematurely into the adult world, he responded with the single-minded drive, energy, and ambition that would characterize the rest of his life. He rarely if ever questioned his motives or methods but rather pressed forward, confident in the correctness of his actions.

Shepherd's paternal grandfather, Thomas, died in 1817 in Charles County, Maryland, leaving the family relatively well off, with an estate worth $4,000 (exclusive of land holdings) that included nine slaves.[1] This was at a time of

---

[1] Will of Thomas L. Shepherd, Charles County, Md., HBBH 313, August Term 1816, pp. 475–78; Estate of Thomas Shepherd, April Term 1817, Maryland Hall of Records,

significant migration from the Tidewater region, when an estimated 250,000 whites abandoned the area between 1790 and 1820 as a result of the depletion of the tobacco fields.[2] Perhaps this was the reason that Alexander Robey Shepherd's father, Alexander Shepherd Sr., left in 1822 to seek his fortune in Washington, D.C. Why he chose to migrate to the nation's capital is conjectural, but he may have been attracted to the business potential of the infant city—only a quarter-century old—that President George Washington had envisioned as both the commercial center and the seat of government of the new nation.

Shepherd Sr. returned to Charles County in 1833 to marry Susan Davidson Robey, daughter of Townley Robey, a wealthy planter. Robey had seen military service in the War of 1812, was an Episcopal Church vestryman, and served as sheriff of Charles County, all roles associated with the county's financial and social elite.[3] Later, Alexander Robey Shepherd would remember his maternal grandfather as "a tall old gentleman in a white beaver hat, coming from church on a Sunday and drawing water from the well, in a bucket with a long pole."[4] The marriage to Susan Robey gave Alexander Shepherd Sr. enhanced social standing and the wealth she inherited after her father's death in 1844. This wealth consisted of land and money from an estate totaling almost two thousand acres and physical property valued at $5,000 (including eighteen slaves), a considerable sum at the time.[5]

Shepherd's father developed coal and lumberyards near his Washington City residence at Twelfth Street and Maryland Avenue SW and in Market Square, the area next to Center Market on Pennsylvania Avenue NW, adjacent to the Washington Canal. He was a director of the Georgetown-based Potomac Insurance Company and active in public life, serving as an assistant commissioner for Ward 5, responsible for overseeing public improvements such as streets and walkways.[6] He remained a slave owner; the

---

pp. 312–14; Estate of Thomas Shepherd, Accounts and Inventories, Thomas Shepherd, 1817, Charles County (Md.) Courthouse, pp. 312–14.

[2]Allan Kulikoff, *Tobacco and Slaves: The Development of Southern Cultures in the Chesapeake, 1680–1800* (Chapel Hill, 1986), p. 77.

[3]F. Edward Wright, *Maryland Militia: War of 1812*, 7 vols. (Silver Spring, Md., 1979–86), 5:37.

[4]Photocopy of typescript and unsigned note to Grant Shepherd (son of Alexander Shepherd), both apparently written by his mother, Mary Grice Shepherd, n.d., courtesy of Shepherd granddaughter Mary Wagner Woods.

[5]Townley Robey Inventory, Inventories 1844–1846, Townley Robey Will, December Term 1844, Charles County (Md.) Courthouse.

[6]*National Intelligencer* (Washington, D.C.), Sept. 25, 1837.

1840 District of Columbia census recorded five slaves in the household, although in 1841 he sold a thirteen-year-old slave, with instructions for manumission at age twenty-five.[7] At Shepherd's death in 1845 he still owned seven slaves, although he left instructions for their eventual manumission.[8]

Turning his back on the family's Episcopalian tradition in Charles County, Shepherd's father joined and played a leadership role in two of Washington's Presbyterian churches, the First and the Fourth. While the Episcopal Church was the church of the upper classes, Presbyterianism was a fast-growing Protestant faith in Washington. Alexander Shepherd Sr. significantly increased his participation in church affairs after joining Fourth Presbyterian, being elected to the board of trustees and then elected its president the following year. It is likely that he had developed a group of friends among the young businessmen of Washington who were already Presbyterians and that he became a Presbyterian more as a social than a religious decision. This would be a pattern his eldest son would also follow.

After the birth of the couple's second child, Alexander Robey Shepherd, on January 30, 1835 (their first child, Anna, was born in 1832), four other children—Bettie (1837), Thomas (1839), Wilmer (1841), and Arthur (1842)—followed in quick succession. The family continued to live in southwest Washington City until Shepherd, in failing health, purchased a farm in neighboring Washington County adjacent to St. Paul's, the Rock Creek Episcopal parish, where the family lived for a little more than a year before his death from an undisclosed illness in June 1845. In the period that he owned the farm, he turned it into a showcase, no doubt assisted by the wealth inherited following the death the previous year of his father-in-law.[9]

---

[7] *U.S. Census, 1840 Population Schedules, District of Columbia*, microfilm roll 11, microcopy T-5, p. 33, Martin Luther King Jr. Memorial Library, Washington, D.C.; Washington, D.C., Recorder of Deeds, Liber WB, folio no. 88/1841. William Tindall, long-time aide to Alexander Robey Shepherd, wrote that Shepherd's father manumitted "a number of slaves" before the Civil War for whom he provided "in a large measure, as they resorted to him in every exigency of privation or disaster and were never refused" (William Tindall, "A Sketch of Alexander Robey Shepherd," Records of the Columbia Historical Society 14 [1911]:50).

[8] Last Will and Testament, Alexander Shepherd, Office of Register of Wills, 1845, Probate Clerk's Office, Washington, D.C.

[9] *National Intelligencer*, July 15, 1845; for information on Shepherd's purchase of the farm in Washington County and subsequent residence there, see Robert Isherwood to Alexander Shepherd, Dec. 20, 1842, Washington, D.C. Recorder of Deeds, Liber WB, Folio #99/1843); Robert Tweedy to Alexander Shepherd, Jan. 16, 1844, D.C. Recorder of Deeds, Liber WB, Folio #107/1844.

The time Alexander Robey Shepherd passed as a youngster on a working farm must have had an impact on him, since there was always work to be done, and he demonstrated an early willingness, even eagerness, to engage in it. As a man, he was often remarked to outwork his employees.

Alexander Shepherd Sr.'s will directed that his eldest son, Alexander, upon reaching the age of twenty-one, be advanced the sum of $4,000 (approximately $127,000 today) "to enable him to prosecute advantageously such business as he may select for his future support." The will also directed the executors to provide a suitable education for the children to prepare them for business, adding that if any of the sons demonstrated a talent for the "learned professions," funds should be made available for university studies.[10] A newspaper column a few days after Shepherd's death paid tribute to his sterling character and dedication to the church, describing him as industrious, honest, and enterprising and pointing out his kindness not only to his own family but also to anyone in need.[11]

The Young Capital

The Washington, D.C., area to which Alexander Shepherd Sr. came in 1822 as a young man seeking a better life was a young, straggling place with a total population of some thirty-three thousand, composed of two-thirds whites and one-third slaves and free blacks.[12] James Monroe had been re-elected president two years previously, and Washington was in the early stages of defining itself physically and socially. The most striking characteristic of Washington in the first half of the nineteenth century was the discrepancy between its untidy reality and the grandiose scale of the original intent of the founders. Peter Charles L'Enfant, the French-born architect and engineer chosen by President Washington in 1791 to plan the city, had envisioned a magnificent city of grand avenues, sweeping vistas,

---

[10]Will of Alexander Shepherd, dated Apr. 28, 1845, D.C. Recorder of Wills, Washington, D.C., Office of the Probate Clerk; the estimated current value of the advance to Alexander is from measuringworth.com, a nonprofit website providing U.S. currency equivalents from 1776 to the present.

[11]*National Intelligencer,* June 6, 1845.

[12]*U.S. Census, 1820, District of Columbia,* microcopy no. 33, reel 5, Washingtoniana Room, Martin Luther King Jr. Memorial Library, Washington, D.C.

and magnificent public monuments and buildings.[13] Published maps of the District of Columbia portrayed L'Enfant's plan, but the city experienced by visitors and residents fell far short. Scattered but imposing government buildings stood alongside undistinguished hotels and commercial establishments, graceful row houses alongside undistinguished frame houses and squalid shanties. These differences were the more dramatic because of long, undeveloped spaces separating the "arc of settlement."[14] The streets were muddy when wet and dusty when dry, and the Washington Canal was polluted. Many of the city's roads were still only lines on the plan drawn by L'Enfant in 1791, and almost all those in use were unpaved. Only a few major public buildings had been erected, among them the White House, Post Office, and Patent Office; repair work on the Capitol, which had been burned during the British invasion in 1814, was ongoing. Congress was the principal institution in the city, but evident only when it was in session. Boardinghouses for members of Congress were numerous, as were taverns and restaurants catering to the legislators. Georgetown, across Rock Creek to the west, was the center of organized local society and had been a river port before L'Enfant laid out Washington City in 1791. Georgetown boasted elegant brick homes and a social set; Washington City suffered by comparison.

When one thinks of modern Washington, D.C., with its elegant public buildings, parks, avenues, and Potomac River vistas, it is almost inconceivable that, for the first seventy years of the city's life sporadic efforts were made to "remove" the capital from Washington or to retrocede pieces of it to Maryland and Virginia. Yet this debate was only a continuation of intense discussions prior to the selection of the site for the capital in 1790.[15] Washington's residents, who believed that the decision by Congress to site the national capital in a ten-mile square on the Potomac River would put the location debate to rest, were to be proved wrong time and again.

The starting point for Washington's development was the original plan for the city by L'Enfant. Drawn after consultation with President George

---

[13]Robert Harrison, *Washington during Civil War and Reconstruction: Race and Radicalism* (Cambridge, 2011), p. 2.

[14]Ibid.

[15]Kenneth Bowling, *The Creation of Washington, D.C.: The Idea and Location of the American Capital* (Fairfax, Va., 1991), pp. 127–60.

Washington, the plan envisioned an elegant, continental design imitating the grandeur and aesthetic coherence of European planning without overlooking the republican values of the new country.[16] Key to L'Enfant's plan was a vision of a capital city that would serve as both political symbol and commercial hub, reflecting the views of President Washington, who foresaw the city's potential access to maritime traffic as well as to overland routes to the interior.[17]

The uneven, haphazard development of Washington during Alexander Robey Shepherd's youth was traceable to a flaw in the planning process centered on the role of Congress, which under the Constitution wielded total authority over matters in the District of Columbia. The problem was that Congress, the "mother" of the District of Columbia, barely acknowledged its obligations to its "child" for a number of historical reasons, the most important being that members looked primarily to the interests of their home states and districts and considered Washington more as a place to visit when Congress was in session. Thomas Jefferson's antipathy toward the creation of a major metropolis as the national capital was based on his concern that a large city would become a center of corruption and would be inimical to the agrarian American ideals he so deeply held. The famous drawing of Jefferson's vision for Washington showed a small town he intended as the seat of Congress and the presidency rather than a capital from which the central government would dominate national life. This view reinforced the concept of multiple political-cultural-commercial centers around the county, unwittingly providing encouragement to New York City to become the commercial capital of the country at the expense of Philadelphia and other East Coast cities.[18]

The Young Shepherd

If "the child is the father of the man," so it was with Alexander Robey Shepherd. Shepherd's secretary in later years, who knew him well, described

---

[16]Harrison, *Washington during Civil War and Reconstruction*, p. 3; Scott W. Berg, *Grand Avenues: The Story of the French Visionary Who Designed Washington, D.C.* (New York, 2007), pp. 78–80.

[17]Berg, *Grand Avenues*, pp. 97–100.

[18]Bowling, *Creation of Washington, D.C.*, p. 12.

Shepherd's father as small and his mother as large and strong, noting that Shepherd came naturally by his exceptional physical and mental powers from his two parents.[19] The house of his birth in southwest Washington City was a modest, two-story home with a dormer window attic and ample grounds.[20] Before the move to the farm in Washington County, from whence he rode a pony down Rock Creek Road to school in the city, Shepherd was an active boy, with an attachment to the Perseverance Hose Company, a nearby firehouse. He showed up every time there was a fire alarm, encouraging the company and sometimes participating in its conflicts with rival firehouses, bringing away occasional scars as testament to his zeal.[21] He was watched over and protected by one of the family's older slaves, Henry Magruder, whom Shepherd's father assigned to keep his rambunctious son from getting into too much trouble.[22] While his early education took place under a private tutor, Shepherd's brief encounter with formal education ended after three years at Rittenhouse Academy School (located at what is now Indiana Avenue near John Marshall Place NW), run by the Nourse brothers, and a short term at the Preparatory Section of Columbian College (Fourteenth Street NW, above Florida Avenue).[23]

After Shepherd Sr.'s death, widow Susan Shepherd, Alexander, and his five siblings should have been able to continue life in the comfortable fashion to which the family had become accustomed. Nevertheless, within a

---

[19]Tindall, "A Sketch of Alexander Robey Shepherd, pp. 49–50.

[20]This information is from a biographical fragment from Mary Grice Shepherd, narrated in Mexico in the 1880s and dictated to Fred Martin, based on information provided by Shepherd. Mrs. Shepherd noted, "In earlier years I had driven past the home which Mr. Shepherd pointed out as his birthplace, a statement his mother confirmed" (copy courtesy of Shepherd granddaughter Mary Wagner Woods). Identifying the location of Shepherd's birthplace has generated controversy, which is all the more surprising since it was misidentified by no less an authority than Dr. William Tindall, author of *A Standard History of the City of Washington* (Knoxville, Tenn., 1914) and "A Sketch of Alexander Robey Shepherd," as well as personal secretary to Governor Shepherd and his successors. Tindall named another birth location in southwest Washington, for which there is no land deed showing it was owned by Shepherd's father. Much later, Tindall identified his source for the incorrect birthplace address as Thomas Shepherd, Alexander Shepherd's somewhat unreliable younger brother (*Evening Star* [Washington, D.C.], May 8, 1919).

[21]Tindall, "Sketch of Alexander Robey Shepherd," p. 50.

[22]Ibid.

[23]Typescript account written in Mexico in the 1880s by a family member, possibly Mary Grice Shepherd, pp. 1 and 50, copy given to the author by Shepherd great-grandson W. Sinkler Manning Jr. (hereafter Mexico Typescript).

year, Susan Shepherd and her six young children were confronted with the as-yet-unexplained loss of most of the estate, probably due to mismanagement. Susan Shepherd and local grocer Sylvanus Holmes were coexecutors of the estate, but within a year Holmes had closed his business and left Washington. There is no demonstrated link between Holmes's abrupt departure from Washington and the failure of the Shepherd estate, but a negative implication remains. There is also no record of commentary by any member of the Shepherd family about the circumstances surrounding these events. While seriously affected financially, the Shepherd family was not destitute; Susan Shepherd is recorded as having bought and sold several properties in the years following her husband's death.

His father's death and the change in the family's finances had a marked impact on ten-year-old Alexander Robey Shepherd. Within three years he had dropped out of school and gone to work to help support the family, perhaps a consequence of being the eldest child. But his course of action was also indicative of an early willingness to act decisively when the situation required. As an adult who would surround himself with the trappings of wealth, he would have remembered his mother's swift descent from a comfortable lifestyle to becoming a boardinghouse keeper at her new residence at 440 Ninth Street W. (between G and H Streets N.) within a year after his father's death.[24] The collapse of family fortunes no doubt steeled Shepherd's resolve to create a level of wealth that would protect his family from such an occurrence ever again. The questionable role of Sylvanus Holmes, who may have contributed to the family's financial problems, could also have been a factor in Shepherd's lifelong commitment to giving loyalty to friends and colleagues and expecting similar loyalty in return.

Young Shepherd, thrust rudely into the adult world, began work as a store clerk. Seeking a new trade after two years, he became a carpenter's apprentice, but the restless boy became discontented with his employer and left after two years.[25] In April 1852 Shepherd made one of his most important

---

[24]Although the Mexico Typescript says only that the widow Shepherd supported the family by her own exertions, the 1850 city directory (Edward Waite, *The Washington Directory and Congressional and Executive Register for 1850* [Washington, D.C., 1850]) cites a boardinghouse operated by a Mrs. Shepherd at a slightly different address on Ninth Street, but no doubt refers to the same person. A new Washington quadrant and house-numbering policy in 1869 dramatically altered house numbers.

[25]Mexico Typescript, p. 1.

life decisions: on the recommendation of his pastor at Fourth Presbyterian Church, the seventeen-year-old became an employee of J. W. Thompson's plumbing and gas fitting establishment.[26] The role of Shepherd's pastor in brokering a clerkship at the Thompson firm suggests that the young Shepherd was an active member of the church where he, his sister Anna, and a future brother-in-law, William P. Young Jr., had been accepted in December 1848. It also implies that Shepherd was considered worthy of special attention.[27] By turning his back on carpentry and accepting a position as a clerk—soon to become head bookkeeper—Shepherd demonstrated that, where opportunity presented itself, he preferred to use brain over brawn.[28]

In many respects John Thompson would serve over the years as the father Shepherd had lost. He was not only an employer but a social mentor and a fellow sports enthusiast and investor in local businesses. Thompson was a respected, successful businessman who opened doors for the young and ambitious Shepherd and no doubt smoothed out incidents when the hot-tempered young man offended members of Washington's business establishment. Plumbing and gas fitting were important trades in the growing city of Washington, since piped water and rudimentary sewerage links were becoming available and sought by homeowners. Shepherd did not disappoint John Thompson, and by 1859 he had become a partner in the firm that he would eventually own.[29]

As Shepherd rapidly demonstrated his ambition at John Thompson's plumbing firm, he also grew into the athletic body that would be a subject of mention by virtually every commentator. A close observer referred to Shepherd's broad forehead as "the most impressive feature of his countenance" and described him as "an Apollo in form, a giant in strength."[30] Shepherd's friend, personal attorney, and lifelong defender William Mattingly described him as "a magnificent specimen of manhood . . . tall, large of frame, with remarkable strength, broad forehead, rugged features,

---

[26]Tindall, *Standard History of the City of Washington*, p. 262.

[27]"Sessions Book, Fourth Presbyterian Church, Washington, D.C., First Book, Session 1828–1878," National Presbyterian Church, Washington, D.C.

[28]George W. Evans, *The Master Mind and Rebuilder of the Nation's Capital: A Paper Read before the Society of Natives of the District of Columbia, October 20th, 1922* (Washington, D.C., 1922), p. 6.

[29]Mexico Typescript, p. 1.

[30]Tindall, "Sketch of Alexander Robey Shepherd," p. 66.

firmness expressed in mouth and chin."[31] Besides physical dominance, Shepherd had a dramatic voice, described by one writer as having "a richness and fullness of tone as an implement of conversation [and] a laugh that was . . . musical and unconstrained. If he had studiously applied his talents to public speaking he readily could have attained distinction as an orator."[32]

As a young man, Shepherd combined impressive physical attributes with extracurricular interests that he carried into maturity: social-religious on the one hand and sporting on the other. By 1857 the twenty-two-year-old school dropout was a director of two literary groups, the Metropolitan Literary Association and the Washington Library Company, in both of which his mentor, John Thompson, played a leading role.[33] No doubt self-conscious about his shortage of formal education, Shepherd would have valued these links with books and literary discussion. In later life he was an avid reader and consumer of information. In the sporting world, Shepherd was a founder of the Undine Boat Club and a regular in its racing shell. Undine—named after a famous Philadelphia club—was one of several local boat clubs that rowed on the Potomac River and engaged in friendly rivalry with other clubs. Shepherd was one of the most active Undine promoters, telling prospective members, "We want to get up a good crew, with plenty of beef in the boat." The members were athletic and as a general rule heavyweights. The club boat was in demand for holiday picnics, and the members would take it to event sites, bringing along other sporting gear.[34]

Shepherd used the boat club to begin assembling the nucleus of a group of friends and colleagues who would, almost without exception, play significant roles in Washington political and social affairs and provide support as Shepherd weathered storms and political controversies. John Thompson was the boat club president, and other members close to Shepherd included William G. Moore (business partner), A. C. Richards (longtime Washington City chief of police), and Lewis Clephane (editor, real estate broker,

---

[31]William F. Mattingly, "The Unveiling of a Statue to the Memory of Alexander R. Shepherd in front of the District Building, Washington, D.C., May 3, 1909," pp. 24–25, Kiplinger Research Library, Historical Society of Washington, Washington, D.C.

[32]Tindall, "Sketch of Alexander Robey Shepherd," p. 62.

[33]*Evening Star*, May 16, 1857; and Walter Clephane, "Lewis Clephane: A Pioneer Washington Republican," *Records of the Columbia Historical Society* 21 (1918):276.

[34]*Evening Star*, July 3, 1885. The article went on to say that silting up of the Potomac River flats created a major problem for reaching deep water. The onset of the Civil War saw the boat club forgotten, and members fought for one side or the other.

and founder of the local Republican Party). Most of the boat club members were also involved with Shepherd in the Metropolitan Literary Association and Washington Library Company. William Moore was to enlist with Shepherd in the National Rifles in 1861. As he matured, Shepherd practiced and honed the social and organizational skills he would bring to bear on his adult activities. His profession as a plumber and gas fitter, however, was no boost to his social standing, despite becoming a lucrative source of income.

Washington's Adolescence

The city that Shepherd would eventually transform had slow and bumpy early years, some of which his father before him had also experienced. Washington, D.C., made an early and unsuccessful attempt to achieve the dream of Washington and L'Enfant for becoming a commercial as well as political national capital. The first goal was to serve as a gateway to the interior of the new country via the Chesapeake and Ohio Canal, for which President John Quincy Adams famously turned the inaugural shovel of dirt the same day (July 4, 1828) that the Baltimore & Ohio Railroad received congressional approval to open a line to Washington. The canal would be a failure, while canals and railroads in other cities, supported by state legislatures and private capital, took advantage of Washington's inertia. Washington was to remain on the margins of America's northern industrial core throughout the nineteenth century.[35]

Ridiculed by American and European visitors and residents alike for its run-down appearance and lack of development, Washington, D.C., reflected Congress's ambivalence toward the nation's capital. To some observers, who would come to include Shepherd, the lack of congressional investment in the city implied a lack of commitment to a strong federal government, more recently embodied in the two terms of President Andrew Jackson, who shared Jefferson's profound distrust of concentrated power.[36]

Underdeveloped as it was, Washington was not radically dissimilar to other American cities of similar size, with the exception of the congressional

---

[35]Carl Abbott, "National Capitals in a Networked World," in *Berlin-Washington, 1800–2000: Capital Cities, Cultural Representation, and National Identities,* ed. Andreas Daum and Christof Mauch (Cambridge, 2005), p. 112.

[36]Bowling, *Creation of Washington, D.C.,* p. 12.

stranglehold on the city.[37] Philadelphia was often compared with Washington because Philadelphia had been a power base for American revolutionaries who favored strong central government. Philadelphia was cosmopolitan, urbane, and religiously diverse, with a vibrant social and intellectual life.[38] It also was a city of personal interest to Shepherd because it was the home of his bride-to-be, Mary Grice Young.[39] Shepherd would turn to Philadelphia numerous times throughout his business and political life, purchasing gas lighting and plumbing fixtures for the firm as well as studying the city's paving system and borrowing the plan for the future Washington Board of Trade from the example of its Philadelphia counterpart.

As Baltimore, Philadelphia, New York, Boston, and other cities outpaced Washington's development in the first half of the nineteenth century, it became evident that a powerful constraint on Washington was Congress's refusal to acknowledge the reality that the modest population had no way to underwrite the cost of creating, let alone maintaining, the city's wide streets and boulevards, which thanks to L'Enfant's plan occupied more than 50 percent of the total land space in the city.[40]

The unwillingness of Congress to provide adequate appropriations to develop and maintain the nation's capital was evident from the beginning. The city charter of 1820, authorized by Congress, called on Congress to pay its share of improvements around federal property but failed to provide the necessary funds.[41] Only a few legislators attempted to address the issue. In 1835 Senator Samuel L. Southard of New Jersey acknowledged Washington's persistent "pecuniary embarrassments" and stated in a report to Congress his conviction that it would be "utterly impossible" for the city to meet its obligations without congressional assistance. Southard exonerated the city fathers of responsibility for the problem while conceding individual indiscretions because of their governing views "of a liberal and public-spirited

---

[37]Harrison, *Washington during Civil War and Reconstruction*, pp. 4–6.

[38]Kenneth Bowling, "Siting Federal Capitals," in Daum and Mauch, *Berlin-Washington, 1800–2000*, pp. 37–38.

[39]The Grices were from Philadelphia and the Youngs were from Portsmouth, Virginia; ancestors from both families had served with distinction in America's early wars.

[40]Alan Lessoff, *The Nation and Its City: Politics, "Corruption," and Progress in Washington, D.C., 1861–1902* (Baltimore, 1994), p. 5.

[41]Howard Gillette, *Between Justice and Beauty: Race, Planning, and the Failure of Urban Policy in Washington, D.C.* (Baltimore, 1995), p. 18.

character."[42] Southard reviewed the history of the city and made special note of the "unusual magnitude and extent" of its streets and avenues, which the city's population (just over twenty thousand in 1835, of whom almost seven thousand were free and enslaved blacks) was much too small to maintain: "The plan of the city was formed by the public authorities; the dimensions of the streets determined by them, without interference by the inhabitants, or regard to their particular interest or convenience."[43]

The results of congressional negligence were apparent to all, and out-of-town visitors excoriated the nation's capital for its shabbiness and uncompleted character. Lionized during his 1842 American tour, English author Charles Dickens later painted a withering, oft-cited portrait of the city: "[Washington] is sometimes called the City of Magnificent Distances, but it might with greater propriety be termed the City of Magnificent Intentions. . . . Spacious avenues that begin in nothing, and lead nowhere; streets, miles-long, that only want houses, roads, and inhabitants; public buildings that need but a public to be complete; and ornaments of great thoroughfare—which only lack great thoroughfares to ornament—are its leading features."[44] Another European visitor noted sagely that it would be impossible to build a real city without "revenues to squander."[45]

The District of Columbia was subjected to further indignity in 1846, when Congress accepted a request from the Virginia delegation for the Alexandria, Virginia, portion of the original ten mile square to be "retroceded" to the state of Virginia. This remarkable development removed one-third of the capital's land mass and created today's oddly shaped Washington. Reasons given by the residents of Alexandria included the demand to be free of congressional scrutiny of its booming slave trade, along with a desire to regain the right to vote. At least retrocession made an impression on the Washington City Council, which soon thereafter passed a resolution calling for the development of guidelines for public improvements, along with priorities and estimated costs.[46]

---

[42]*Report [with Senate Bill no. 136]*, 23rd Cong., 2nd sess., 1835, S. Rep. 97, Feb. 2, 1835, reprinted in full in *Board of Public Works 1872 Annual Report* (Washington, D.C., 1872), pp. 25–32.

[43]Ibid., p. 26.

[44]Charles Dickens, *American Notes for General Circulation*, 2 vols. (London, 1842), 1:281–82.

[45]Walter Erhart, "Written Capitals and Capital Topography," Daum and Mauch, *Berlin-Washington, 1800–2000*, pp. 57–58.

[46]Gillette, *Between Justice and Beauty*, pp. 22–23.

Some progress, at least at the planning level, was generated in other quarters. In 1830 architect Robert Mills sent Congress a report on Washington's need for a reliable water supply for drinking, cleaning, and fire fighting—a need brought home by an 1851 fire in the Library of Congress in the Capitol. Engineer Montgomery Meigs, a captain in the U.S. Army Corps of Engineers, oversaw construction of an aqueduct to supply water from Great Falls in 1853, which required planning for expanded distribution and sewerage systems. Following the establishment of a committee of distinguished residents that included Mayor Walter Lenox, banker William Wilson (W. W.) Corcoran, and Smithsonian Secretary Joseph Henry, architect Andrew Jackson Downing produced a plan for the redesign of the Mall. By the time the Civil War had worn down the city with the demands of war, Washington had created—at least on paper—a framework for modernization.[47]

War Comes to Washington

The country watched with growing concern as North-South tensions escalated in 1860, and Washington, D.C., became a focal point of conflict. The election of Abraham Lincoln as president in November was widely considered a portent that war would surely come, despite Lincoln's protestations in support of an undivided Union. During his unsuccessful bid for a U.S. Senate seat from Illinois in 1858, Lincoln had given his famous "House Divided" speech, in which he said, "I believe this government cannot endure, permanently half slave and half free."[48] Lincoln steadily strengthened his central theme of preserving the Union, the core idea around which Shepherd, as a fledgling politician, would build his political platform when he entered politics. Even though Shepherd came from a slaveholding family and held conservative social views, he was enough of a practical politician to realize that Lincoln and the Republican Party were the wave of the future, and he was determined to conform sufficiently to benefit from the momentum.

On the eve of the Civil War, Washington was a slaveholding city wedged between two slaveholding states, Maryland and Virginia. A vivid portrait of the city described it as "a southern town, without the picturesqueness, but

---

[47]Ibid., pp. 25–26.
[48]In Ronald C. White Jr., *A. Lincoln: A Biography* (New York, 2009), p. 251.

with the indolence, the disorder and the want of sanitation."[49] The city's
water supply was augmented by wells and by springs in the hills. With only
scattered sewer lines, privies were plentiful. In 1860 Washington had a population of 75,080, with 60,793 (81 percent) whites and 14,316 (19 percent)
blacks, of whom 3,185 were slaves and 11,131 free.[50] The whites were mostly
southern born: 57 percent had been born in the city, 13 percent in Virginia,
and 18 percent in Maryland.[51] An easy social alliance existed between Tidewater families and southern politicians in Washington; moreover, southern
members of Congress were more likely than those from the North to bring
their families to Washington, reinforcing the southern ambiance of the city.[52]
Congress had imposed a partial ban on the slave trade as part of the package of legislation making up the Compromise of 1850, but residents could
still buy and sell slaves for personal use. Newspapers advertised slave traffic, and the occasional slave coffle still passed through the city.[53]

The gloom in Washington over the worsening national political situation
also affected the economy: the real estate market had virtually collapsed in
the wake of Lincoln's election as president. Many would-be sellers retained
their property, fearing that they would be unable to obtain the desired price,
while others traded D.C. properties for western lands. As 1861 dawned, the
Evening Star reprinted an article from a Philadelphia newspaper sure to cast
a pall over the expectations of the Washington business community by
linking political chaos and economic failure with the threat of the physical
removal of the capital: "If there is the slightest danger or disturbance at
Washington, the ultimate result will be, and before any far distant day, the
removal of the seat of government." The article predicted that any disturbance of public tranquility would deal a body blow to real estate values.
It further predicted that any reverse for the Union in a conflict with the
South would make transfer of the capital to the safe and growing West a
certainty, leaving Washington "a waste, howling wilderness."[54] As a young
businessman who would make his fortune building and outfitting houses in

---

[49]Margaret Leech, *Reveille in Washington, 1860–1865* (New York, 1941), pp. 9–10.

[50]Lessoff, *The Nation and Its City*, p. 18.

[51]*U.S. Census, 1860: Recapitulation of the Tables of Population, Nativity, and Occupation*
(Washington, D.C., 1864), pp. 616–19.

[52]Carl Abbott, *Political Terrain: Washington, D.C., from Tidewater Town to Global Metropolis*
(Chapel Hill, 1999), pp. 64–65.

[53]Ibid., p. 11.

[54]*Philadelphia Ledger*, Dec. 29, 1860, quoted in *Evening Star,* Jan. 2, 1861.

Washington, Shepherd would have been sensitive to anything that would have a negative impact on the local economy.

The tone of Washington society on the eve of the war was set by the larger property owners, many of whom were linked by marriage to aristocratic, slave-owning families of Maryland and Virginia. It was common for George-town residents to refer to themselves as Marylanders, but they were known locally as "old citizens" or "antiques," and money alone was not sufficient to gain admission to their circle. At the national level, the male residents were primarily government officials, military officers, and businessmen. Democrats had controlled Congress for several years prior to 1860, and southern-leaning Democrats held many of the top appointive positions, along with a large percentage of the clerkships in the federal bureaus.[55] To the small, Georgetown-based clique that dominated Washington life, Shepherd would always be a parvenu seeking acceptance and respectabil-ity that they were determined not to give to a self-made, school-dropout plumber.

By the eve of the Civil War, the twenty-six-year-old Shepherd, by then a partner in the J. W. Thompson firm, was making his mark as an ambitious young member of Washington's business community. Still a bachelor, he supported his widowed mother and siblings while living in the family home on Ninth Street. For young, patriotic men like Shepherd yet to make their mark, the political tension resulting from southern secessionism be-came nerve-wracking as 1861 began. Rumors of sedition in Washington became standard fare. Government clerks, often emboldened by whiskey at the Willard Hotel and elsewhere, proclaimed that Lincoln's inauguration on March 4 would never take place.[56]

Concern was widespread that the secession of two slave states—Virginia and Maryland—from the Union would make it impossible for Washington to continue as the capital of the United States. Governor Thomas Hicks of Maryland—who ultimately stood with the Union and blocked a special ses-sion of the legislature expected to vote for secession—received anonymous letters describing plans to capture Washington and convert it into the capi-tal of the Southern Confederacy by seizing the federal buildings and archives

[55]James Whyte, *The Uncivil War: Washington during the Reconstruction, 1865–1878* (New York, 1958), p. 104.

[56]Leech, *Reveille in Washington*, p. 4.

before exacting de jure and de facto recognition from foreign governments.[57] On Christmas Day 1860 the *Richmond Examiner* published an editorial calling for Maryland men to join with Virginians in seizing the federal capital.[58] In response to rumors of sedition swirling around Washington, a nervous Congress convened a select committee at the end of January to investigate but found no evidence of a serious conspiracy.[59]

As winter turned into spring in 1861, the lines between North and South were drawn, and the Confederate attack on Fort Sumter in Charleston Harbor on April 12 marked the onset of hostilities. On April 15 President Lincoln called for seventy-five thousand volunteers to defend the Union, and Shepherd and his younger brother Thomas enlisted with the National Rifles. This volunteer Washington militia unit reflected political tensions in Washington over the future of the Union. Events earlier in the spring had revealed seditious scheming in the National Rifles, whose pro-Southern captain had molded a sympathetic unit and amassed weaponry far in excess of need. The unit was purged, and disloyal members, including the leader, dismissed, which meant that the National Rifles were under strength at the first call for volunteers on April 10.[60] By April 15, however, the unit listed seventy-five privates enrolled, plus sergeants and officers—exceeding the minimum forty per unit established by the War Department. The National Rifles claimed to be the first Washington militia to muster that day, thanks to marching double-quick to the War Department.[61]

The Alexander Shepherd who heeded his president's April 15 call for volunteers was ready for personal testing. He had been shaped through years of hard, physical work and sports, as well as his own combative personality. He was still unmarried and had progressed from clerk to partner at John Thompson's plumbing establishment. He had become active in Washington Republican Party politics on a pro-Union ticket. Shepherd's National Rifles mustering-in card for Company A, Third Battalion, gives a snapshot of inductee number 49, who signed on as a private for a standard ninety-day enlistment: Washington-born plumber, twenty-six years of age

[57]*Evening Star,* Jan. 1, 1861.

[58]Leech, *Reveille in Washington,* p. 23.

[59]House Select Committee of Five, *Alleged Hostile Organization against the Government within the District of Columbia,* 36th Cong., 2nd sess., Feb. 14, 1861, H. Rep. 79.

[60]*War History of the National Rifles, Company A, Third Battalion, District of Columbia Volunteers, of 1861* (Wilmington, Del., 1887), p. 11.

[61]Ibid., p. 17.

and six feet tall, with light blue eyes, dark brown hair, and sallow complexion.[62] Shepherd's fellow enlistees that day were a varied lot, with a wide range of employment: clerk, draughtsman, lawyer, bank teller, law student, upholsterer, patent lawyer, pharmacist, mechanical dentist, printer, soldier, architect, tobacconist, reporter, sawyer, jeweler's clerk, civil engineer, carpenter, editor, stenographer, student, physician, and messenger.[63] Among the volunteers was William G. Moore, a reporter who became Shepherd's decades-long friend and business partner.

After initial tasks that included guard duty and seizure of a steamer suspected of sending military supplies south, the National Rifles were tested following riots in Baltimore when prosecessionist mobs attacked a Massachusetts regiment transiting the city by train to Washington on April 19.[64] Baltimore officials—ostensibly to avoid further hostile demonstrations—did not stop the mob from burning the railroad bridges linking Washington with New York and Boston. Not only was it now impossible for people to travel between Washington and the north by train; newspapers stopped, and then the telegraph. For the next five days the nation's capital was isolated from the rest of the Union, until Maryland's governor agreed to allow federal troops to land at Annapolis by water.[65]

South of Baltimore, however, the tracks to Washington were intact, and a spur ran from Annapolis Junction to Annapolis, where the Seventh New York and Eighth Massachusetts regiments had just arrived by ship. Shepherd was part of a detachment of National Rifles volunteers who on April 23 reconnoitered the track with an engine and two cars and confirmed that sections of the spur had been torn up. At Annapolis Junction the detachment pushed through a belligerent crowd and forced the telegraph operator to communicate with Annapolis, confirming that the Seventh New York was still there. The engine and two cars backed all the way to Washington, and arrangements were made to assemble a train to bring the troops in Annapolis to Washington.

---

[62]Third Battalion, D.C. Militia, "Description and Morning Report," vol. 1, Record Group 94, National Archives and Records Group, Washington, D.C. (hereafter NARA).
[63]Ibid.
[64]*War History of the National Rifles*, pp. 17–18, 24.
[65]Constance McLaughlin Green, *Washington*, vol. 1, *Village and Capital 1800–1878* (Princeton, N.J., 1962), p. 241.

On April 25 the Shepherd brothers and forty other National Rifles soldiers volunteered to accompany the special train to get as close as possible to Annapolis and retrieve the soldiers of the Seventh New York. Approximately one thousand New York troops met the train at Annapolis Junction that morning, having marched from Annapolis but slowed in order to repair tracks torn up by hostile local elements that shadowed the soldiers along the route. After safely delivering the troops to Washington, the train, with its National Rifles guards, returned to Annapolis Junction and retrieved approximately eight hundred members of the Eighth Massachusetts Regiment. Both Shepherd brothers mounted guard overnight at Annapolis Junction, in addition to escorting the troops to Washington.[66] The city heaved a collective sigh of relief now that a large number of regular army troops had taken up residence in the city, where the Seventh New York Regiment was assigned to the House wing of the U.S. Capitol. Desks and gallery branches were allotted to the men, while the less lucky occupied corners and lobbies. Staff used the committee rooms, and the colonel occupied the Speaker's suite.[67]

As April gave way to May, life in the nation's capital adjusted to a new reality of massive dislocation from the thousands of Union troops billeted in the city's structures. Besides taking part in drills and parades, the young soldiers amused themselves by insulting residents and taking over many of the eating and drinking establishments for their own use. Critical to Washington's sense of security was the political stance of Virginia, and on May 23 Virginia's residents ratified the Virginia Convention's April 17 vote to secede, except for the loyal counties west of the Alleghenies that would later become the free state of West Virginia.[68] Although Alexandria remained quiet, it was committed to the Confederacy: it was easy to spot a Confederate flag atop Marshall House, a local hotel, and Confederate campfires could be seen at night. Arlington Heights, on the Virginia side of the river, was within artillery range of the White House and other government buildings

---

[66]*Evening Star*, Apr. 25, 1861; *War History of the National Rifles*, pp. 20–22; an interesting sidelight to the troop retrieval story is that one of the Pennsylvania Railroad employees detailed by the railroad's vice president, Thomas Scott, to assist was Andrew Carnegie, "a dapper little flaxen-haired Scotchman" who was Scott's private secretary and personal telegrapher (Leech, *Reveille in Washington*, p. 67).

[67]Leech, *Reveille in Washington*, p. 67.

[68]Ibid., pp. 79–80.

in Washington, while militants in Alexandria represented a potential challenge to free navigation of the Potomac River.

After the Union decision to neutralize the Virginia side of the Potomac, Washington's militias responded to the call for volunteers, since they were obliged to serve only within the District of Columbia. The National Rifles signed on, and the Shepherd brothers were part of the group that assembled at the National Rifles armory on the second floor of Temperance Hall at Tenth and G Streets NW the evening of May 23. At about 10:00 p.m., the unit marched down Twelfth Street SW and passed Maryland Avenue SW, yards away from Shepherd's birthplace two doors west. The troops—regulars and militia—closed the draw span of the Long Bridge (now the Fourteenth Street bridge), and soon after midnight the National Rifles, led by Captain John Smead, advanced across the bridge into Virginia. According to the National Rifles official history, the unit was the first company to march onto the "sacred soil" of Virginia.[69]

Shepherd and his fellow militiamen met no armed resistance; the Confederate pickets abandoned their positions as the Union forces arrived. The National Rifles participated in patrolling, mounting guard, and guiding out-of-state regular army units before leaving a contingent of five soldiers at the Aqueduct Bridge (now the site of Key Bridge) and returning to Washington on the morning of May 24. That day, however, saw the dramatic incident at Alexandria's Marshall House in which Colonel Elmer Ellsworth, leader of the dashing Fire Zouaves of New York, was killed by the hotel proprietor after Ellsworth had torn down the offending Confederate flag on the roof. The death of Colonel Ellsworth, an associate of President Lincoln and a colorful figure in his own right, was a shock to Washington, since the Zouaves were bivouacked in the city and Ellsworth cut a glamorous figure in local society. Funeral services in the Executive Mansion were attended by the president.[70]

---

[69]*War History of the National Rifles*, pp. 26–27; *Evening Star*, May 24, 1861. Shepherd's Civil War service on the Virginia side of the Potomac River was attested by a military pass dated June 8 from Head Quarters, Military Dept. of Washington, authorizing him to pass over the bridges within the lines. Shepherd signed his name beneath the text on the back of the pass (copy courtesy of Shepherd granddaughter Mary Wagner Woods).

[70]Leech, *Reveille in Washington*, pp. 80–81; *Evening Star*, May 24, 1861; *War History of the National Rifles*, p. 31.

Civil War Politics

Against the backdrop of war, Washington politicians struggled to adjust their positions to changing realities. Party politics were in a state of flux, with all distinctions complicated by the departure of Democratic representatives and senators from the South, which created opportunities for new groups. The Republican Association of Washington had been formed under the leadership of Shepherd associate Lewis Clephane and four others.[71] The organizing principle was opposition to permitting slavery in the new territories. The association was active in promoting the candidacy of the first Republican presidential candidate, John C. Frémont, in 1856, before choosing Abraham Lincoln in 1860.[72] The Unconditional Union Party (UUP) emerged as a supporter of the war effort, but its chief, former mayor Richard Wallach, opposed general emancipation efforts.[73] Elsewhere, the UUP stood strongly for emancipation.[74] Among Democrats, the War Democrats came to the support of the Union, and the Peace Democrats/Union Democratic Party criticized the administration and opposed the war. The opposition was composed of those who, according to the *Evening Star*, "are . . . radiant with joy when news of a secesh victory reaches the city." Its supporters denounced the Unconditional Union Party as allied with the Radical Republicans, a powerful group in the House and Senate who coalesced around opposition to slavery.[75] Radical Republicans were consistently in the forefront of legislation to advance the rights of black Americans.

Although Shepherd was faithful to his military obligations, he was also in the process of launching a political career in Washington by seeking and winning a seat on the Fifty-Ninth Washington City Common Council on June 4 on the Unconditional Union ticket.[76] Shepherd was a latecomer

[71]Clephane, "Lewis Clephane," pp. 263–77.

[72]Bryan, *History of the National Capital*, 2:392–93.

[73]Kenneth J. Winkle, *Lincoln's Citadel: The Civil War in Washington, D.C.* (New York, 2013), p. 204.

[74]Salmon P. Chase, *Going Home to Vote: Authentic Speeches of S. P. Chase* (Washington, D.C., 1863), pp. 27–28.

[75]Leech, *Reveille in Washington*, pp. 242–43; Eric Foner, *Reconstruction: America's Unfinished Revolution 1863–1877* (New York, 1988), pp. 228–29.

[76]*Evening Star*, June 4, 1861.

in deciding to run for the council, and the UUP organizers were late in adding him to their ticket, since it was not until May 31—only four days before the election—that a newspaper announcement for the Unconditional Union ticket included Shepherd as a candidate for a Ward 3 Common Council seat.[77] No doubt Shepherd had commended himself to local political power brokers through his gregariousness and military service. Shepherd's commitment to the Unconditional Union ticket was to launch him as a lifelong Republican, a party to which he gave great energy and from which he was to benefit personally and politically. Shepherd was new to politics, but from his vantage point at the J. W. Thompson plumbing firm, he was in contact with a wide swath of Washingtonians, since almost everyone needed home improvements and plumbing. All the Unconditional Union candidates for City Council were elected, including A. C. Richards, a Shepherd ally and later the city's chief of police, to the Board of Aldermen (the upper house) and Shepherd to the Common Council (the lower house). Newspaper accounts of the election noted that it was a quiet one and that all voters had free access to the polls, a polite way of confirming that less than 50 percent of eligible voters went to the polls.[78]

Still on active military duty, Shepherd attended the organizing session of the Fifty-Ninth City Council on June 10 and was appointed to a committee to certify election results for citywide officials.[79] At the next weekly meeting of the Common Council, Shepherd offered a resolution to instruct the Council's Ways and Means Committee to reduce expenses of the City Corporation and fix the local tax rate not to exceed fifty cents.[80] During the month of June Shepherd continued to carry out National Rifles duties in the Washington area, having made arrangements to remain in Washington when the majority of the unit was sent to Rockville, Maryland. Upon completion of the ninety-day term of enlistment, Shepherd mustered out on July 15.[81]

Shepherd's military service in the Civil War was over. When a drawing was held in August 1863 to determine which Washingtonians would be

---

[77]Ibid., May 31, 1861.

[78]Ibid., June 4, 1861.

[79]Ibid., June 10, 1861.

[80]Ibid., June 17, 1861. Considering Shepherd's later massive expenditures, including taxing Washington residents for public improvements, his attention to tax reduction in his initial term on the Common Council is noteworthy.

[81]*War History of the National Rifles*, pp. 36–37; Third Battalion, D.C. Militia, "Description and Morning Report," vol. 1, RG 94, NARA.

drafted, 607 names were drawn for the draft out of 2,035 eligible men in Shepherd's Ward 3. Both Alexander and Thomas Shepherd were selected despite prior service. Thomas later reported that he paid $800 for a substitute for himself and his brother.[82] Neither man was required to serve again.

Church Issues

The Shepherd and Robey families had been faithful churchgoers in Charles County and in Washington. By nature drawn to established social practice, Shepherd developed a close relationship with his father's old church, Fourth Presbyterian, whose pastor, Rev. John Smith, had recommended him for a job in John Thompson's plumbing firm. However, Shepherd left the church due to a dispute over whether Pastor Smith had broken church rules by authorizing church renovations without consulting the building committee. The trustees supplied a report documenting affairs during their tenure and submitted their resignations at a November 1860 church meeting, charging that they had not been supported and that their orders had been disputed and ignored. During a heated discussion, Shepherd weighed in, defending Pastor Smith's right to be heard and objecting to interruptions by other members. The meeting chairman supported Shepherd, who sarcastically dismissed a reference by one speaker to the church's book of government, saying there might be difficulty in finding it.[83] The incident in all likelihood left Shepherd feeling that while he had done the right thing in defending Pastor Smith, he had generated enough hard feelings that he would no longer feel at home at Fourth Presbyterian (which was directly across the street from his mother's home). Shepherd's defense of the pastor for having taken decisions without consulting the church fathers was a harbinger of charges that would be leveled against Shepherd as chairman of the Board of Trade.

The row caused Shepherd to decamp to the newly formed New York Avenue Presbyterian Church, which he attended for a time before asking

---

[82]Certificate no. 893.510, Civil War and Later Survivors' Records, RG 15, NARA. Since commutation via cash payment cost $300, not the $400 recollected by Thomas Shepherd fifty years later, his statement about paying for "both" could be taken to mean that he paid for substitutes for himself and for his brother, Alexander. Why the less well-off brother would have paid for the wealthier one is unknown, but it is possible that Alexander wished not to be on the record as having paid for a substitute to avoid further military service.

[83]*Evening Star*, Nov. 11, 1860.

its rector, Dr. Phineas D. Gurley, to officiate at his wedding and formally joining the church in the spring of 1862. In January 1862 Shepherd married Mary Grice Young, whom he knew from Fourth Presbyterian Church, where her father, William Probey Young, was an elder. Dr. Gurley performed the wedding ceremony at the Young family home on Ninth Street NW.[84] Like his father before him, Shepherd gained social standing from his marriage, since the Youngs were well known in the community, and William Young was a decorated veteran of the War of 1812. As noted earlier, the Grice side of the family came from Philadelphia, where they had settled in the eighteenth century and fought in the War of the American Revolution.

Shepherd's relationship with Dr. Gurley and New York Avenue Presbyterian Church provides possible insights into Shepherd's religious as well as social views. New York Avenue was an "Old School" congregation, from the 1837 split in the national Presbyterian Church over theological and organizational issues. Both traditions were grounded in the Bible, but the Old School favored a rational doctrinal approach, whereas the "New School" was more open to religious experience expressed in the revivalism of the Second Great Awakening then sweeping the country. The New School was also committed to political reform, especially antislavery, while the Old School held that the church should not involve itself in political questions. Gurley stood squarely in the Old School Presbyterian understanding of Reformed theology.[85] A theologian and student of Washington Presbyterianism has observed that slavery was the hidden agenda for the split in the Washington Presbyterian churches, although it was not usually discussed in those terms.[86]

Abolitionist sentiment was widespread among New School Presbyterians, while Old School Presbyterians ranged from southern defenders of slavery to northerners who deplored slavery but cautioned against the social and

---

[84]"Sessions Book, Fourth Presbyterian Church, Washington, D.C., First Book, Session 1828–1878." Shepherd Family Bible, courtesy of Shepherd great-granddaughter Alexandra Wyatt-Brown Malick; photocopy of marriage certificate courtesy of Shepherd granddaughter Mary Wagner Woods.

[85]White, *A. Lincoln*, pp. 403–4; Mitchell Snay, *Gospel of Disunion: Religion and Separatism in the Antebellum South* (Chapel Hill, 1997), is an excellent source for understanding the break between the two wings of the Presbyterian Church.

[86]Dewey D. Wallace, George Washington University, conversation with the author, Mar. 3, 2006.

political disruption that abolition would bring. Many Old School church-goers were not proslavery or politically reactionary, although they were in general more socially conservative than New Schoolers. Some Old School Presbyterians were supporters of the American Colonization Society, whose platform was transportation of freed slaves to Liberia and their coloniza-tion there. Dr. Gurley was a leading figure in the society and hosted its na-tional meetings in 1861 and 1864. Gurley was also a strong Unionist who was considered a reconciling voice toward the South, paralleling the views of President Lincoln, who attended but was not a member of the church.[87]

Besides the row over the pastor's actions at Fourth Presbyterian, Shep-herd's move from a New School to an Old School Presbyterian church may have been motivated by a desire to find a more socially conservative insti-tution. Making the change had required leaving the long-standing church of his father, his own youth, his future wife and in-laws, and his siblings; only his future wife transferred with him. Gurley's New York Avenue Church not only appealed to Shepherd's conservative nature; Dr. Gurley also had the kind of active, virile personality to which Shepherd was drawn.

In the midst of the Civil War, young Alexander Shepherd was ready to take his place in the uncertain worlds of Washington business, politics, and society. An ambitious and rising businessman, he had developed a network of friends and associates not only in business, but in a variety of social, civic, and political organizations. His service in the National Rifles and his elec-tion to the Common Council demonstrated his commitment to the local and the national government. In spite of a limited education, he had demon-strated an early promise of high achievement, and the roads he had chosen lay open ahead of him.

---

[87]Dewey D. Wallace, "The New York Avenue Presbyterian Church: Context and Overview," unpublished draft, 2006, pp. 22–23.

Chapter Two

"The Great Work of Improving and Beautifying Our Beloved City"

First Steps in Business and Political Leadership, 1862–1865

BY 1862, TWENTY-SEVEN-YEAR-OLD Shepherd—married, a Union war veteran, and a partner in the plumbing firm of John W. Thompson— had entered the first phase of his political life in Washington. He quickly demonstrated leadership skills and began to build the case for political themes he would eventually see through to completion, although with consequences he had not imagined, for both himself and the city.

Civil War Washington was not much to look at. Almost every street in use was dirt and would remain so for several more years. Washington's streets, such as they were, took an endless beating during the war from the stream of horses, wagons, carts, and soldiers, becoming a quagmire in winter and a dustbowl in summer. The capital's public buildings were set amid open spaces or surrounded by unappealing wooden structures. The Washington Monument, not completed until 1884, was an ugly stump. The war overwhelmed Washington in every way. Aside from the constant threat of Confederate attack, the war brought tens of thousands of Union soldiers, healthy and wounded, into the city. The Capitol and the Patent Office became temporary barracks, with soldiers bunking in the Capitol rotunda and between Patent Office glass cases filled with inventions. The Capitol basement briefly became a bakery. Hospitals, a vital element in Union hopes of healing and returning soldiers to the front, sprang up everywhere, including in private homes and wooden structures erected for the purpose. Sixty-eight forts were built around the city's perimeter to defend against

Confederate attack, although only one, Fort Stevens, was needed to resist a July 1864 assault. The Civil War was a horse war, and thousands of horses had to be corralled, fed, and paraded in the city. Trees were a major casualty: the need for firewood for cooking was insatiable, forests were replaced by military camps, and the forts needed clear sight lines for their weapons.

After the departure of the southern Democratic members of Congress at the outbreak of war, some Republican members welcomed the opportunity to make the District of Columbia a testing ground for social and political engineering that would result in significant gains for Washington's black residents. Known as Radical Republicans, these legislators proposed racial policies for the District that were still illegal or politically anathema in their home states. Senator Charles Sumner (R-Mass.) was the most persistent congressional advocate for emancipating blacks in the nation's capital and for providing black children with educational opportunities equal to and integrated with those of the District's white children. The senator, brutally caned on the Senate floor in 1856 by Democratic congressman Preston Brooks of South Carolina for antislavery remarks, continued to introduce progressive legislation for black rights in Washington until his death in 1874.

The most dramatic early demonstration of Radical Republican political clout was passage of the District of Columbia Emancipation Act on April 16, 1862, eight months before President Lincoln's Emancipation Proclamation. The new law, which provided compensation to slave owners for freeing their slaves, was joyously welcomed by Washington's black residents but had been anticipated by many white Washingtonians with a mixture of apprehension and dread. Local politicians began to speak up in protest shortly after Senator Lot Morrill (R-Maine), chairman of the Senate District Committee, introduced the emancipation bill in February; no effort was made to seek the consent of local voters. Regardless of whether congressional Republicans were influenced by abolitionist pressure at home, were made aware of the new political conditions created by the war, or were influenced by the demands of their own consciences, they took a step that not only initiated a wider legislative war against slavery but also marked a decisive change in the practical relationship between the national government and the capital city in which it sat.[1] Opposition within the local population to freeing the

---

[1]Robert Harrison, "An Experimental Station for Lawmaking: Congress and the District of Columbia, 1862–1878," *Civil War History* 53 (Mar. 2007):33.

District's slaves created friction that Shepherd would exploit for his own political gain.

Slavery had traditionally defined race relations in the nation's capital. Washington's black codes—applied to free as well as enslaved blacks—imposed fines for being on the street after 10:00 p.m. or engaging in card games, as well as six-month jail sentences for anyone arrested at a "nightly and disorderly" meeting.[2] Two incidents in the recent past had heightened racial fears among Washington's white residents. The first was an 1835 attempt by a slave on the life of Anna Maria Thornton, widow of the former architect of the Capitol, William Thornton. This incident triggered the Snow Riot, when a white mob assaulted a free black restaurateur, Beverly Snow, and led to a three-day-long attack on Washington's black residents.[3] The second incident, in 1848, was a bold escape attempt by seventy-six slaves on board the schooner *Pearl*, led by the ship's abolitionist captain. Freedom for the escapees was short-lived, however, and they were brought back to jail for subsequent sale in the Deep South.[4] In response, whites stiffened the black codes, aiming for constant surveillance of the black population.

During the war the District attracted escaped slaves from plantations in neighboring Maryland and Virginia as well as farther south; consequently, the number of so-called contraband blacks in the District of Columbia mounted steadily. The black population, which made up less than 20 percent of the total District population in 1860, grew dramatically by 1870, with blacks, now freedmen, constituting 33 percent of the total population of 131,700.[5] Most contrabands were illiterate, having served mainly as plantation field hands. However, the District's freedmen had established a self-conscious community that seized educational and commercial opportunities whenever they presented themselves. This resulted in a number of the city's black residents becoming prosperous businessmen and property owners as the capital's demands for goods and services skyrocketed during the war.[6] After

---

[2]Constance McLaughlin Green, *The Secret City: A History of Race Relations in the Nation's Capital* (Princeton, N.J., 1967), p. 18.

[3]Jefferson Morley, *Snow-Storm in August: Washington City, Francis Scott Key, and the Forgotten Race Riot of 1835* (New York, 2012), pp. 144–56.

[4]Josephine F. Pacheco, *The Pearl: A Failed Slave Escape on the Potomac* (Chapel Hill, 2005), pp. 53–57, 92, 112.

[5]Alan Lessoff, *The Nation and Its City: Politics, "Corruption," and Progress in Washington, D.C., 1861–1902* (Baltimore, 1994), p. 18.

[6]Green, *Secret City*, pp. 89–90.

the war, blacks also were represented in government clerkships and had access to higher education at Howard University, which opened in 1867. Particularly after receiving the vote in 1867, they sought to translate these gains into increased liberty. The emancipation of the District's slave population in 1862 proved a blessing to the Republican Party; in gratitude for their freedom, former slaves handed the Republicans a virtually solid voting block for more than ten years.

Other than his obsession with streamlining governance of the District of Columbia and making Congress own up to its responsibility to help pay the bills for the capital, the most vexing issue for Shepherd was the status and role of Washington's black population. Like many of his white business and political associates, he opposed social equality for blacks in spite of his support for President Lincoln and for emancipation, once it became law in January 1863.[7] During the spring of 1862 Shepherd voiced opinions about race questions on several occasions during Common Council debates, strongly opposing the black suffrage movement that was gaining ground among Radical Republicans in Congress. In early March he made his first official commentary on race. This occurred following resolutions by the Metropolitan Police Board that requested repeal of the Washington and Georgetown black codes restricting the movements of blacks after 10:00 p.m. Shepherd introduced an unsuccessful amendment for review of the ordinances, noting that he did not desire to stir up agitation on the subject or to offend any member of the board. Shepherd said that his resolution was not meant to anticipate repeal by the board but rather to show respect for the police.[8] The intent of the amendment is not clear, although Shepherd's proposal to review police ordinances might imply that he was raising a question of whether or not the police board had the authority to call for revision of the black codes, all of which were in any event repealed that spring.[9] At the end of March he joined a 14–4 Common Council majority in passing a joint resolution with the Board of Aldermen opposing the congressional emancipation bill.[10]

---

[7]Social equality was "a container for everything that (opponents) considered anathema." Kate Masur, *An Example for All the Land: Emancipation and the Struggle over Equality in Washington, D.C.* (Chapel Hill, 2010), pp. 9–10.

[8]*Evening Star* (Washington, D.C.), Mar. 11, 1862.

[9]Green, *Secret City*, p. 60.

[10]*Evening Star*, Apr. 1, 1862; *National Republican* (Washington, D.C.), Apr. 1, 1862.

In April, during a council debate on an education bill, Shepherd observed that he hoped that the discussion of the "negro question" was at an end, adding that he considered the subject a "hobby [horse]" that politicians ought not to ride in seeking office; he wished to see agitation on the subject ended.[11] Shepherd made one of his most categorical statements on the black vote in 1864, in response to reports that he supported a congressional bill to provide the franchise for adult male residents of the District, regardless of race. The press reported that Shepherd

> was opposed to the principle of allowing negroes to vote, *in toto*. A certain class of people were now trying to force the negroes to sit in the [horse] cars, with white people, but he . . . was not quite up to that standard. This negro-equality question was now being forced upon the people by the red-mouthed abolitionists in the United States. He . . . could not favor it, and yet he considered that his unionism was of a high standard. He was in favor of the President's proclamation to free the slaves, but he was not in favor of putting them on an equality with white men.[12]

During his first term on the Common Council, Shepherd pushed hard but unsuccessfully to include a loyalty oath as a voting requirement. Failing this, he later proposed changing the Washington City charter to include such an oath. Shepherd linked his support for a loyalty oath with opposition to a congressional bill regarding residency requirements for Washington voters. During a congressional debate about the proposal to require only a six-month residency for Washington City voters, without regard to property ownership, he objected, again unsuccessfully, on the grounds that it would be unjust to property holders to permit recent residents to influence elections.[13] Furthermore, he argued that such a short residency requirement would also be unjust to property holders since "it would be abused by a class, such as teamsters, etc.," who would take advantage of it for whiskey and money.[14]

Despite the failure of these initiatives, they strengthened Shepherd's public image as a member of the Unconditional Union faction on the council and as a spokesman for property owners. He was a self-made businessman who had seen the disappearance of his father's estate and subsequent

---

[11] *National Republican*, Apr. 29, 1862.
[12] Ibid., Mar. 22, 1864.
[13] *Evening Star*, Apr. 11, 1862.
[14] Ibid., Apr. 18, 1862.

family difficulties, and as a result he had developed firm views on the centrality of property as a qualification for political participation, a position on which he never wavered. Realizing that he was creating a political image that resonated with voters, Shepherd continued to stake out hard-line positions on loyalty to the Union, winning a third term on the Washington Common Council in 1863.

During this period Shepherd drew criticism from some Washington politicians who complained that they were being branded insufficiently loyal to the United States. They accused Shepherd and his supporters of having labeled them "copperheads," a derogatory term for Southern-leaning Northerners. By taking a leading position on the Unconditional Union ticket and dramatizing the loyalty issue, Shepherd created an awkward situation for local, conservative, often Georgetown-based figures whose political sympathies were frequently with the South.

Shepherd's debating style was always confident and occasionally aggressive. From the beginning he demonstrated a willingness to use his imposing physical presence to support a legislative position; one challenge during his term on the Elections Committee brought the response that he would allow no one to "asperse" him. Speaking in a loud tone and with a belligerent attitude, Shepherd told the other speaker to take his seat, and both men appeared ready to fight. Nothing ensued, however, and Shepherd closed by defending the members of his committee from the charge of unfairness.[15] During one debate he contended that he did not care about "appearances, ridiculous or not. . . . The only question was whether it was right," adding that he would do his duty and let others think what they might.[16]

During his three terms on the Common Council, Shepherd maintained a steady criticism of Congress's refusal to provide local government with taxing authority while at the same time providing concessions and franchises to outside corporate investors in the capital. Responding to an article in a local paper critical of the District for neglect of Pennsylvania Avenue, he commented bitterly that "when a railroad franchise, or gas company, or anything of that sort was asked [of Congress], it was rushed straight through; but when the city asked for power to tax property for necessary improvements, to make this city a pride for its people, instead of a disgrace,

---

[15]Ibid., Nov. 12, 1861.
[16]Ibid., Sept. 24, 1861; Mar. 18, Mar. 25, Apr. 18, May 13, 1862.

we were snubbed or kicked out until the adjournment of Congress."[17] Among Shepherd's targets was the Baltimore & Ohio Railroad. He saw the railroad, which had a rail station near the Capitol and tracks across the mall that disfigured the vista of the Capitol, as a corporate bully that had political influence with Congress and would be an obstacle to his plans to rationalize the development of the city.

Balancing family life with his business and political affairs, Shepherd married Mary Grice Young in January 1862, and he and his bride moved into their first home, a comfortable brick row house at 358 Tenth Street W.[18] Shepherd's Washington residences would reflect his growing financial success, culminating in the mansion at 1705 K Street some ten years later. Although his mother remained in her nearby Ninth Street residence until after the end of the war, she helped the newlyweds settle into their new home. The couple's first child, Mary Young Shepherd, was born in early December 1862 at their new home, where Shepherd's mother no doubt was able to help out with the growing family.

Because Shepherd was a businessman whose major activities were equipping homes with heating, lighting, and plumbing systems, as well as developing real estate and constructing homes, he understood the importance of optimism and stability to encourage investment in local real estate. The constant attacks on Washington for its shortcomings were a threat to such local investment and encouraged attempts to "remove" the capital to some other part of the country. Local newspapers, informed observers such as the recorder of deeds, and the principal real estate brokers and developers of the time were vocal in attributing stuttering investment—public as well as private—in Washington to the threat of retrocession to Maryland and "removal" of the capital to the West. Retrocession had already occurred once, when Congress returned the Alexandria City and County portion of the original ten-mile square across the Potomac River to Virginia in 1846. Agitation and uncertainty had a negative influence on attitudes and property values, something Shepherd well understood.[19] Consequently, as early as the Civil War, Shepherd had begun to take steps to identify and

---

[17]*National Republican*, May 1, 1864.

[18]*Hutchinson's Washington and Georgetown Directory* (Washington, D.C., 1863). Due to a map adjustment in 1869, 358 Tenth Street W. would become 1125 Tenth Street NW.

[19]Wilhelmus Bogart Bryan, *A History of the National Capital from Its Foundation through the Period of the Adoption of the Organic Act*, 2 vols. (New York, 1914), 1:448.

respond to the threat of capital removal, which he believed would crush the life out of Washington and his growing investments in land and buildings.

Article I, section 8, of the Constitution gave Congress exclusive jurisdiction over an area of up to ten miles square anticipated for cession by the states. Early debates over local governance of the nation's capital were united on one key point: executive authority should be vested in an appointee of the president of the United States, not an individual elected by the residents. As an appointee, the mayor, it was thought, "could not fail to administer local affairs in harmony with the national administration."[20] Nonetheless, by 1802 this concept had shifted to a congressional decision to delegate administration of local affairs to the local government, thereby granting limited freedom to residents to manage what concerned them more than it did the general government. However, Congress reserved the right to recall any or all of these privileges if at any time they were neglected or abused.[21] The 1820 charter of Washington City made the City Corporation responsible for urban improvement, including streets, but from the outset the national government showed little interest in beautifying its creation. For many years the only aesthetic embellishment was Thomas Jefferson's planting of four rows of poplar trees on Pennsylvania Avenue, in imitation of the famous Unter den Linden in Berlin.[22]

Shepherd was not alone in grasping the magnitude of the challenge facing Washington if it was to overcome its status as a stepchild of the national government, but he developed a special ability to convert anger and frustration into concrete results through coalition building. Shepherd realized that Washington's residents were simply unable to underwrite the physical development expected of the capital of a fast-growing nation without congressional support and funding. He would therefore have to convince Congress that its financial support for the improvement of the nation's capital was in its own best interest.

Shepherd made use of his election speech as president of the Sixtieth Common Council in 1862 to identify themes to which he would return time and again: (1) supporting Unconditional Union (UU), the bedrock of his

---

[20]John Addison Porter, *The City of Washington: Its Origin and Administration*, Johns Hopkins University Studies in Historical and Political Science, 3rd ser., nos. 11–12 (Baltimore, 1885), p. 19.

[21]Ibid., p. 19.

[22]Ibid., pp. 20–21.

views; (2) downplaying what he called "unnecessary agitation" and division; (3) maintaining and developing Washington's urban infrastructure; and, most important, (4) obtaining a commitment from Congress to participate fully in the city's development. He exhorted his listeners, "Let us in all things uphold our government and by our acts and discussions secure the aid of our national legislature in the great work of improving and beautifying our beloved city."[23]

Building Blocks for Consolidation

The first step in Shepherd's long campaign to create a new Washington was revision of the city charter to give the City Council authority to generate tax revenues adequate to pay for urban improvements. An 1862 joint council resolution calling for Congress to revise the Washington City charter led with the statement that the current charter limited the powers of the corporation to such an extent that carrying out substantial improvements was impossible. Shepherd explained his resolution in debate, saying that the corporation needed the power to provide for improvements, including sewerage, river dredging, a new city asylum for the poor, and, above all, paving of the streets. In order to determine where matters stood legally, the City Council approved Shepherd's proposal for a digest and codification of corporation laws, which had become "incorrect and faulty" as a result of numerous amendments.[24] As part of his campaign to create greater awareness of Washington history, Shepherd also called for purchasing an original map of the District of Columbia and requested that General Montgomery Meigs donate photos of the Washington Aqueduct, which Meigs had designed and built in the 1850s to bring an adequate water supply to Washington from farther up the Potomac River.[25]

---

[23]*Evening Star,* June 9, 1862. Another newspaper added, "Let us labor, fellow-councilmen, to make this metropolis worthy [of] the hallowed name it bears, and worthy to be the capital of the 'Great Republic' of the world" (*National Republican,* June 10, 1862).

[24]*Evening Star,* June 30, 1863; *Journal of the 61st Council* (Washington, D.C., 1863), p. 25. The resultant digest of Washington City laws was completed in the fall of 1863, and the Common Council approved purchase of fifty copies in January 1864 (*Journal of the 61st Council,* pp. 326–27).

[25]*Evening Star,* Apr. 12 and 19, 1864.

In 1863, his final year on the Common Council, Shepherd's principal legislative initiative remained the reform of the Washington City charter. For reasons that are unclear, Shepherd was absent from most of the council meetings in the summer and early fall of that year. He may have become disenchanted with the influence of the Common Council; he could also have been focusing more on building what was becoming a very successful plumbing and gas-fitting business. He had reason to devote more time and energy to his business dealings.

During the first half of 1864 Shepherd undertook a "private war" with Joseph F. Brown, who ran the Washington Gas Light Company and represented Shepherd's Ward 3 constituency on the Board of Aldermen. The controversy was a combination of personalities, business, and politics. Shepherd took aim at the company's pricing policies and supported a proposed bill in the Common Council to create a charter for a new gas company.[26] Throughout the spring Shepherd and Brown swapped heated exchanges in the press. Shepherd challenged the quality of the gas company's work, and Brown countered with allegations about J. W. Thompson's gas lines. It was clear that each man's personal integrity was on the line. In a letter to the *Evening Star*, Shepherd accused Brown of slandering the Thompson firm in order to bring in more business for Brown's newly launched plumbing establishment, adding that his own antagonism toward the gas company was due to his opposition to all monopolies that "oppress" the people.[27] Although the spat was officially resolved at a meeting arranged by friends, it resurfaced in a bitter dispute over which man should be the official candidate to represent Ward 3 in the June election for alderman. Shepherd stepped down as president of the Sixty-First Common Council (1863–64) in June 1864 in order to run for Brown's Ward 3 Board of Aldermen seat. After a series of no-holds-barred public exchanges, Brown defeated Shepherd by a vote of 483 to 395.[28] After the legislative defeat, Shepherd may have decided that his bid to move to the higher legislative chamber was too ambitious, and he took the opportunity to shift his focus to building his fortune and laying the groundwork for the grand plans that were to be unveiled a few years later.

---

[26]Ibid., Feb. 2, 1864.

[27]Ibid., Feb. 2–3, 1864.

[28]Ibid., June 1–4 and 7, 1864.

In 1864 Shepherd was twenty-nine years old and the de facto head of the J. W. Thompson plumbing establishment, although the original name remained in use until Shepherd purchased the firm the next year. Even during the dark days of the war, Shepherd and his wife quickly established a lively social presence, making their home a focal point for merrymaking and building political relationships. At their Tenth Street residence they hosted events that were to fill the social pages of Washington newspapers for years to come. The Shepherds loved to show off their means through elaborate and expensive entertainments. A typical party in February 1864 was described in the *Evening Star* as among the most agreeable parties of a season distinguished for the number and brilliancy of such affairs.[29]

Shepherd was also becoming a leader in church affairs at New York Avenue Presbyterian Church. He was appointed chairman of the church's Northern Presbyterian Mission, which was successful at raising money, purchasing land, and establishing a chapel just north of Boundary Street (now Florida Avenue).[30] Shepherd's public generosity was expressed in his gift of a white marble pulpit for the Metropolitan Presbyterian Church on Capitol Hill.[31] The church had just completed construction of a major edifice, and President Ulysses S. Grant would attend the dedication.[32] Shepherd was becoming astute in linking charitable contributions with high-visibility political situations.

Shepherd was also in the process of launching an investment initiative in local street railroads. Among the first was the Metropolitan Railroad, which was planned as a double track from near the Capitol, along D Street to Fifteenth Street NW, and a single or double track back along New York Avenue to Ninth Street, then south to the Washington Canal. Following the railroad's incorporation by Congress, a July meeting of shareholders elected seven directors: Shepherd and six friends and business associates who would remain in his inner circle for years to come.[33]

---

[29]Ibid., Feb. 17, 1864.

[30]"Minutes of Session of the F St. Church 1819–1859 and the New York Ave. Presbyterian Church 1859–1871," p. 177, National Presbyterian Church Archives, Washington, D.C.

[31]*Evening Star*, Dec. 5, 1872.

[32] Ann Nickel, "A Church on the Hill," *Hill Rag Magazine* (Sept. 2011): 60–61.

[33]*Evening Star*, Jan. 28, July 27 and 29, 1864. In addition to Shepherd, the directors were William B. Todd, Matthew G. Emery, Lewis Clephane, John R. Semmes, J. W. Thompson, and S. P. Brown.

Two weeks after Shepherd lost his bid for the Ward 3 alderman seat in June 1864, his first son, also named Alexander, died at the age of six months, the first of three Shepherd children to die in infancy. Shepherd purchased a plot of ground in Oak Hill Cemetery in Georgetown, a favorite project of banker and philanthropist William Wilson Corcoran. Eventually the plot would hold the graves of several members of Shepherd's immediate family, although he and his wife are buried in a granite mausoleum in Rock Creek Cemetery across town. Following the death of his son, Shepherd, his wife, and his brother Tom joined his sister-in-law Susan Young and other members of the Young family on a vacation in New England, visiting the White Mountains of New Hampshire and New York's Niagara Falls and Saratoga, among other stops, before returning through New York City and Philadelphia. The change of scenery appeared to do Alexander and Mary good, although Mary said pointedly in one letter home, "Yankee land is horrid."[34] One of Shepherd's few surviving personal letters from the vacation is worth quoting because of the unusual glimpse it gives into his spirituality. Writing to his mother from Niagara Falls, he spoke at length of the moving nature of the experience, demonstrating a naïve and unquestioning acceptance of the divine:

> One has only to view such grand proofs of old dame nature to feel what a terribly small and despicable thing man is. What a tiny atom in the great work of creation and what a kind and merciful being *Our God* is in putting in man that spirit from on high which makes him the superior of all other created beings. I assure you that I have never heard a sermon which so inculcated humility and thrilled me with a sense of my own utter insignificance as that which thundered over the rocks of Niagara Falls . . . as I stood for the first time and looked upon this wonderful work of God. Oh, what a powerful sermon was preached in its thunder tones. How any atom like man could stand here and doubt the existence of a God is more than I can comprehend. As I stood on the shore at the Cave of the Winds and looked upward at the rocky cliffs which overhung one and seem about to fall and overwhelm me, I experienced a feeling of terror such as I have never before felt.[35]

---

[34]Mary Shepherd to her parents, Shepherd Papers, box 2, Manuscript Division, Library of Congress, Washington, D.C.

[35]Alexander Shepherd to his mother, Aug. 21, 1864. Shepherd Papers, box 2, Manuscript Division, Library of Congress, Washington, D.C. Shepherd Papers, donated by the family, appear to have been extensively edited.

The Union is Preserved

In April 1865 the Civil War ended, and President Lincoln was assassinated. In the wake of these two major events, the United States struggled to establish a new equilibrium. Two critical issues faced the nation: reintegration of the devastated former Confederacy into the national polity and the future of millions of unskilled or semiskilled and vulnerable freedmen. The Union victory had affirmed the unity of the nation and brought a renewed sense of national power and a dramatic shift in the relationship between the states and the national government.[36] Like the nation as a whole, the District of Columbia was reeling, its primitive streets having been churned into mud and dust by soldiers' horses, its trees cut down for firewood, and former Confederate sympathizers straggling back to reestablish their lives in a hostile social environment. Blacks now made up one-third of the District's population, and their political and civil rights would be a vexing political issue for leaders such as Shepherd. After its first sixty-one years of halting progress, the nation's capital had experienced four war years of disruptive change. The stage was set for the next act in the postbellum human drama, with Radical Republicans in Congress arguing that denial of rights to blacks was an insult to the enlightened sentiment of the age.[37]

The chief business of the capital was government, and local government, such as it was, ultimately rested in the hands of Congress, where District residents had no representation, and local elites could not bring the crucial spheres of economic and political power under their control. The Confederate defeat was a disaster for the city's old southern elite, who were dispersed, defeated, disgraced, or impoverished, and sometimes all four. Into the vacuum created by the demise of the old southern aristocracy rushed a host of newcomers eager to fill the vacancies they left behind.[38] In the decades before the war, the unfinished capital had been the physical embodiment of American distaste for centralized government, but the Civil War brought new vigor and a vastly expanded scale to the federal bureaucracy

---

[36]Robert Harrison, *Washington during Civil War and Reconstruction* (Cambridge, 2011), pp. 56–57.

[37]Ibid., p. 112.

[38]Kathryn Allamong Jacob, *Capital Elites: High Society in Washington, D.C., after the Civil War* (Washington, D.C., 1995), p. 8.

in Washington. Only a strong, centralized government could provide the leadership that the war effort ultimately demanded. The same war that strengthened the federal government, however, had left Washington a physical mess. The immediate postwar capital was the ugly antithesis of the almost mythic image of the "Great Republic," "the Nation," and "the Union" that was filling the print and oratory of the day. The new crop of federal officials who wanted the scope of government enlarged also insisted on a capital that would project its grandeur to the rest of the nation.[39]

The gap between reality and expectations was vast. Pennsylvania Avenue, the one paved street between the White House and the Capitol, was home to "cheap saloons, gambling houses, and pawnshops. Ford's Theatre, notorious for President Lincoln's assassination, had been requisitioned by the government. The National Theater and Wall's Opera House provided what meager legitimate entertainment options as were available; high- and low-class gambling establishments still flourished. Unpainted wooden buildings that had served as barracks and stables for army mules still stood mute, months after the end of the fighting."[40]

Taking Care of His Business Interests

Shepherd remained out of elective politics for several years and devoted his energies to two principal goals: becoming a successful, wealthy businessman and advancing the cause of Washington's transformation. The long-expected transition at the J. W. Thompson plumbing firm took place in mid-May 1865, when newspaper announcements confirmed the company's dissolution and the elevation of Shepherd, the former junior partner, to owner of Alexander Shepherd & Brothers.[41] The firm then consisted of five shops for gas fitting, plumbing, brass finishing, carpentry, and blacksmithing.[42] Much of the merchandise boasted a Philadelphia pedigree, and advertisements in Washington papers for current lighting models frequently cited their having been brought from Philadelphia. This became a Shepherd trademark to be

---

[39]Ibid., pp. 9, 58.
[40]James Huntington Whyte, *The Uncivil War: Washington during the Reconstruction, 1865–1878* (New York, 1958), pp. 14–15.
[41]*Evening Star*, May 17, 1865.
[42]Ibid., Sept. 12, 1865.

repeated in his later development work, when he made use of the text of the Philadelphia Board of Trade document in his next major civic venture, the Washington Board of Trade. Aside from any intrinsic superiority, Philadelphia was also the home of Mary Shepherd's maternal ancestors, and it would have been natural for Shepherd to strengthen family ties while conducting personal or public business.

A key element in Shepherd's plans for Washington was the Board of Trade, which he helped launch at a meeting at City Hall on October 17, 1865, bringing together some fifty leading businessmen and twenty-one firms. He understood the nexus between commerce and politics and saw a business development organization as a useful tool to address political issues indirectly. Shepherd was one of the first speakers at the meeting, and he eloquently described the advantages of a merchants' exchange and urged cooperation among members of the business community, including those in Georgetown, in order to make it happen. Not surprisingly, Shepherd was spokesman for the planning committee, whose draft preamble noted that a lack of unity had been a detriment to the interests of the community and that commercial advantages were best obtained by united action.

The Board of Trade's initial skirmishes included criticism of a proposed license for a Washington and Alexandria Railroad line through the city as "a gross outrage upon the industrial interests of this city; of incalculable harm to the interests of its citizens; and calculated to destroy the business prospects of this Metropolis."[43] At a meeting with the Washington Board of Aldermen in November, Shepherd argued against the license because, he asserted, it would further monopolize control of local rail lines by outside interests and degrade vital parts of the city with tracks, water towers, and parked rail cars. Employing a technique he would use effectively throughout his career, Shepherd arranged for an elegant repast at the end of the meeting in an effort to create goodwill.[44] Always a gregarious figure, Shepherd had become adept at using the leverage afforded by his wealth, more than his physical size and aggressive personality, to influence others to his way of thinking.

Shepherd's strategic objective with the Board of Trade became clear in November 1865. He returned to a favorite topic by proposing to create a new,

[43]Ibid., Oct. 31, 1865.
[44]Ibid., Nov. 16, 1865.

single charter for the whole of the District of Columbia built around consolidation of the capital's three fragmented and separately governed jurisdictions (Georgetown, Washington City, and Washington County). He argued that Congress should be persuaded to create an "efficient and harmonious" government for the District through consolidation and that the Board of Trade, which represented such a large proportion of the District's commerce, was the proper vehicle for advancing the project.[45] A number of board members objected to using a business promotion organization for political purposes, but Shepherd framed the issue differently: the resolution was only a business necessity that "should not be mixed up in any degree with politics, negro suffrage, or anything else. . . . We have nothing to do with politics in this District, and they should never be dragged into matters of District interests."[46]

At the December 6 meeting to discuss consolidation, Shepherd provided insights into his thinking about how the consolidated entity might be governed: "Whether the Government should be territorial or be vested in appointed commissioners, or a ruler to be elected by the people, are questions which might cause a diversity of opinion, but the advantages [are] fully recognized by businessmen and taxpayers." He went on to argue that "there are no politics here, and we had no political rights," assuring his audience that the initiative would not be viewed by the people as political and asserting that nine-tenths of the residents would favor consolidation.[47] Despite general agreement that Georgetown would also support the move, one participant noted that the people, not the Board of Trade, should initiate such an important change in local government. Shepherd retorted that he expected the cry of politics to be raised, "as is always so when something of benefit to the District of Columbia is proposed." He reiterated his view that consolidation was a pure business issue, "and if the municipalities were placed under one good man, and Congress pay the Government's portion," there would be positive results and reduced corruption. "As for political rights, we haven't any, and are not as good as darkies."[48] Shepherd pressed the point by noting, "The City has few privileges, and Congress may at any time enact obnoxious laws, and it would therefore seem much better if

---

[45]Ibid., Nov. 23, 1865.
[46]Ibid.
[47]Ibid., Dec. 8, 1865.
[48]Ibid., Dec. 8, 1865.

Congress had entire control."[49] To give additional weight to the initiative, Shepherd also offered a resolution for the Board of Trade to urge Congress to consolidate the District of Columbia. With these assurances from its most forceful member, the board passed the resolution unanimously.

Shepherd was playing a sophisticated political game. He used the newly established Board of Trade to advance a radical political initiative while maintaining that it was nonpolitical and that business promotion alone was the focus. He was able to identify an issue that combined commercial development with an implicit appeal to the conservative "old citizens'" rejection of black enfranchisement. He was well aware of but not sympathetic to the rapidly changing goals of black Washingtonians. Although blacks were not to receive the vote until January 1867 and their votes were not yet in play, class and politics mattered a great deal. As businessmen and loyal Republicans, members of the board had the ear of Congress. The board made no explicit case for or against voting rights and steered clear of inflammatory language. Instead, it emphasized the vocabulary of progress and prosperity to make the case against black voting rights and, more generally, against democratic government.[50] Board members wanted a unified District above all, and Shepherd's formula for charter consolidation avoided addressing the racial issue.

Deploying the Board of Trade, a nonpolitical entity, as a tool of influence to achieve political ends was a tactical if not a strategic change because in the years before 1864 Shepherd had made every effort to use his initiatives in the Common Council for the same purposes. He may also have realized that his defeat for a seat on the Board of Aldermen provided him with an opportunity to change gears. For the next several years he would work officially outside the political system in order to bring about change within.

---

[49]*National Intelligencer,* Dec. 7, 1865.
[50]Masur, *An Example for All the Land,* pp. 195–96.

Chapter Three

"We Want an Honest Board of Commissioners and No Broken-down Political Demagogues"

Building His Business and Political Base for Civic Reform, 1865–1868

WITH THE COUNTRY struggling to find a new equilibrium in the aftermath of the Civil War, Shepherd—and Washington—faced numerous challenges. Shepherd used the years after the war to build his fortune and establish himself as a major player on the local scene while crafting a strategy to consolidate the District of Columbia and change its form of governance. An additional distraction—and spur to action—was the persistent campaign to "remove" the nation's capital closer to the geographic center of the expanding nation. Membership on the Levy Court[1] would provide Shepherd with a vehicle for launching trial political balloons on Washington's future.

Shepherd's tactics, if not his strategy, on one issue—the civil rights aspirations of Washington's black citizens—appeared to change after he resigned from the Common Council and was defeated in his bid for alderman in 1864. He had repeatedly offered views on racial issues in the past, opposing both the black franchise and attempts to put blacks "on an equality" with whites. His use of what would today be considered racist language (e.g., "darkies"), while not uncommon at the time, suggests a paternalistic attitude at minimum. As the 1860s drew to an end and the District's black

---

[1]The Levy Court was the governing body for Washington County. A relic of archaic Maryland law, it consisted of nine judges appointed by the president, including three from Washington City, of whom Shepherd was one.

citizens obtained the vote, Shepherd downplayed his racial views by promoting consolidation of the District of Columbia charter in the name of government efficiency and economic prosperity. He abandoned explicit calls for black subordination, despite continuing to champion policies that would eliminate black suffrage.

Washington's black residents were well aware of the changed political environment brought about by the defeat of the Confederacy. Following the District of Columbia Emancipation Act of April 16, 1862, the city's black population intended to push for full rights as Americans. Black Washingtonians, with Radical Republican congressional support, fought for the vote.[2] More than 2,500 of the city's leading black residents petitioned Congress in fall 1865, arguing for political equality on the grounds that "we are intelligent enough to be industrious, to have accumulated property, to build and sustain churches and institutions of learning. . . . We are intelligent enough to be amenable to the same laws and punishable alike with others for the infraction of said laws. . . . Without the right of suffrage we are without protection and liable to combinations of outrage."[3] Partly in response to such pleas, the Thirty-Ninth Congress opened its first session in December 1865 with submission of bills in both houses to extend the franchise to all black male D.C. residents over the age of twenty-one.

White Washingtonians overwhelmingly opposed black voting rights and in a December plebiscite voted resoundingly against it. In Washington City, whites were 6,591 against and 35 in favor, while in Georgetown, the vote was 712 against, with only one in favor. Washington mayor Richard Wallach complained that supporters of black voting rights had "little association, less sympathy, and no community of interest with the city of Washington," describing them as only temporary residents who "claim and invariably exercise the right of franchise elsewhere."[4] Radical Republicans in Congress were outraged by such views. Representative George Julian (R-Ind.) summarized the Radical perspective in a House speech: "The ballot should be given to the negroes as a matter of justice to them. It should also be done

---

[2]See Thomas R. Johnson, "Reconstruction Politics in Washington: 'An Experimental Garden for Radical Plants'," *Records of the Columbia Historical Society* 50 (1980):180–90.

[3]U.S. Senate Records, 38th Cong., District Committee, cited in James Huntington Whyte, *The Uncivil War: Washington during the Reconstruction, 1865–1878* (New York, 1958), p. 50.

[4]William Tindall, "A Sketch of Mayor Sayles J. Bowen," *Records of the Columbia Historical Society* 18 (1915):33–35.

as a matter of retributive justice to the slaveholders and rebels. . . . That contempt for the negro and scorn of free industry which constituted the mainspring of the rebellion cropped out [in Washington] during the war in every form."[5]

While he followed these matters closely, Shepherd had other, pressing concerns. He had set his sights on using his plumbing and gas fitting as well as his home construction operations to make himself a major economic force in Washington. What motivated him to pursue this goal is unknown, but it is not a stretch to think that the premature death of his father, the collapse of family finances, and the necessity for his mother to open a boardinghouse to pay the bills played an important part. It was already apparent that he was by nature an active and determined person. Shepherd demonstrated a talent for business that suited the freewheeling era after the Civil War that came to be known as the "Gilded Age." This period, given its nickname by Mark Twain and Charles Dudley Warner in their novel of the same name published in 1873, was characterized by weak or ineffectual presidents, congressional malleability, and the creation of some of the nation's largest fortunes at the time. It was a time when ambitious men (and women) would reject waiting their turn or for approval from their social betters to pursue personal ambition.

New interest in the nation's capital made it attractive to newcomers, many from the North or West, with money, ambition, or both. Shepherd was among the most consequential of this new generation of Washingtonians. Despite his financial success, the "old citizens" of Washington, whose families were not necessarily more than a generation or two older than his, closed their social ranks to him. Boston, Philadelphia, New York, even Baltimore, all had urban pedigrees going back much farther than Washington, so Shepherd considered himself an ideal candidate to thrive in the changing environment in Washington.[6]

While he concentrated on building his commercial and social base, Shepherd continued to devote time and energy to laying the groundwork for his vision of remaking Washington. He was well suited in several respects for this role: he was a staunch Republican but socially conservative, thus able

---

[5]Quoted in Constance McLaughlin Green, *The Secret City: A History of Race Relations in the Nation's Capital* (Princeton, N.J., 1967), p. 299.

[6]Kathryn Allamong Jacob, *Capital Elites: High Society in Washington, D.C. after the Civil War* (Washington, D.C., 1995), pp. 2–3.

for a while to bridge the gap between the Radical Republicans in Congress pushing for integrating blacks into the mainstream of America and the hostile but influential Washington white population who wanted nothing to do with the political equality of the races. Through his tenure on the Levy Court, Shepherd carried on, as he had during his three terms on the Washington City Common Council, experimenting with forms of local government.

Shepherd's business efforts were rewarded with success. His rapidly increasing wealth tracked closely with his growing influence in Washington affairs. He first made the list of well-to-do Washington taxpayers in 1865, with reported taxable income of $3,350 (local banker George Washington Riggs topped the list with $54,681). Shepherd was in a group of up-and-coming businessmen that included gas company president Joseph F. Brown, contractor John O. Evans, builder Moses Kelly, *Evening Star* part owner Samuel H. Kauffmann, and John H. Semmes, a prominent local political figure.[7] Among influential local Washington residents, attitudes toward Shepherd were tolerant, if not congenial, as long as he focused on business and advocated reforming local government from the sidelines.

The group of leading Washington income earners was diverse: Riggs, a banking partner of William Wilson (W. W.) Corcoran, had become wealthy from marketing bonds to fund the Mexican-American War. Moses Kelly, a contractor-builder, partnered frequently with Shepherd in building homes in the District of Columbia and was politically supportive. Samuel H. Kauffmann, originally from Ohio, where he published a small newspaper, became a part owner with Shepherd of the *Evening Star* in 1867 and also supported Shepherd's political endeavors. John Evans, a builder who was to receive many contracts from the Board of Public Works, was a trustee of Shepherd's Washington Club.[8] John Semmes, sharing a Charles County family background with Shepherd, had served as alderman on the Washington City Council during the Civil War while Shepherd was on the Common Council.[9] Only Joseph Brown, head of the gas company, was a thorn in Shepherd's side, and the two had clashed repeatedly on the City Council.

---

[7] *Evening Star* (Washington, D.C.), July 26, 1866.

[8] Wilhelmus Bogart Bryan, *A History of the National Capital from Its Foundation through the Period of the Adoption of the Organic Act*, 2 vols. (New York, 1916), 1:608, n. 2.

[9] Wilhelmus Bogart Bryan, *Forms of Local Government in the District of Columbia* (Washington, D.C., 1903), pp. 45–47.

By 1866 Shepherd's taxable income had jumped dramatically, to $29,244, placing him between Riggs, the banker ($12,296), and financier Henry D. Cooke ($69,659).[10] Shepherd's taxable income in 1867 ranked seventh among thirty-six individuals making more than $10,000 a year.[11] By 1870 Shepherd was listed as the fourth wealthiest Washingtonian, with personal property of $117,000. Only Corcoran ($228,000), A. H. Herr ($177,000), and Cooke ($152,000) exceeded him.[12] In keeping with his increasing wealth and business stature, Shepherd made sure to present an image of wealth and success. Daughter Grace captured the private man in a charming reminiscence written after her father's death:

> Father was bodily, next to Mother, the cleanest mortal I ever knew. Water, soap, toilet vinegar and bay rum! He was as finicky as a fastidious girl about linen and clothes, a dandy in fine shirts made to order, thin ribbed silk underclothes, finest linen handkerchiefs, usually embroidered with his A.R.S. . . . always, perhaps since his children vied for gifts suitable for him.
>
> No one darned skillfully enough to mend his fine lisle hose except Mother. His shirts were made to order . . . in New York and his outer clothes by Brooks, N.Y. The exception, the morning suit made in London by Poole when he took us to Europe on that most memorable trip of our lives [1895–96], and in which posterity views him today in bronze on the corner of Penn Ave. and 14th St., never fit him, as did Brooks's garments.[13]

By 1870 Shepherd was or had been intimately associated with some twenty-five different business ventures in addition to ownership of Alex. R. Shepherd and Bros., the plumbing firm that now included his younger brothers Thomas and Wilmer. Most of the business activities with which Shepherd became associated during this period were new initiatives. Not all came to fruition, let alone made money, but they show the range of his business interests, most of which contributed to the growth of Washington's economic and financial base. Combining personal capital and a progressive business outlook, Shepherd was invariably an investor and director once

---

[10] *Evening Star*, May 22, 1867.

[11] *National Intelligencer* (Washington, D.C.), May 8, 1868.

[12] Shepherd Papers, box 6, Manuscript Division, Library of Congress, Washington, D.C. (hereafter DLC). (This undated newspaper clipping, along with other clippings, is pasted between items from October 1871 and probably was dated Oct. 7, 1871.)

[13] Grace Shepherd Merchant, typed reminiscence post–1909, Shepherd Papers, DLC. The statue is now located at the northwest corner of the Wilson Building, yards from its original location.

he became involved. His business involvement included banking, railroads, shipping, insurance, and building, as well as part ownership of the *Evening Star*, which became one of Washington's leading newspapers. The *Star* adopted a probusiness policy while maintaining a conservative approach toward black aspirations and support for political changes in Washington that would reduce the franchise for blacks as well as whites.[14] The newspaper, which mirrored Shepherd's own conservatism and probusiness outlook, was a major supporter of his political and development goals. Its editor, Crosby Noyes, who had come to Washington as a young man from Maine, was friends with Shepherd and would use his influence to support Shepherd's public activities.

Shepherd's business initiatives included insurance companies such as the National Capital Life Insurance Company[15] and the Washington Insurance Company.[16] Banks included the National Safe Deposit Company of Washington,[17] National Metropolitan Bank,[18] and National Savings Bank.[19] Shepherd was also committed to improving rail access to Washington. His opposition to the monopolistic Baltimore & Ohio Railroad led him to participate in organizing several local railroads: the Metropolitan Railroad Company,[20] National Junction Railroad,[21] as well as the stillborn New York and Washington Railway Company, which proposed to construct a rail line from Washington to New York and on to Cincinnati.[22] A supporter of expanded and improved regional shipping, Shepherd was an organizer of the

---

[14] *Evening Star*, Nov. 9, 1867.

[15] With future mayor Matthew G. Emery, real estate investor Lewis Clephane, Levy Court colleague George H. Plant, and architect Thomas M. Plowman, *Evening Star*, Apr. 1, 1869.

[16] With J. W. Thompson, local businessman W. G. Metzerott, developer and Board of Public Works colleague S. P. Brown, *Evening Star* co-owner Samuel Kauffmann, and architect Henry R. Searle, *Evening Star*, Dec. 15, 1868.

[17] With banker William S. Huntington and later opponent George W. Riggs, *Evening Star*, Mar. 1, 1866.

[18] With banker John B. Blake, a later opponent, *Evening Star*, Apr. 11, 1867.

[19] With hotelier Henry W. Willard, Georgetown businessman William H. Philip, and Matthew Emery, *Evening Star*, Nov. 26, 1870.

[20] With William B. Todd, former mayor Matthew Emery, Lewis Clephane, John Semmes, J. W. Thompson, and S. P. Brown, *Evening Star*, July 27, 1864.

[21] With future governor Henry D. Cooke, banker William Huntington, and real estate developer Hallet Kilbourn, in William M. Maury, *Alexander "Boss" Shepherd and the Board of Public Works*, GW Washington Studies, no. 3 (Washington, D.C., 1975), p. 23. (Maury cites *Congressional Globe*, June 5, 1871.)

[22] *Evening Star*, Feb. 10, 1870.

New York and Washington Steamship Company, intended to strengthen shipping between the two cities.[23] Through it all, his flagship plumbing and gas fitting firm, Alex. R. Shepherd and Bros., remained the basis for his fortune, and Shepherd used his wealth to take advantage of Washington's dramatic growth in the post–Civil War period by building one thousand homes for wealthy as well as middle-class residents.[24] In 1868 Shepherd owned 182 residential lots in Washington.[25]

L'Enfant's Washington City Canal, which virtually split the capital down the middle, was to play a major role in Shepherd's later public improvements program, but at this point it became a target for privatization. Shepherd and his colleagues organized the Washington City Canal Company, and Noyes introduced a bill in the Board of Aldermen to sell the canal to a consortium of local businessmen.[26] The sale, which required congressional approval, would have required the new owners to develop a sixty-foot-wide canal in which four feet of water would be maintained at all times; the City Council declined to endorse it.[27] The project failed to gain congressional support, perhaps because the existing canal was seen as an integral part of the capital's infrastructure.

Corruption?

In light of later allegations of corruption, several of Shepherd's involvements in the postwar years were to raise questions about his colleagues', if not his own, conduct. The most notorious connection was the Maryland Freestone Mining and Manufacturing Company, better known as the Seneca Sandstone Company, organized in 1867 by Shepherd supporters, including Senator William Stewart of Nevada and General Ulysses S. Grant. Shepherd joined the board of the company in 1868, along with local investors Henry D. Cooke, Lewis Clephane, and William Huntington.[28] Seneca Sandstone was

---

[23]Ibid., Nov. 14, 1866.

[24]Joseph West Moore, *Picturesque Washington* (Providence, R.I., 1861), p. 51.

[25]District of Columbia Corporation property assessment books (O–Z), 1868, Record Group 351, National Archives and Records Administration (courtesy of Richard Hage).

[26]Henry D. Cooke, publisher William J. Murtagh, William H. Philip, and Samuel Norment.

[27]Washington, D.C., City Council, *Journal of the 65th Council*, 1869, pp. 101–4, 622.

[28]Maury, *Shepherd and the Board of Works*, pp. 88–89.

accused on numerous occasions of using political influence to gain government contracts, and as a senior officer of the Freedman's Bank, Huntington
was shown to have approved loans to the company in exchange for stock that
became worthless.[29] Shepherd was also a player in the Portland Stone
Company (Lewis Clephane, Hallet Kilbourn, publisher William Murtagh)
and the Metropolis Paving Company, which later became a center of attention over charges of a "paving ring" intended to monopolize street paving
during the territorial government. Shepherd sold his stock in Metropolis
Paving when he became a public official, although allegations of conflict of
interest were to surface later. Shepherd sent contracts in the direction of the
firm, and it was revealed that representatives of two Washington newspapers
were among the stockholders, despite having paid nothing for their shares.[30]

Another of Shepherd's business ventures that raised questions of conflict
of interest was the Vaux Anti-Freezing Pipe and Roofing Company, headed
by Ethan P. Vaux, a talented but alcoholic craftsman. Vaux obtained
contracts for roofing federal buildings in a number of cities thanks to his
friendship with Alfred B. Mullett, supervising architect of the Treasury
Department and a close associate of Shepherd. Mullett was for several years
secretary and treasurer of the Vaux firm.[31] Shepherd directed the teams of
workmen, including Vaux, who were dispatched across the country to
replace iron roofs with Vaux's patented copper roof. Mullett's control over
lucrative government contracts for local construction projects proved irre-
sistible to President Grant's inner circle, which pressured Mullett to favor
particular localities with projects.[32]

Developing Social and Cultural Connections

Shepherd's involvement in organizing social and cultural activities in
Washington was as wide and eclectic as his business ventures. Such
connections—not counting special events such as the 1871 Pennsylvania

---

[29]Whyte, *Uncivil War*, pp. 176, 255–56; Mark Summers, *The Era of Good Stealings* (New
York, 1993), p. 201.

[30]Summers, *Era of Good Stealings*, p. 141.

[31]Antoinette J. Lee, *Master Builders: A Guide to Famous American Architects* (New York,
1985), pp. 74–75; *Columbia Historical Society Newsletter* (July–Aug. 1983):18–20.

[32]Lee, *Master Builders*, p. 75.

Avenue gala, presidential inaugurations, and charity balls—numbered more than twenty, albeit not all at the same time and not all continuous. From his youthful association with the Undine Boat Club, the Metropolitan Literary Association, and the Washington Library Company, Shepherd significantly broadened the range of his involvements as he matured. He remained a longtime lay leader in the Presbyterian Church, initially at Fourth Presbyterian and later at New York Avenue Presbyterian. He was also a force in New York Avenue's outreach program, having provided a chapel for the Gurley Mission School, named after his religious mentor, Dr. Phineas Gurley, and served as chairman of the Northern Presbyterian Mission.[33]

Being an intensely social—and sociable—person, Shepherd was drawn to men's club life. Always desirous of acceptance by the Georgetown social set, Shepherd, sponsored by Lewis Clephane, joined the recently established Metropolitan Club a few months after stepping down as president of the Common Council in 1864.[34] The Metropolitan Club, then, as now, drew on Washington's governmental, military, commercial, and social elites. Riggs was the club's first treasurer, and Corcoran became president when the club resumed operations in 1872 after a five-year hiatus.[35] Uncharacteristically, there is no mention of participation by Shepherd in Metropolitan Club records from 1864 to 1867, whereas in every other activity with which he was associated, he was among the most active members. It is possible that having just lost his bid for a seat on the Washington City Board of Aldermen, Shepherd chose to take a lower profile in the Metropolitan Club.

Shepherd's charitable activities in this period included leading roles in the Provident Aid Society, formed to meet the needs of Washington's poorest residents through soup kitchens and donations of firewood; he moved on to become president of the newly formed Association for the Poor, whose officers were higher up the social ladder and included Supreme Court

---

[33]Shepherd Papers, box 5, DLC; and "Minutes of Session of the F St. Church 1819–1859 and the New York Ave. Presbyterian Church 1859–1871," p. 177.

[34]"Metropolitan Club Members, 1863–1867," Records of Metropolitan Club, Washington, D.C.

[35]John-Manuel Andriote, *The Metropolitan Club of the City of Washington* (Washington, D.C., 1997), p. 23. It is noteworthy that when the club did resume operations in 1872, Shepherd was not a member—possibly because he chose not to be, but more likely because he was not invited by its new president, W. W. Corcoran.

justice Salmon P. Chase, Riggs, Corcoran, and Cooke.[36] Shepherd's social and humanitarian work included directorships of the YMCA, the Humane Society, Columbia Hospital, the American Printing House/National University for the Blind, the Washington National Monument Society, plus a brief stint as a director of Corcoran's Oak Hill Cemetery.[37]

In 1870, the Jefferson Baseball Club, an amateur Washington team, elected Shepherd as its nonplaying president; otherwise, the youthful sportsman of the Undine Boat Club participated little in organized sports in these years. It is likely that the election had followed a generous financial contribution, based on a letter from the team secretary noting, "I am instructed also, to say the club fully appreciates your kindness."[38]

Spring 1867 brought significant personal and professional change for Shepherd when he was approved by Congress for the Levy Court, the governing body for Washington County. The county was not a corporation like Washington City and Georgetown, and the Levy Court was based on a law inherited from the original Maryland land grant to the national government. The court, composed of nine judges appointed by the president for three-year terms, governed a large, thinly populated area consisting of farms and occasional grand houses. Shepherd was one of the three judges appointed from Washington City.[39] His duties no doubt brought back memories of living on the farm next to Rock Creek Church before his father died. If, perhaps, the affairs of Washington County seemed far removed from the concerns of Washington City and Georgetown, development was pushing out into the county. The Levy Court experience was useful for Shepherd in working closely with men whom he would encounter professionally in the future, as well as providing a complement to his earlier work with the Washington City Common Council.

In 1867, when Alexander and Mary Shepherd decided to build an out-of-town home for their growing family, they returned to the vicinity of the old family farm in the county north of Rock Creek Cemetery. Consistent with his new wealth and embrace of conspicuous consumption, Shepherd

---

[36]*Evening Star*, Dec. 20, 21, 1867; Dec. 30, 1870.

[37]Ibid., Oct. 8, 16, 1866; Feb. 24, 1868; and Aug. 30, 1870; Shepherd Papers, box 5, DLC; Oak Hill Cemetery Records, Washington, D.C.

[38]Shepherd Papers, box 5, DLC.

[39]Walter Fairleigh Dodd, *The Government of the District of Columbia: A Study in Federal and Municipal Administration* (Washington, D.C., 1909), pp. 33–34.

Mount Pleasant, Shepherd family home in Charles County, Maryland. (Courtesy of Samuel Ward Collection, College of Southern Maryland)

Union troops parading on an unpaved Washington street, ca. 1865. (Courtesy of Prints and Photographs Division, Library of Congress)

Long Bridge, 1865 (from Washington side of Potomac River). (Courtesy of Prints and Photographs Division, Library of Congress)

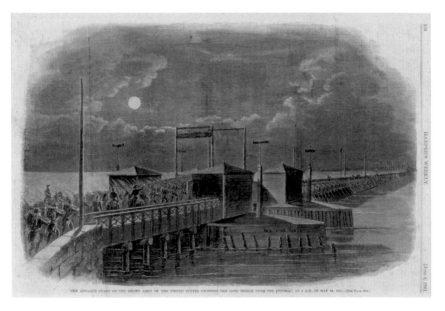

Harper's Weekly (June 8, 1861) print depicts Union troops crossing Long Bridge into Virginia in May 1861. (Courtesy of Kiplinger Library, Historical Society of Washington)

Union soldiers on the Mall (unfinished Washington Monument in background). (Courtesy of Prints and Photographs Division, Library of Congress)

Downtown Washington road scene (F Street NW) before Shepherd's paving operations. (Courtesy of Kiplinger Library, Historical Society of Washington)

Shepherd Building, Pennsylvania Avenue NW, during an 1871 parade celebrating paving of the avenue. (From the collection of Robert A. Truax)

Bleak House, Shepherd's suburban Washington residence north of Walter Reed Hospital, was built in 1868. (Courtesy of Kiplinger Library, Historical Society of Washington)

Shepherd seated portrait, 1880. (Courtesy of Kiplinger Library, Historical Society of Washington)

Shepherd residence at 1125 Tenth Street NW, where the family lived before completion of the K Street mansion. (Courtesy of Kiplinger Library, Historical Society of Washington)

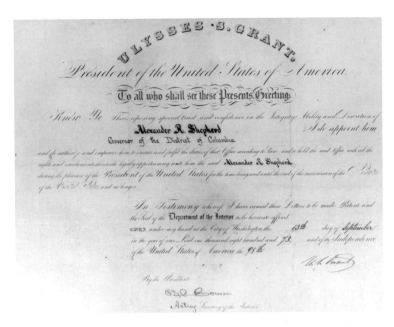

This certificate signed by President Grant appointed Shepherd governor of the District of Columbia in 1873. (Courtesy of Kiplinger Library, Historical Society of Washington)

Sayles J. Bowen, former Washington City mayor and Shepherd critic. (Courtesy of Kiplinger Library, Historical Society of Washington)

(*left*) William Wilson Corcoran, influential Washington banker and Shepherd opponent. (Courtesy of Prints and Photographs Division, Library of Congress)

(*right*) Mary Grice Shepherd, 1880. (Courtesy of Kiplinger Library, Historical Society of Washington)

built an elegant house that the family named "Bleak House" from the title of the Charles Dickens novel the children were reading at the time. A family account described the approximately 260 acres as the highest spot in the District, with old apple trees, meadows, and woodland running back to Rock Creek.[40] The Second Empire–style wooden main house was one of the show-places of this remote suburban district and considered large in its time. The estate contained a bowling alley and gymnasium, a barn and overseer's house, as well as trout ponds and a cherry orchard.[41] The formal entrance to Bleak House was a stone porter's lodge on Seventh Street Road (today Georgia Avenue) at some distance from the residence.[42] Bleak House was to hold many memories—both happy and sad—for the Shepherd family. Daughter Grace Shepherd Merchant later described Bleak House as meaning much more to the family than the mansion Shepherd later built on Farragut Square.[43]

Drive for Change in Governance

The five years before 1870 saw the unfolding of a complex political process to determine the future governance of the District, and Shepherd was well positioned to be a major player, even though he held no elected legislative position. As an ambitious, self-made businessman from a conservative social tradition, Shepherd understood the importance of remedying the dysfunc-tional nature of the District's governance if the city was ever to move beyond haphazard, piecemeal development. An advocate of giving the decision-making responsibility to those who paid the taxes, Shepherd was able to justify his campaign for a commissioner government, which had a platform of removing authority from newly enfranchised blacks and other non-landowning residents and giving it to presidentially appointed commis-sioners, who, under a conservative Republican president would be expected to favor a conservative course of action.

---

[40]Typescript, probably written by daughter Grace Shepherd Merchant, Shepherd Papers, DLC. The site is in the neighborhood currently known as Shepherd Park, immediately north of Walter Reed Army Hospital.

[41]*Evening Star*, ca. July 1916, Feb. 17, 1880; Shepherd Papers, box 4, DLC.

[42]James M. Goode, *Capital Losses: A Cultural History of Washington's Destroyed Buildings*, 2nd ed. (Washington, D.C., 2003), p. 98.

[43]Typed Reminiscences, most likely by Grace S. Merchant, Shepherd Papers, DLC.

During 1865 and 1866, blacks in Washington had in effect transformed the public spaces of the District of Columbia, strengthening new prerogatives such as access to streetcars.[44] Encouraged by Shepherd and the Board of Trade, Senator Lot Morrill (R-Maine), chairman of the Senate District Committee, introduced a bill in January 1866 calling for cancellation of the District of Columbia's corporations and replacement by three presidentially appointed commissioners.[45] Morrill argued, "The District of Columbia never was designed to be a government. It is a seat for the Government of the United States; and that is all it ever was designed to be."[46] The same day Morrill's bill was presented, Representative William Kelley, a Democrat from Pennsylvania, introduced a bill in the House of Representatives that called for giving blacks in Washington the vote. Kelley quoted from a petition submitted to Congress by a delegation of Washington blacks that said, "Without the right of suffrage we are without protection and liable to combinations of outrage."[47] Enfranchising blacks in Washington would have little meaning if elected local government was replaced by an appointed—not elected—form of government.

The Board of Trade resolution that supported the Morrill bill had the backing of important Washington civic leaders, including Riggs, Corcoran, and Cooke, and provided a focus for the charge that supporters of presidentially appointed commissioner government sought a means of denying black voting rights by taking them away from all voters. The timing of these bills provided a striking and tense contrast between the two political perspectives. However, Morrill's bill went nowhere at this session, in part because members of Congress objected to depriving Washington's voters of their suffrage and, more crucially, because Radical Republicans in Congress wanted to try out the politically important experiment of black suffrage, which would be nullified if commissioner government went into effect.[48] Legislation providing for universal adult male suffrage in Washington, D.C., was passed by Congress over President Johnson's veto in January 1867,

---

[44]Kate Masur, *An Example for All the Land: Emancipation and the Struggle over Equality in Washington, D.C.* (Chapel Hill, 2010), pp. 125–27.

[45]Whyte, *Uncivil War*, p. 52.

[46]*Congressional Globe*, 39th Cong., 1st sess., June 15, 1866, p. 3192.

[47]Whyte, *Uncivil War*, pp. 50, 52.

[48]Masur, *An Example for All the Land*, p. 294; Green, *Secret City*, p. 333; Whyte, *Uncivil War*, p. 52.

and Washington blacks, supported by Radical Republican allies, opposed having it snatched away by the imposition of government by appointed commissioners.

In February 1867 the Board of Trade petitioned Congress to repeal the existing city charters and impose presidentially appointed commissioner government on the District of Columbia.[49] Despite his conservative instincts, Shepherd avoided the bitter struggle between Radical Republicans and President Andrew Johnson over the president's determination to block equality before the law for African Americans. Johnson, in so doing, alienated moderate and conservative Republicans who might have supported him as the successor to the martyred President Lincoln.[50] Although not all Republicans agreed on black suffrage, they did come together on basic civil equality short of suffrage for blacks, thus moving what had been a radical position to a moderate one by 1866.[51] Shepherd would have been reluctantly supportive of this middle-of-the-road stance.[52] For opponents of black suffrage, it was a short step to realize that in order to block this unwelcome development, Senator Morrill's commissioner bill—endorsed by Shepherd and the Board of Trade—must succeed, even though it would cost all D.C. residents the right to vote.

During the early months of his tenure on the Levy Court, Shepherd was learning how to put this remnant of the Maryland legal system to work for his own purposes. By the end of 1867 he had turned the court into a vehicle for floating his own views on governmental reorganization in the District of Columbia. In December Shepherd offered a resolution in two parts, the first calling for consolidation of the District of Columbia into one government and the second calling for introduction of a territorial government for the District.[53] The territorial government concept, based on the congressional Ordinance of 1787 governing the Northwest Territory, ordinarily entailed an appointed governor, an elected house of representatives, and a

---

[49]Whyte, *Uncivil War*, p. 61.

[50]LaWanda Cox, "Civil Rights: The Issue of Reconstruction," in *Freedom, Racism, and Reconstruction: Collected Writings of LaWanda Cox*, ed. Donald G. Nieman (Athens, Ga., 1997), p. 99; see also Michael Les Benedict, *A Compromise of Principle: Congressional Republicans and Reconstruction, 1863–69* (New York, 1974), p. 69.

[51]Cox, "Civil Rights: The Issue of Reconstruction," p. 105.

[52]Ibid., p. 112.

[53]*Evening Star*, Dec. 2, 1867.

legislative council appointed from candidates recommended by the House of Representatives.[54]

Considering Shepherd's public advocacy on behalf of commissioner government and objection to voting rights for anyone in the District, this resolution—conveniently covered by his *Evening Star*—may have been a trial balloon in response to growing sentiment in favor of territorial government in the District of Columbia. The resolution passed unanimously. Considering how distant Washington County affairs were from most Washington and Georgetown residents, it is also possible that Shepherd thought the proposal would go unnoticed and surface only if he found it useful to raise it again in future.

Momentum for change in the District's form of government picked up early in 1868 when Senator Morrill and the Senate District Committee invited twenty leading citizens, Shepherd among them, to meet with the committee to explore a unified government for the District and to draft a bill for the purpose. Shepherd was appointed a member of the drafting committee and reported that after a long conversation the evening of January 16, Senator Morrill told him that the Senate would listen to suggestions from the taxpayers, and that the bill would be passed in a shape to give satisfaction; Morrill would "take off his coat" and go to work to ensure passage.[55]

On the heels of these exchanges, Shepherd and other supporters of governmental change convened a meeting January 17 of some one hundred prominent Washington residents at Metzerott Hall. Shepherd ally C. H. Nichols, director of the National Hospital for the Insane, was elected chair. There was sufficient difference of opinion among the participants to require two subcommittees, one to draft a bill based on the Morrill commissioner bill and the other to draft a bill for a territorial government, although the majority appeared to favor commissioner government.[56] Several participants, including Shepherd, offered slight changes in the commissioner bill, such as increasing the number of commissioners from three to five or more. More significantly, they asked the federal government to pay its

---

[54] An Ordinance for the Government of the Territory of the United States Northwest of the River Ohio (Northwest Ordinance of 1787), July 13, 1787. The act was passed by the Confederation Congress to provide a mechanism for governing federal territory prior to statehood.

[55] *National Republican* (Washington, D.C.), Jan. 13, 1868; *Evening Star*, Jan. 18, 1868.

[56] *Evening Star*, Jan. 18, 1868.

share for street improvement and its share of tax revenue. Shepherd was well aware that efforts underway within the City Council for a long-term extension of the city's charter would create an additional obstacle to the push for commissioner government. Shepherd attempted to distance District governance from black voting rights: "It might be claimed that [the commissioner bill] was a blow aimed at colored suffrage, but it could be readily shown that the objection had no validity. This bill had been carefully proposed by Senator Morrill some years ago, when colored suffrage was not a matter in question, and it was advocated now without distinction of party."[57] Despite Shepherd's assertion, Congress had excluded black voting rights from the 1866 Civil Rights Act, despite the inclusion of broad protections in the Fourteenth Amendment.[58]

Shepherd then dropped any pretense of a conciliatory attitude and spelled out how he saw charter extension proposals in the City Council. Noting that both chambers (the Board of Aldermen and the Common Council) had all but approved a twenty-year charter extension, he said that if the citizens present were to vote for harmonization of views with the City Council, it would take not twenty, but one hundred, years:

> The taxpayers of this city did not want elections of any kind, and had not wanted them for 20 years. If the people trifled with these petty little elections, the city never would come to anything. . . . We want an honest Board of Commissioners and no broken-down political demagogues. . . . A board of Commissioners of men of the right stamp could do better than any elected officials . . . in ten years the oldest inhabitants would hardly recognize the city.[59]

Shepherd added a cautionary note: "In regard to the chances for the passage of the bill, there might be some difficulty, owing to the peculiar circumstances in which we are placed," referring no doubt to congressional intention to preserve black voting rights in the District.[60]

---

[57]Ibid.

[58]Masur, *An Example for All the Land*, p. 126.

[59]*Evening Star,* Jan. 16, 1868.

[60]Ibid. Another paper recorded Shepherd's comments as follows: "(D.C. taxpayers) want to see (their money) go toward improving the streets of the city. They wanted a Board of Commissioners with a presidential head . . . to carry on their beautifying of the city, and in 20 years it would not be known by those who know it now" (*National Republican,* Jan. 18, 1868).

Black Push for Rights

The advent of black suffrage in Washington in 1867 had put social and political change in the District of Columbia on the fast track. Washington's
black residents were almost unanimously Republican, reflecting their commitment to the party of Lincoln and to the congressional Radical Republicans who had passed the emancipation and black suffrage laws for the
District. Local Republican clubs were at the heart of black political activ-
ism and were a conduit for that community's concerns about education, civil
rights, and jobs.[61] Although no blacks were elected to municipal office until
1868, voter registration in 1867 was dramatic: 9,800 whites and 8,200 blacks,
despite the fact that blacks constituted only one-third of the total population.[62] One informed estimate is that in Washington in 1868 there were four
black Republican voters for every white Republican voter, and a two-to-one
ratio in 1871.[63] An article from the *New Orleans Standard*, quoted in the black-
owned *National Era*, communicated the passion felt on this topic: "within
the last ten years . . . the great Republican Party . . . has been the chief in-
strumentality of our deliverance from an awful and cruel oppression, both
physical and mental, and we pray God to blot us out of existence whenever
we raise a hand against its life and prosperity in this or in any other country. For a colored man to repudiate the Republican Party—the party that
made him a free man and a full citizen—is the very climax of human
ingratitude."[64]

Against the backdrop of massive black Republican registration in Washington, the active role played by blacks in ward politics, and his own strong
identification with the national Republican Party, it is striking that Shepherd was largely absent from grassroots Republican politics in Washington
in 1868. He was a staunch supporter of the party, but despite extensive
coverage given by Washington newspapers to Republican ward political
meetings, Shepherd's name did not appear in a single related news story.
Speculation on this point goes in several possible directions; for example,

---

[61]Robert Harrison, "Race, Radicalism, and Reconstruction: Grassroots Republican
Politics in Washington, D.C., 1867–74," *American Nineteenth Century History* 3 (Fall
2002):74.

[62]Green, *Secret City*, p. 301.

[63]Harrison, "Race, Radicalism, and Reconstruction," p. 79.

[64]*National Era* (Washington, D.C.), Feb. 24, 1869.

Shepherd's preference was to work with small groups of influential Washing-tonians in support of mutual goals, where his impact would be felt more strongly, whereas the wards were less manageable from his perspective. On the other hand, in light of his racial views, it is at least as likely that Shep-herd simply did not want to associate with blacks in politics, regardless of their significant influence on elections. It is also possible that he considered the black vote "in the bag" for the Republicans, and given his personal in-clination and intense practicality, he may have calculated that personal en-gagement would not make a difference in the outcome.

The first racially integrated Washington municipal elections took place in 1867; the first integrated mayoral election took place in 1868, when Sayles J. Bowen was the unanimous Republican nominee and election win-ner. Born in Scipio, New York, Bowen had worked in Washington since 1845, starting as a clerk in the Treasury Department, where he was fired for circulating tracts against the expansion of slavery. He campaigned for Republican candidates in the 1856 and 1860 elections and was rewarded by President Lincoln with a series of appointments, culminating in post-master of Washington in 1863. He also served alongside Shepherd on Washington County's Levy Court.[65] Bowen's long record of support of schools for black children and integrated schools, along with his appoint-ment of blacks to responsible positions and extension of their rights to serve as witnesses and jurors in courts of law, made him a hero to the black community, although they had already let him know that they expected a fair share of contract work in street-building and other trades.[66]

Bowen also enjoyed initial support from white Republican businessmen, despite having signed the petition opposing commissioner government. While having drawn a line against the Shepherd-led business community, Bowen retained their support because at this point he was still speaking for the twin agendas of the national Republican Party: free-market economic development and civil rights for blacks. When nominated for mayor, he said, "It will be my purpose . . . to rescue the city from its present degraded posi-tion, and to make it what it should be in the eyes of the nation and the world. It will also be my aim to perfect a system of public schools in this Dis-trict that will secure to every child within its limits a good education." He

---

[65]Tindall, "Sketch of Mayor Sayles J. Bowen," pp. 26–27.
[66]Ibid., p. 28; *Evening Star*, Feb. 4, 1867, in Bryan, *History of the National Capital*, 2:562.

added later that the scant attention Congress paid to District development needs was due to congressional lack of confidence in the local government, and he promised to remedy the deficiency.[67] Reflecting growing uneasiness in Washington over attempts to remove the capital to the Midwest, one of Bowen's campaign slogans was, "A vote for Bowen is a vote to keep the capital in Washington."[68] Along with the radical *Chronicle* and the *National Republican* newspapers, the *Evening Star* also endorsed Bowen's candidacy, reflecting the probusiness orientation of its owners. The tactical alliance between Washington's radical and conservative Republicans would put Bowen over the top, albeit by a scant eighty-three-vote margin.[69] The election was marred by racial violence, and incumbent mayor Richard Wallach initially refused to acknowledge Bowen's victory because of alleged voter fraud. The newly elected mayor was forced to break open the door to his office, since outgoing Mayor Wallach refused to give him the keys.[70]

Governance problems for Bowen started immediately, with Republican loss of control of the Common Council by a margin of twelve Democrats to nine Republicans, while the Board of Aldermen was equally divided, nine to nine.[71] Two black candidates for Common Council were elected, but only four out of the seven city wards were in Republican hands, and the stalemate blocked progress on legislative issues throughout the summer.[72]

The election of 1868 reflected a political calculation by Shepherd and his business colleagues that Sayles Bowen could make good on his promises to bring about physical development of the city. Bowen's inaugural message to the City Council seemed attuned to business concerns and was cautious on the sensitive topic of racially integrated schools, calling for keeping them separate "at present," on the grounds that whites would boycott mixed schools and that blacks were also opposed.[73]

During this time Shepherd continued vigorous activity in his personal and business life. Bleak House was completed in the spring of 1868, and the Shepherds made frequent use of it to escape the heat and distractions of downtown. In June 1868, William Young Shepherd was the first child born

---

[67]*National Republican*, May 9, 1868.
[68]Green, *Secret City*, p. 312.
[69]*Journal of the 66th Council*, 1868, vol. 1, p. 7.
[70]Whyte, *Uncivil War*, pp. 67–69.
[71]Ibid., p. 67.
[72]Ibid.
[73]*Journal of the 66th Council*, 1868, vol. 1, p. 22.

at Bleak House, but he lived only a month.[74] By 1869 six children had been born to the family, of whom three died in less than a year. The four children born at Bleak House after 1869 all lived to adulthood.

Like his family, Shepherd's home-construction business was also growing. In addition to his plumbing firm's involvement in much of the capital's private construction work in this period, and besides his being a major buyer and seller of land in the District, Shepherd's impact on the home construction business can be seen in snapshots in the local press of some of the houses he built during this period. The *National Republican* reported twelve "handsome" houses he built opposite St. Aloysius Church on I Street NW, between North Capitol and First Street NW, each with fourteen rooms and made of pressed brick with marble trim,[75] and the *Evening Star* cited three "elegant" row houses plus plumbing work for nine others on East Capitol Hill (First and C Streets SE).[76]

Capital Removal

With so much invested in the District, Shepherd's fears of seeing the nation's capital moved from Washington grew in 1868. No major attempt at removal had been made in Congress since the fall of 1814, after the British had burned many of the public buildings. Nevertheless, the issue had not disappeared from the national discourse. Proposals to move the capital closer to the westward-shifting center of the country and away from proximity to the former Confederate rebels who attempted to capture Washington in 1864 gained popularity. Anxiety in Washington rose when a former Union general, Representative John A. Logan (R-Ill.), offered an incendiary resolution in Congress on June 15 that called for removal, citing the alleged "disloyalty" of D.C. residents as the main reason. He played on festering anger at the perceived pro-Confederacy attitudes of Washington residents during the Civil War, describing them as "adverse" to the authority of the

---

[74]William Tindall, "Governor Alexander R. Shepherd's Photograph," *Records of the Columbia Historical Society* 24 (1922):194; Oak Hill Cemetery Record Book and gravestone, Washington, D.C.; Shepherd Family Bible, courtesy of Alexandra Wyatt-Brown Malick.

[75]*National Republican*, Jan. 7, 1868 (an announcement the next year for sale of the land referred to seventy-two "dwellings" that had been erected in the previous twelve months, although it is not clear if Shepherd built all of them (*Evening Star*, June 15, 1869).

[76]*Evening Star*, Sept. 14, 1867.

Congress of the United States, determined to defy Congress, and in general to work against the interests of the nation. Besides these charges, Logan accused D.C. residents of "render[ing] the city undesirable as a residence, and an unsafe and unfit place for Congress to assemble." Logan cited the standard midwestern arguments for removal, including better railway access and "a populous region and a rich and highly cultivated country where obstructions to access and free communications are not interposed by the hostile legislation of neighboring States." Logan's motion to suspend the rules was defeated 67–43, with a surprising seventy-nine members not voting, but Shepherd's worst fears were in danger of being realized.[77] Logan's characterization of Washington as an unsafe and unfit third-rate city struck home.

The Washington press responded quickly and substantively to Logan's provocative charges. The *National Intelligencer* said, "Nothing more mean or monstrous has yet been conceived here," and the *Evening Star* opined that removal could not be dismissed with a wave of the hand but must be considered a contingency: "As the West increases relatively over the East in population and wealth, year by year this idea takes firmer hold in that section, and the public mind there is getting familiarized with it as an event that must happen at no distant day." Retention would require "making Washington so attractive as a place of residence, its society so congenial and agreeable, and the relations of the municipal government so much in harmony with Congress that there shall be no motive for a removal." The editorial closed, "Any form of municipal government that will take us out of the arena of politics and start the city upon the path of progress will be welcome."[78]

The challenge to Washington and its advocates, in politics as well as business, was becoming more sharply drawn. If the nation's capital were to stay where it was, whoever was chosen to lead the city in the immediate future would play a critical role. Sayles Bowen, the man to whom the lead role was given with the blessing of Shepherd and the business community, started off strong but proved unequal to the task. Bowen's failure would make Shepherd's arguments more appealing.

---

[77] *Congressional Globe*, 40th Cong., 2nd sess., June 15, 1868, p. 3174.
[78] *Evening Star,* June 15, 1868.

Chapter Four

"The Necessity for a Change in the Form of Government for This District"

Promoting Territorial Government, 1869–1870

B Y S AYLES B OWEN's second year as mayor, it was apparent that he would be unable to accomplish the dual goals of promoting rights for Washington's black residents and obtaining congressional support for the development of the city's infrastructure. A campaign to bring an international industrial exposition to Washington, intended as a counterthrust to the campaign for capital removal, provided Shepherd with a short-lived distraction. The conservative wing of the local Republican Party, with Shepherd in the lead, established the Citizens Reform Association (CRA) in early 1870, which became the spearhead in the campaign to reorganize municipal government. A tug-of-war ensued between supporters of commissioner and territorial government.

The June 1869 municipal elections in Washington raised questions about Mayor Bowen's black supporters, who attacked members of the "Colored Citizens Movement," an anti-Bowen group, and tried to prevent them from voting. In the ensuing violence, Police Chief A. C. Richards was injured by stones thrown by Bowen supporters. The police fired into the crowd, killing one person and injuring a number more; order was restored only when Bowen went to the scene. This violence confirmed the split in the black community in Washington, all of whom were Republicans but who now mirrored the white Republican divide between Bowen's Radical wing and the conservative wing led by the business community, including Alexander Shepherd. The established black community in Washington dominated black

63

society, although distinguished newcomers like Frederick Douglass; Reverend Sella Martin, a prominent minister; Dr. Alexander R. Augusta (a former Union Army surgeon); and Dr. Charles B. Purvis, a Howard University professor and surgeon at Freedman's Hospital, played important roles in strengthening black Washington's claims to acceptance by the larger community on the grounds of individual accomplishment.[1]

Election results brought a Republican sweep in the Common Council and virtually so in the Board of Aldermen, 11–3. One black was elected from each of the seven city wards, roughly proportional to their numbers in the city.[2] Excess of zeal among his supporters was to plague Bowen and was a factor in the swift drop in his popularity, contributing to the subsequent adoption of territorial government for the District of Columbia in 1871.[3] The 1869 election was closely watched elsewhere because it pointed to intraparty factionalism, and Democratic newspapers, particularly in New York, cited the violence as an inevitable result of giving black men the vote.[4]

In his second inaugural address to the City Council, Bowen for the first time as mayor called for integrated schools, having declined to do so the year before. This time he told the council, "In my judgment the time has arrived when these schools should be incorporated with our other public schools. The distinction of color is no longer recognized in our charters, nor at the ballot box. . . . It should be eliminated as soon as possible from our school system."[5] Determined to make good on Bowen's civil rights initiatives, the City Council passed a law in June requiring places of public entertainment to provide access to orderly patrons paying regular ticket prices and to allow patrons to sit anywhere regardless of color.[6] No action was taken on school integration.

---

[1]Constance McLaughlin Green, *The Secret City: A History of Race Relations in the Nation's Capital* (Princeton, N.J., 1967), pp. 97–99.

[2]James Huntington Whyte, *The Uncivil War: Washington during the Reconstruction, 1865–1878* (New York, 1958), p. 73.

[3]Ibid., pp. 72–73.

[4]Kate Masur, *An Example for All the Land: Emancipation and the Struggle over Equality in Washington, D.C.* (Chapel Hill, 2010), p. 294; Green, *Secret City*, p. 172.

[5]"Message of the Mayor to the Boards of Aldermen and Common Council of the City of Washington, D.C., by Sayles J. Bowen, Mayor, Delivered June 29, 1869," D.C. Community Archives, Collection 60, Artificial Collection, Washingtoniana Division, Martin Luther King Jr. Memorial Library (hereafter MLK Library). Integrated schools were not to come to Washington until the 1954 *Brown v. Board of Education* Supreme Court decision.

[6]Whyte, *Uncivil War*, pp. 73–74; Green, *Secret City*, p. 321.

The newly elected City Council also showed strong interest in the physical improvement of the nation's capital. Matthew G. Emery, president of the Board of Aldermen and future mayor, pointed out "the miles of streets, avenues, alleys, and footways, and gutters to be graded, graveled or paved, sewers to be constructed, bridges to be built." He also took aim at the Washington Canal, calling it "a mere cesspool or place of deposit for the debris of the city . . . wholly useless" that must be either improved for commercial benefit or removed altogether.[7] Mayor Bowen also picked up on the theme, proposing "to arch the canal and convert it into a main sewer across the city [as] doubtless the most feasible plan of disposing of this troublesome and vexatious subject. . . . In its present condition the canal is unquestionably a festering nuisance, and I trust that some action may be taken without delay looking to an abatement of this evil."[8]

Mayor Bowen's administration, closely watched by friend and foe alike, did not do well as he moved into his second year. Hoped-for congressional support for improvement and beautification of the capital failed to materialize. Bowen was able to employ a large number of blacks as laborers for grading and leveling streets, but few were paved and most only graveled. Evidence of the precarious state of Washington finances was revealed when the mayor's office furniture was repossessed because of unpaid bills for the District Asylum. A sofa and five office chairs were held hostage against the bills but eventually returned.[9] For Alexander Shepherd and his allies, underperformance by the Bowen administration—made more alarming by the unwillingness of the Radical Republican-dominated Congress to support the Radical Republican mayor of Washington—pointed to the necessity to seize the reins of power in order to insure that public improvements were made on a scale sufficient to silence the calls to remove the capital from Washington.

The pace of movement toward change in the form of governance in the nation's capital slowed somewhat in 1869, with many residents and members of Congress following Mayor Bowen's efforts to make good on his promises to advance civil rights and public improvements in Washington. On the racial front, Congress in early 1869 passed a bill proposing to merge white

[7]Washington, D.C. City Council, *Journal of the 67th Council* (Washington, D.C., 1870), 1:5–6.
[8]Mayor Bowen Address, June 29, 1869, MLK Library.
[9]*Evening Star* (Washington, D.C.), Jan. 1, 2, 1870.

and black schools in Washington, but black residents, fearful of losing what little control they had over their community and their children's lives, persuaded President Johnson to veto it. The City Council took no action.[10] Local racial relations appeared stalemated, with neither side able to persuade the other.

In spring 1869, Senator Hannibal Hamlin (R-Maine), Lincoln's vice president and now chairman of the Senate D.C. Committee, offered a bill calling for repeal of the city charters and replacement with commissioner government. The press noted that the bill was prepared at the citizens' meeting at Metzerott Hall in January, when the citizens committee had drafted two bills, one favoring commissioner government and one favoring territorial government.[11]

Relations between the conservative social power brokers in Washington and the reformers were still cordial. The spring saw a brief collaboration between Shepherd and William Wilson (W. W.) Corcoran, the legendary banker, philanthropist, and conservative Georgetown figure. The setting was Oak Hill Cemetery in Georgetown, which Corcoran established on fifteen acres of land he purchased in 1848 from a descendant of George Washington and donated to the cemetery corporation a year later. Corcoran commissioned distinguished architect James Renwick to design the iron enclosure and Gothic chapel, and it is likely that Andrew Jackson Downing, designer of the Mall in Washington, prepared the landscape design for Oak Hill.[12] Shepherd had purchased a plot in the cemetery in 1864 for his firstborn son and namesake, who died as a baby.[13] It is likely that Shepherd's decision to buy a plot in Oak Hill rather than in Rock Creek Cemetery (where his parents, other relatives, and he and his wife would be buried) reflected a desire to curry favor with Corcoran, who dominated the Washington business and social scene. To Corcoran, Shepherd was an up-and-coming Washington businessman who merited a look by the city's conservative power brokers, several of whom were also members of the cemetery board. Corcoran appointed Shepherd to the Oak Hill board of directors in 1869 for a four-month period to fill an unexpired

[10]Green, *Secret City*, pp. 319–20.

[11]*Evening Star*, Mar. 27, 1869.

[12]Oak Hill Cemetery Brochure, 1987, author's collection.

[13]Oak Hill Cemetery Records, plot 524, Georgetown, Washington, D.C. Between 1864 and 1868 a total of three Shepherd children would be buried in the family plot.

term.[14] Whether this brief personal interaction between Shepherd and Corcoran helped or hindered Shepherd's later relations with him is not clear. In any event, Shepherd was not asked to extend his director's term. After the later falling-out between the two men over public improvement plans, all Shepherd family members would be interred at Rock Creek Cemetery.[15]

Shepherd was well aware of the double jeopardy in which Washington found itself: on the one hand it suffered underdevelopment and unhealthy conditions, and on the other it suffered the constant threat of the capital's removal for the same reasons. The Common Council reflected this concern with a resolution in August calling for paving Pennsylvania Avenue and asserted that such improvement, plus construction of a new market house, cleaning out the "pestiferous" canal, deepening the Potomac River channel, and in general paving and beautifying the streets and avenues would be required to defeat the constant agitation for removal.[16]

International Industrial Exposition

Always inclined to go on the offensive, Shepherd was an enthusiastic promoter of a proposal to hold an International Industrial Exposition in Washington in 1871. Intended to showcase American industrial progress as well as—presumably—an improved Washington, the exposition would deflect removal efforts. At an organizing meeting held at the Kirkwood House hotel, Shepherd said that he was willing to give his time, influence, and money to make it a success. He added that if Congress was willing to help, it would be all the better, but the idea should go forward regardless.[17] Exercising a familiar talent for persuasion, Shepherd chartered the steamer *Keyport* for a Potomac River cruise on September 16, inviting a number of prominent Washingtonians, including General O. O. Howard and his family.[18]

---

[14]Ibid., 1869.

[15]John P. Richardson, "A Tale of Two Cemeteries," *American Cemetery* (June 2014):16–19.

[16]*Evening Star*, Aug. 10, 1869.

[17]Ibid., Sept. 11, 1869.

[18]Shepherd to Howard, Sept. 10, 1869, O. O. Howard Papers, Bowdoin College Library, Brunswick, Me.

Planning for the exposition moved forward, and a committee of fifteen was named to report an operational plan. The distinguished group, of whom Shepherd was a part, included Corcoran, naval gun designer Admiral J. A. Dahlgren, jeweler M. W. Galt, the mayors of Washington and George-town, developer Moses Kelly, former mayor J. G. Berret, and developer Hallet Kilbourn.[19] Six donors committed at the $10,000 level: Corcoran, Shepherd, and future mayor Matthew Emery were among them. President Grant was reported to have pledged $5,000. Shepherd said he was pre-pared to double his contribution in order to make the exposition a success, noting that Washington had been held up as a "national almshouse." Si-mon Wolf, D.C. recorder of deeds and a friend of Shepherd's, said that "since the subject of removing the capital had been agitated, transfers of real estate had fallen off rapidly. . . . The only way to silence the question of removing the Capital is to make the exhibition a success." General Howard supported the same theme, saying that "removal of the capital . . . could not be done while there remains the United States, and while the people of this country love the name of Washington and cherish the records of the past, it shall never be removed."[20] By the end of the meeting, the chair announced new donations of $170,000, totaling $400,000, which "with the small taxation proposed" reached an amount of $1 million.

Despite a unanimous City Council resolution endorsing the proposed International Industrial Exposition, the planners knew they must turn to Congress if the necessary funding was to be obtained. Legislation was introduced in both houses of Congress to incorporate the exposition, but Congress quickly quashed hopes for success. Senator William Stewart of Nevada, a future investor in Alexander Shepherd's new Washington, spoke plain truth in his remarks on the exposition: "The idea of inviting the world to see this town, with its want of railroads and its muddy streets, seems to me to be altogether out of the question. Let us have a city before we invite anybody to see it. . . . I hope the whole thing will be abandoned."[21] Senator Justin Morrill, also a backer of Washington and Shepherd, commented that, absent major local funding, the exposition would be bankrupt.[22]

---

[19] *Evening Star*, Sept. 28, 1869.
[20] Ibid., Nov. 25, 1869.
[21] *Congressional Globe*, 41st Cong., 2nd sess., Dec. 22, 1869, p. 304.
[22] Ibid.

Climax of Removal Campaign

It was understandable that Washington residents would be looking over their shoulders in the fall of 1869, when a convention of enthusiasts who supported planting the nation's capital in the Mississippi Valley met in St. Louis in October for a boisterous, self-congratulatory event. The argument was the same: Washington might have been centrally located in colonial America, but the Louisiana Purchase, the Mexican War, and westward expansion had redefined the country geographically, and the center was now the Mississippi Valley, in or near St. Louis, Missouri.[23] The capital should follow the admonition popularized by newspaperman Horace Greeley to "Go West, young man, and grow up with the country!" Not so often stated were less idealistic arguments against the capital remaining in Washington: vulnerability to foreign attack, as in the War of 1812, and vulnerability to treasonous neighbors, as in the Civil War. As always, the trump card was the deplorable condition of the city's streets and living conditions.

It was one thing for Washingtonians to endure the bluster and drum beating of capital removal enthusiasts, but it was another when they demanded cancellation of funding for future public buildings in Washington, scorned in the final resolution of the St. Louis convention as "a useless and wanton waste of the property of the people." Linkage of the positive (westward movement) with the negative (cancelling public funding) struck fear into Shepherd and others dedicated not only to keeping the capital where it was but also making it a place the nation could be proud of. The *Evening Star* pleaded that the $40 million investment in recently completed buildings not be given to "rats and bats." "The only present danger . . . is that this capital-removing question will be made a political question. . . . Don't put the capital 'on wheels.' "[24] Congressional approval in spring 1870 of funding for the new State, War, and Navy Building (now the Eisenhower Executive Office Building) next to the White House would demonstrate congressional intention to remain in Washington. Nonetheless, uncertainty, then as now, was the enemy of investment, and in post–Civil War Washington, one new

---

[23] *Evening Star*, Oct. 22, 1869.

[24] Ibid., Nov. 16, 1869.

building alone was not enough to persuade the residents that the capital was no longer in danger of donning wheels.

Shepherd understood the importance of presenting a dramatic, positive front to his money-making ventures. Maintaining business momentum, he completed construction of the flagship Shepherd Building in fall 1869 (at 910 Pennsylvania Avenue NW, between Ninth and Tenth Streets) as headquarters for his plumbing firm. The four-story brick building, reportedly fireproof, was the finest structure in the vicinity; a press account described it as "an edifice which will be an ornament to the avenue." The structure contained sixteen thousand square feet of space for the Shepherd plumbing establishment and upper-floor offices for rent to other businesses. Despite initial enthusiasm, it was a disturbing sign of the times that almost a year after the building's opening, there were still six unrented offices on upper floors.[25]

Push for Territorial Government

If the four years since the end of the Civil War saw skirmishing over possible change in Washington's form of governance, 1870 was the year that the battle was fully joined, with Alexander Shepherd at the center. At this juncture, Shepherd and other activists realized that there was no longer great enthusiasm for a presidentially appointed commissioner government, in large part because it would be opposed by many Washingtonians, including the entire black population, who would lose their hard-won right to vote. Conservative Washingtonians, including many white residents of Georgetown, were still content to lose the vote if it would mean that blacks would be kept from influencing elections.

Public opinion had swung to support some variant of territorial government, which would still sharply curtail the impact of the voters on government decisions. Following informal encouragement by the House District Committee, a group of Washington political activists emerged in early January 1870 to take the lead in defining the direction that governmental change in Washington should take. Recognizably in the lead was Shepherd, along with his close associates, including Hallet Kilbourn, James A.

---

[25]Ibid., Nov. 12, 1870.

Magruder, S. P. Brown, and Dr. Charles H. Nichols.[26] The movement that would be known as the Citizens Reform Association (CRA) held an organizing meeting January 12 at which there was "entire unanimity" on "the necessity for a change in the form of government for this District and a majority call for a territorial form of government, with one House or both elected by the people and a Governor appointed by the President."[27] A follow-up session was held the next day at Kilbourn's office to develop a "more efficient" form of District government, where Shepherd spoke in favor of a "modified" form of territorial government, with the upper house appointed by the president and the lower house elected, which met with general approval.[28]

Momentum for change in District governance accelerated through the early spring of 1870. Reflecting uncertainty about the preferred version of territorial government for the District, Representative Shelby Cullom (R-Ill.), chairman of the House District Committee, introduced a bill in late January calling for an appointed governor, with both branches of the legislature elected. A congressional role in providing funding for the District was not included in the draft legislation. In the Senate, only John Sherman (R-Ohio) spoke in favor of territorial government, adding that Congress ought to establish a rate of compensation for the general expenses of the District. In the House, William Niblack (D-Ind.) said that Congress should contribute in the same proportion as the value of property in the District of Columbia owned by the federal government. Only the Senate took action, passing a much-altered version of the bill.[29]

The CRA held its first public meeting at Lincoln Hall on February 2. The distinguished residents present included two strong advocates for elected officers of the proposed territorial government, General O. O. Howard and Judge George P. Fisher of the District Supreme Court. Howard also urged Congress to pay the equivalent of taxes on its share of District property. A number of blacks were present, including Frederick Douglass Jr.,

[26]Allan B. Slauson, ed., *A History of the City of Washington: Its Men and Institutions* (Washington, D.C., 1903), p. 66.

[27]*Evening Star,* Jan. 13, 1870.

[28]Ibid.

[29]Wilhelmus Bogart Bryan, *A History of the National Capital from Its Foundation through the Period of the Adoption of the Organic Act,* 2 vols. (New York, 1916), 2:575–76.

son of the distinguished civil rights activist. Only Alfred M. Green, a black assistant commissioner for Ward 4, challenged the sense of the meeting by saying that fear of Republican and black power motivated the consolidators. Green pointedly asked if the consolidators "were in favor of the extradition of the blacks from the District, whereby the Republican ranks here would be depleted."[30]

Divisions in the Black Community

At this point, prochange local activists were working hand in glove with the House District Committee, which was encouraging District of Columbia governmental reform. A meeting of concerned citizens on January 17 at the offices of S. P. Brown and Company represented blacks and whites. The whites included Shepherd and a number of his supporters; prochange blacks included the Reverend Anthony Bowen, Robert Hatton, Jerome and John Johnson, and George F. Coakley. A letter from General O. O. Howard was read, insisting that both houses and the congressional delegate must be elected by the people. Several of the blacks present opposed any measures that would restrict suffrage. Shepherd explained the thinking behind having an appointed upper house, which was "to obtain the cooperation of the federal authorities. The United States had so many interests here as to justly entitle it to representation in the local government." Shepherd said that "individually" he favored the election of all officers but was sure that Congress wouldn't permit such latitude in the District of Columbia.[31]

Black Washingtonians were divided. While some, like those who met with Shepherd and the organizers of the CRA, were willing to accept a new form of local government provided that it preserved voting rights, most were deeply troubled by what they considered a retrograde political step. Black activists, who played a major role in Republican ward politics, met early on with the reform leaders but voiced their strongest complaints in the ward clubs. Shepherd attended one such First Ward meeting, where the dominant

---

[30]*Evening Star*, Feb. 2, 3, 1870.
[31]Ibid., Jan. 18, 1870.

view was that the territorial government proposal would effectively remove the black vote. Shepherd defended himself, admitting having had "something" to do with the draft legislation but denied being its author and insisted he favored everyone being elected to office. He attempted to reassure his audience about his respect for working men by citing his own struggle upward from poverty as a boy, adding that "he wanted no office because it does not pay." Shepherd concluded, "What was wanted was a single government for the District, with powers to deal with District matters."[32] The black-owned *National Era*, edited by the Reverend Sella Martin, pulled no punches, saying that "the old fogies are opposed to negro suffrage" despite strong support from black Republican voters since 1867: "As they cannot withdraw [the suffrage], they seek to diminish, if not destroy, the opportunities for its exercise. Here is the whole secret of the recently inaugurated movement to take away our municipal government. We want no Territorial Government. It would be a useless and expensive machine, wholly inapplicable to a Territory, every foot of which can be seen from the dome of the Capitol."[33]

Mayor Bowen, who had publicly opposed replacement of the District corporation charters, which were initiated by the Shepherd group, made every effort to rally his Radical Republican supporters against the proposed changes, including hosting a dinner party at his residence January 20 for members of the House and Senate District of Columbia Committees, plus the presidents of the Washington Board of Aldermen and Common Council.[34] The gap within the local Republican Party was widening, however. The Bowen faction received strong support from a large portion of the black community, Democrats, and Georgetown residents, the latter two politically conservative but opposed to Shepherd's proposed government changes. The Shepherd faction, drawing strength from the business community and—less publicly—the Grant administration, became more vocal in charging Bowen with malfeasance and came to call for his replacement by Emery and eventually by a territorial government.[35]

---

[32] *National Republican* (Washington, D.C.), Jan. 18, 1870.
[33] Kate Masur, *An Example for All the Land: Emancipation and the Struggle over Equality in Washington, D.C.* (Chapel Hill, 2010), p. 200.
[34] *National Era* (Washington, D.C.), Jan. 27, 1870.
[35] *National Republican*, Jan. 20, 1870.

A citizens meeting of Reform Republicans at Union League Hall on January 20 was met with rowdyism by pro-Bowen forces, including a number of blacks, and was broken up by a well-organized gang of toughs.[36] The conveners retreated to a private location, where they passed a competing resolution deploring that "colored men recently freed from the thralldom of slavery should join with venal politicians to crush out free speech, and forcibly prevent the holding of a meeting by those who have been their early and steadfast friends, and who are tried and true Republicans."[37]

The CRA became a wedge dividing the black community. Just as had occurred in the debate about consolidation of the school boards, African Americans again found themselves caught between factions of the Republican Party and uncertain about the definition of party.[38] The *New Era* came out in opposition to territorial government, defending General Howard's reputation with blacks by pointing out that his support was contingent on election of all officers in such a government.[39] The article predicted the defeat of Republicanism in the District should territorial government be approved. The paper did, however, reiterate a constant theme: government of the nation's capital could succeed only if the federal government paid taxes on its holdings in the District or set aside an equivalent sum to relieve the District's financial dependence on congressional handouts.

The consolidators' determination may have been spurred by a series of editorials in the local press in February warning Washingtonians once again about the dangers inherent in the capital removal campaign. While confident that the removers would fail, the paper put its finger on the negative impact of the campaign on local investment: "when [removal talk] became frequent and apparently earnest, men of property became timid and hesitated to build liberally or invest largely in the city. And since a city depends much on its builders for its advancement and beauty, it is difficult to over-estimate how greatly Washington has suffered from the removal agitation."[40]

By the end of February, Shepherd and his group brought in the territorial government bill, which called for an appointed governor and

---

[36]Ibid.

[37]Ibid.

[38]Masur, *An Example for All the Land*, p. 309.

[39]*New Era*, Feb. 10, 1870.

[40]*Evening Star*, Feb. 2–4, 1870.

eleven–member upper house; an elected, twenty–five–member lower house; and an elected District delegate to Congress. The powers of the corporations of Georgetown and Washington City, along with the Levy Court, were to cease with the appointment of the governor and council; Congress would retain the right to annul any law passed by the local legislature.[41]

Shortly thereafter, Senator Hamlin introduced Senate Bill 594, "An Act to change the form of government of the District of Columbia."[42] This time the District of Columbia leaders appeared to have gotten the mix right. At a meeting March 7, Senator Hamlin told the group, "I introduced in the Senate a bill for the government of this District by a commission, and another bill providing a Territorial form of government for the District, neither of which met my views. Since then, another bill, the one now before us has been presented, which very nearly meets my approval."[43] The local participants in the meeting were not unanimous, however. Reverend Sella Martin, standing in for the absent Mayor Bowen, spoke against the bill, noting that he had not found a Radical Republican who identified with it: "None of those who advocated it were among those who stood by the negro."[44] Press coverage acknowledged that Mayor Bowen had been "crippled and hampered" by the constraints of the current governing system.[45]

In an effort to raise the issue above the local level, a select group of prominent Washingtonians called on President Ulysses S. Grant on January 22 to present the case for the District. Led by banker Corcoran, the group included Shepherd, Republican publisher John W. Forney, banker W. S. Huntington, former mayor James G. Berret, and other leading businessmen. Corcoran told the president that the group represented the business community "regardless of the political complications of the day" and that "the continued agitation for the removal of the capital was affecting their interests and paralyzing the development of the District." The president said that "he wished to see the seat of Government made such as to arouse the pride of the citizens of the Republic, and acceptable at least to the

[41]Ibid., Jan. 15, 1870.

[42]William Tindall, *A Standard History of the City of Washington* (Knoxville, Tenn., 1914), p. 247.

[43]*Evening Star*, Mar. 7, 1870.

[44]Ibid.

[45]Ibid.

proper consideration of the people of the Old World." At the end of the interview, Grant added that he "appreciated the disadvantages under which the citizens of the District labored, and that he would help them out to the full extent of his power."[46]

Shepherd's flexibility about the final form of restricted government suggests that he was confident that any outcome would be one in which he would be able to undertake public works development. He may have appreciated that local endorsement of territorial government might well be changed once Congress got its hands on the bill, which is what would happen, with Shepherd's active involvement and approval.

---

[46] *New York Times,* Jan. 23, 1870; Jan. 22, 1870.

Chapter Five

"A Practical Experiment"

Achieving Territorial Government, 1870–1871

B Y SPRING 1870, attitudes in Washington toward the territorial government scheme were changing. Most Washingtonians now believed that this new form of government could—and should—work. It was nearing the time when Shepherd's bold plans would meet the test of implementation.

Shepherd and other similarly minded reform advocates continued pushing for consolidated, development-friendly governance, but many in the black community saw that outcome as a grave threat to their hard-won victory in achieving the vote. Although Shepherd claimed that his objectives were efficiency and public beautification, many opponents believed that his real objective was to subvert democratic principles and dilute the influence of black voters. The split in the Washington black community continued to grow. The *New Era* summarized the problem with two editorials in the month of March. The first, published March 10, described the paper's continuing opposition to charter consolidation and territorial government, noting that "when colored men achieved for the Republican Party its first victory in this city, all the enemies of that party, all of the opponents of impartial suffrage joined hands in efforts to consolidate Washington, Georgetown, and the County in one government." The paper described the "pretended" concern by consolidators in the interests and welfare of local residents that masked hostility to the black franchise. The paper accused the consolidators of subterfuge in gaining congressional support for consolidation. On one point, however, the *New Era* agreed with the consolidators: the paper continued to insist on a congressional contribution to meeting the capital's expenses.[1]

By the end of the month, however, the *New Era* had changed its editorial position and now called for passage of the territorial government bill, citing the changes called for by the Shepherd faction in favor of election of both houses of the local legislature, and said, "The bill . . . is so far altered that it is difficult for Republicans to find fault with it. All we have ever contended for is the submission of the scheme to the vote of the people." The paper applauded congressional Republicans for appearing to support the vote and reiterated its view that without an assured federal payment to the city, real progress was probably doomed to failure.[2]

The Washington mayoral election of June 1870 served as a referendum on a number of issues, among them Radical Republicanism, Reconstruction in the District of Columbia, and the shape of the future local government. These concerns were debated in the larger context of Shepherd's Citizens Reform Association (CRA) and the momentum toward territorial government. A key question was how Washington's majority black Republican supporters would vote. Mayor Bowen's popularity was fast eroding. Municipal-funded debt had risen to $1.5 million, and the floating debt to nearly $900,000, mostly in Bowen's two years as mayor; moreover, results in the form of public improvements were meager. Whites generally blamed Bowen and his black supporters on the City Council for this situation, while blacks claimed that progress in job creation was the result of their labors, not Bowen's.[3]

Bowen was a lightning rod in racially charged Washington, particularly because of his efforts to improve the lives of local black residents. A contemporary observer credited Bowen with preparing with his own hand every law relating to black education that was enacted during his lifetime. Furthermore, Bowen backed up his commitment with his own money, paying an estimated $20,000 for black education when Washington officials refused to do so. He was the first city executive to appoint blacks to offices of public trust and honor and was influential in providing blacks the right

---

[1] *New Era* (Washington, D.C.), Mar. 19, 1870.

[2] Ibid., Mar. 31, 1870.

[3] Constance McLaughlin Green, *The Secret City: A History of Race Relations in the Nation's Capital* (Princeton, N.J., 1967), p. 327.

to serve as witnesses and jurors, as well as obtaining equal punishment under the law.[4]

The opposition Reform Republican wing made its break with Bowen official by nominating Matthew G. Emery for mayor. Emery, a New Hampshire native and master stonemason, was a successful local businessman who had laid the cornerstone for new construction at the U.S. Capitol. Shepherd and his colleagues embraced Emery as a moderate Republican who could unite the business interests of both political parties and garner the black vote. The *Evening Star* and the *National Republican* carried editorials denouncing the Bowen City Hall "Ring" for inefficiency and corruption, comparing the administration with that of the notorious New York politician William Marcy "Boss" Tweed, who would be indicted in 1871 for bilking the city of millions of dollars.[5] Bowen, realizing that his social views were being used against his reelection, became more conservative, emphasizing the right of "intelligent colored men" to vote, and rejecting the support of "ignorant masses" and "contrabands."[6]

For Shepherd, the Bowen vs. Emery election was an opportunity to advance his own views on local governance and public improvements as well as his candidacy for a seat on the Board of Aldermen, his first formal political bid since losing a race for the same seat in 1864. The setting for Shepherd's dramatic intervention was a pro-Emery political rally on May 24, 1870, at City Hall. Some three hundred leading merchants and businessmen were among the large crowd, which included many prominent blacks.[7] Shepherd, who had largely avoided ward politics for several years, was identified as the Ward 3 vice president for the Reform Republicans, a useful step considering his personal candidacy for alderman.

The rally also served to launch the Reform Republican platform, on which Shepherd had worked as a member of the Resolutions Committee, along with close collaborator Lewis Clephane and developer Albert Grant. The Reform Republican platform stated that they stood strongly behind the Fifteenth Amendment, in which "we recognize a wise and final settlement

[4]William Tindall, "A Sketch of Mayor Sayles J. Bowen," *Records of Columbia Historical Society* 19 (1915):28–29.

[5]James Huntington Whyte, *The Uncivil War: Washington during the Reconstruction, 1865–1878* (New York, 1958), pp. 84–85.

[6]*Evening Star* (Washington, D.C.), May 21, 1870.

[7]Ibid., May 25, 1870.

of the question of suffrage and foresee a more rapid progress of the nation as a result of this great act of justice." They also made an appeal to black votes: "we pledge ourselves to bestow upon the colored men of the city a due proportion of the patronage and labor of the corporation." Other planks underscored support for Emery and disdain for Bowen, whose record as mayor they ridiculed for increasing debt without demonstrating positive results in public improvements.[8]

Shepherd's speech at the rally, liberally quoted in the press, was a stinging attack on the Bowen mayoralty and an implicit statement of what Shepherd would do differently and better for the city:

> I stand here as a Republican and as a business man to denounce the present incumbent and corrupt municipal government. . . . It is my firm conviction that nine-tenths of the republicans of this city, who have any interest in its advancement, are convinced that a change in the administration of its affairs is imperatively demanded to save the republican party from disgrace and from consequent disrepute throughout the entire nation. I make this declaration for the reason that here the experiment of universal suffrage was first made, and that Sayles J. Bowen was placed in his present position as a representative man, to demonstrate that our colored citizens were capable of choosing proper men as rulers.

Shepherd went on to contrast the "wealth" of Bowen's promises with the "poverty" of results dealing with schools, streets, the Center Market, the canal, the labor contract system, the jail, and the railroads. He quoted an unnamed Union general—almost certainly O. O. Howard—as telling him, "You cannot do any harm; any change that you make will be for the better." The speech was warmly received.[9]

Senate Passes a Territorial Government Bill

Reflecting popular pressure to expand political opportunity in Washington, a few days later the full Senate passed a version of the territorial government bill that closely paralleled changes proposed by the CRA, establishing a

---

[8]Ibid.
[9]Ibid.

government with an elected governor and both houses of the legislature, along with a nonvoting delegate to Congress. The bill called for approval by District of Columbia residents before enactment; it also included a provision for a proportionate federal payment to the District as its share of expenses. However, the House tabled a similar bill by Representative Cullom (R-Ill.) and took no action until January 1871.[10] What actions Shepherd took behind the scenes between May 1870 and January 1871 are unclear. He had staked out public positions on the bill, but it is conceivable that he lobbied Congress to pass legislation for territorial government that would win over opponents of charter consolidation by calling for an elected government. Nonetheless, he may have intended to undermine the election portion through behind-the-scenes congressional changes. If this was the case, people who endorsed territorial government would be lulled into acquiescence and less able to protest when the final bill, weighted in favor of appointed authorities and minimizing the franchise of the District of Columbia, came into force. This, however, is speculation, even though it is consistent with Shepherd's personal views.

Matthew Emery, with the backing of Shepherd and the business community, waged a vigorous campaign against Bowen, accusing him of emptying the treasury, cashing worthless checks drawn on Jay Cooke and Company, heavily discounting city indebtedness, and triggering lawsuits against Washington for unpaid obligations. When the results were in, Emery had crushed Bowen by 10,096 to 6,877 votes, and Shepherd rode back into local politics with a seat on the Board of Aldermen from Ward 3.[11] Although Emery carried every ward, the Republican-dominated Washington City Council was to suffer short-term paralysis as a result of the Bowen-Emery conflict, since both houses of the local government stood by Bowen and his attempts to block both those who favored consolidation and those who supported a territorial form of government. Although falling well short of expectations, the public improvements executed during Bowen's administration were the inspiration and the object lesson that led to the comprehensive improvements system of the Board of Public Works, for

---

[10]Ibid., May 28, 1870; Green, *Secret City*, pp. 335–36.
[11]Whyte, *Uncivil War*, p. 88; *National Republican* (Washington, D.C.), June 4, 1870; *Evening Star*, June 7, 1870.

which Shepherd customarily receives credit. Bowen was responsible for early efforts in street paving in Washington, including a durable stretch of coal-tar concrete pavement laid on Vermont Avenue NW, in front of Corcoran's Arlington Hotel. Bowen had adopted a uniform system of numbering homes in Washington and, much more important, had looked toward a general sewage system. He also was instrumental in Congress passing a bill in April 1870 that created Washington's "parking" (i.e., planting) system, which permitted narrowing of the capital's wide avenues and streets by placing plantings and service roads on each side. One assessment of Bowen's improvements faulted them for lacking a coordinated plan for "methodical participation of the general government in the expense or management of those public works upon which the appearance, safety, and comfort of the Seat of Government depended."[12] Nonetheless, Bowen was able to provide short-term employment to thousands of laborers, black as well as white, who graded and graveled miles of streets despite opposition to the mayor's plans from the City Council.[13]

Emery's Intentions

After his June 1870 election, Emery left no doubt in Washingtonians' minds about the focus of his administration. In his inaugural address he said, "The great questions of universal freedom and universal suffrage have been settled by the voice of the nation. It is our duty to see that, so far as our power extends, the national voice is obeyed and the Constitution enforced. Further than this, we feel that these questions no longer concern us, and we are glad to be permitted to dismiss them and turn our attention to matters of more immediate local interest."[14] It was clear to Shepherd and his colleagues that, with the mayor's support, Washington's emphasis would now be on local issues such as public improvements, sidestepping the wrenching problems of race and social justice.

The debt accumulated by Mayor Bowen was the first major issue addressed by the Emery administration, since the floating debt had almost

---

[12]Tindall, "Sketch of Mayor Sayles J. Bowen," p. 41.

[13]Kate Masur, *An Example for All the Land: Emancipation and the Struggle over Equality in Washington, D.C.* (Chapel Hill, 2010), p. 154.

[14]*Evening Star*, June 13, 1870.

doubled in the previous two years to nearly a million dollars.[15] One of Shepherd's first actions as a new alderman was a resolution calling for an outside commission "to ascertain the entire amount of indebtedness of the Corporation of Washington [i.e., Washington City] to the first of June 1870."[16] Mayor Emery, Shepherd, and the Washington Corporation Counsel followed up with the Senate District Committee on remedial measures. Shepherd proposed establishment of separate Washington auditor and comptroller positions, the auditor to examine and certify all claims against the corporation, the latter to maintain records of all claims and disbursements. No payments would be made without approval of the comptroller and the mayor's signature. When Congress passed these measures in short order, the Washington press singled out Shepherd for praise, noting that they established a system of controls never before seen in Washington, offering "additional security in our financial transactions."[17] In light of the managerial chaos that descended on Shepherd's public improvements program in 1873–74, it is noteworthy that his early initiatives in support of sound fiscal and monetary management were the right ones. Shepherd also called for issuance of bonds not to exceed $600,000, to be used to pay off old debts of the city.[18] The City Council approved a Shepherd-proposed measure to allow the mayor to "anticipate" revenue of up to $150,000 against future taxes, the amount of the loan the mayor had sought from Washington banks.[19] Had Shepherd the development czar followed the prescriptions of Shepherd the legislator, the benefits to the nation's capital would have been greater and the confusion less.

Early sessions of the Board of Aldermen confirmed the split between a pro-Bowen majority of eight and a pro-Emery minority of five, including Shepherd. This divide weakened the ability of the board to pass legislation and no doubt strengthened Shepherd's determination to minimize the number of elected positions proposed in the territorial government legislation under consideration in Congress. The stalemate on the Board of Aldermen lasted into the fall, with Shepherd usually in the minority and becoming

[15]*Evening Star*, quoting reliable sources on the Senate District Committee, July 13, 1870. The mayoral finance committee looking into the issue later confirmed these numbers (*Evening Star*, July 19, 1870.)

[16]*National Republican*, June 14, 1870; June 13, 1870.

[17]Ibid., July 12, 1870.

[18]*Evening Star*, June 24, 1870.

[19]*National Republican*, June 28, 1870; *Evening Star*, June 28, 1870.

more frustrated all the time. He accused the majority of persistently re-
fusing to act on important measures, saying he had come to do business but
not to filibuster for hours over a handful of nominations. He observed bitterly that "it would be better that there was not an office-holder in the city."[20]

Besides being fully engaged with political and business affairs, in the fall
the Shepherds sold their "elegant" townhouse at 1125 Tenth Street NW for
$25,000 and moved to a larger one on Connecticut Avenue at L Street NW.[21]
By now the Shepherds were the proud parents of three daughters, Mary
(born 1862), Susan (born 1865), and Grace (born 1869).

On the business front, a major commercial project in which Shepherd
became involved was replacement of the old Center Market, located immediately north of the Washington Canal (now Constitution Avenue NW)
between Eighth and Ninth Streets NW and on the current site of the National Archives. A public market had existed in the same location since
1802, and by the end of the Civil War the site consisted of rows of old market sheds crowded along the south side of Pennsylvania Avenue. A vista of
low, patched roofs straggled back from the avenue to the canal, giving the
area a dilapidated and unsightly appearance.[22] In May 1870 Congress—
likely with Shepherd's behind-the-scenes influence—authorized a private
company charter to establish a new Center Market.[23] Shepherd was elected
as one of thirteen company directors; Henry D. Cooke was president. The
distinguished architect Adolf Cluss was engaged to draw up plans for the
new structure.[24] In December a suspicious fire broke out in the old market, spreading so quickly that the entire structure was consumed in two
hours. Shepherd and the directors of the new company, alarmed by allegations that the fire had been set to speed removal of the old market, offered
a $1,000 reward, followed by a $5,000 reward from stall owners, for information about a suspected arsonist, but information emerged to show that
the source of the fire was most likely a fruit dealer's light and a charcoal fire
fueled by a burst gas pipe.[25]

---

[20]*Evening Star*, Oct. 11, 1870.

[21]Ibid., Oct. 31, 1870; *Boyd's Directory of Washington, Georgetown, and Alexandria*, 1870.

[22]Washington Topham, "Centre Market and Vicinity," *Records of the Columbia Historical Society* 26 (1924):76.

[23]Ibid., p. 70.

[24]*Evening Star*, Nov. 5, 1870; Topham, "Centre Market and Vicinity," pp. 70–71.

[25]*Evening Star*, Dec. 19, 20, 1870; Topham, "Centre Market and Vicinity," p. 62.

The new Center Market was to figure later in an eyebrow-raising deal that reduced its required annual rent of $25,000, to support the needs of Washington's poorest citizens, to $7,500, with little to show for it. The crux of the matter was a congressional payment of $75,000 to the city for construction of a new city hall in exchange for the reduced market rent, but the promised city hall was never built, while the lowered rent remained. Other than $5,000 set aside for construction, the board put the balance of the city money to work for municipal improvements by the stratagem of depositing $80,000 worth of sewer certificates (then worth about fifty cents on the dollar) in the bank against the cash. The Board of Public Works treasurer, James Magruder, later testified to a congressional investigation that the board used the money "because it deemed it better to pay its debts to contractors with it, than to use for that purpose the sewer certificates which would bear eight per centum interest."[26]

At the end of 1870 Shepherd would vote with the majority of the Board of Aldermen in rejecting an amendment to a proposed joint resolution urging Congress to pass a law establishing "a general school system," by which it was assumed to mean desegregating the city's public schools.[27] Shortly thereafter, however, Shepherd joined the majority of the board in approving creation of a single board of trustees for black and white students in the capital. At least the management of the system, if not the members of it, would be unified.[28]

The House Responds

On January 20, 1871, the House passed its version of the territorial government bill, substantially similar to Senator Hamlin's S. 594 of 1870—based on the CRA draft—but with important differences: (1) the governor and the upper house of the legislature would be appointed by the president, (2) congressional financial aid to the District of Columbia would be based on the

---

[26]Wilhelmus Bogart Bryan, *A History of the National Capital from Its Foundation through the Period of the Adoption of the Organic Act*, 2 vols. (New York, 1916), 2:597–98; William Tindall, *A Standard History of the City of Washington* (Knoxville, Tenn., 1914), pp. 255–57.

[27]*Journal of the 68th Council of the City of Washington, 1870–1871*, 1871, vol. 1, p. 484. Sewer certificates were a later, desperate Board of Public Works initiative to collect funds for public improvements.

[28]Ibid., p. 506.

assessed value of U.S. property within the District of Columbia at prevailing rates, and (3) a Board of Public Works was to be created.[29] Passage of the bill was smoothed and encouraged by sumptuous dinners and at least one steamboat excursion down the Potomac River—some of which were hosted by Shepherd—intended to woo members of the House.[30]

Countering demands for election of the territorial governor, House District Committee chairman Burton Cook said that only an appointed governor would be able to protect federal government interests in the District and to offset the influence of government clerks from out of state and "a lot of other people who had been thrown here by recent events, during and after the war."[31] Cook acknowledged that language in the House bill calling for creation of a Board of Public Works was a new departure, as no previous legislation or even draft legislation had had such a feature. Because the board was to become Shepherd's vehicle for driving the public improvements process during the life of the territorial government, one must assume that he had a hand in developing the concept and perhaps even the language, although no formal record of his role has emerged.

Once debate shifted to the Senate, Senator William Stewart (R-Nev.) observed, a propos of the dominance of appointed officials, "The District of Columbia should not be entirely under the control of the people who reside here. The government of the United States has so much property here that it is right and proper to allow the President to appoint the Governor, who could have control of the government property to some extent." Language calling for a congressional contribution to D.C. maintenance did not survive the Senate or the reconciling conference committee and was absent from the bill signed into law by President Grant on February 21, 1871.

Territorial Government Established

Implementation of legislation creating the Territory of the District of Columbia was the most dramatic realignment of the system of governance

---

[29]Franklin T. Howe, "Board of Public Works," *Records of Columbia Historical Society* 3 (1900):259, 270.

[30]William Tindall, "A Sketch of Alexander Robey Shepherd," *Records of the Columbia Historical Society* 14 (1911):54.

[31]*Evening Star,* Jan. 20, 1871.

of the nation's capital since the original commissioner form of government gave way to an appointed mayor of Washington and elected bicameral legislature in 1802.[32] The corporate charters of Washington City and Georgetown were cancelled, along with Washington County's Levy Court, and the District of Columbia became a single political jurisdiction for the first time in its history. The consequences of this change were immense, since legislation would now apply throughout the sixty-plus square miles that remained of the original ten-mile square after retrocession of Alexandria to Virginia in 1847. (Even though the territorial government would last only three years, consolidation of the capital's three separate political jurisdictions would remain as an important step forward for Washington.)

In light of the creative roles to which Shepherd would put the Board of Public Works, the wording of Section 37 (Board of Public Works) of the territorial government bill is significant. It spelled out the board's mandate to make regulations to keep in repair the streets, avenues, alleys, and sewers of the city. The board was authorized to disburse all monies appropriated or collected from property holders and to assess on neighboring residents a reasonable proportion of the cost of the improvement, not exceeding one-third of the cost, to be collected along with other taxes.[33] These broad powers, which would be expanded by Shepherd and his board colleagues, were tempered by caveats that became the subject of bitter debate: "The Board shall have no power to make contracts to bind said District to the payment of money except in pursuance of appropriations made by law, and not until such appropriations have been made."[34] By deriving its authority from the overall territorial government legislation, the Board of Public Works was not a *subordinate* but rather a *coordinate* body, and it became for all intents and purposes the government of the District, dwarfing the other branches such as the Board of Health. The governor was an ex officio member of the Board of Public Works, which was not accountable to the local legislature, and its work was of a magnitude never before attempted by any similar body in so short a space of time.[35]

Opposition to change in District governance came from several sectors: blacks upset about virtual removal of the recent, hard-won right to vote;

---

[32]Tindall, *Standard History of the City of Washington*, p. 225.
[33]Text in *National Republican*, Mar. 6, 1871.
[34]Ibid.
[35]Howe, "Board of Public Works," pp. 271–72.

Radical Republicans angry about takeover of local Republican influence by Shepherd and the reformers; and conservative, often Democratic, elements centered in Georgetown who were to demonstrate their ability to harass and delay Board of Public Works' progress in making over the city. Dr. Charles Purvis, a distinguished black physician, chaired a public meeting in early January to express concern that the territorial government would reduce the laboring classes to serfdom and that large property owners would be the principal beneficiaries. Former mayor Emery was critical of the law on the grounds that the voting public would have no voice in either the Board of Public Works or the Legislative Council (the appointed upper house).[36] At a public meeting later in the month, Reverend Anthony Bowen, a black community leader, said he had no other objection to the bill than seeing men advocating its adoption who had no sympathy with Washington's black residents. At the same meeting, Albert Grant, who was developing real estate on Capitol Hill and had been a colleague of Shepherd's in the CRA in 1870, now turned on Shepherd, saying that the law's advocates were really Democrats rather than the Republicans they professed to be. He named Shepherd, Hallet Kilbourn, and R. M. Hall.[37]

Before the new government was installed June 1, thereby cancelling the charters governing different sections of the city, both chambers of the Washington City Council continued to criticize elements of the new legislation. A conservative alderman colleague of Shepherd's, William Moore (not Shepherd's business associate of the same name), said that if Board of Public Works members were appointed, they "would have the power to oppress the people without being accountable to them." Moore was successful in having several resolutions passed, including (1) the majority of Board of Public Works members were to be elected, (2) all improvement monies would be put in the public treasury, and (3) the Board of Public Works would be prohibited from enacting ordinances, assessing taxes, or receiving/disbursing funds.[38] The Board of Aldermen was prescient in identifying and objecting to the practices of the Board of Public Works that were to create resentment in future. The Common Council also weighed in, complaining of "little or no time" for District residents to consider the new legislation.[39] Because of

---

[36] *Evening Star,* Jan. 13, 1871, quoted in Whyte, *Uncivil War,* pp. 103–4.
[37] *Evening Star,* Jan. 25, 1871.
[38] *Evening Star,* January 24, 1871; *68th Council Journal,* vol. 2, pp. 565–67.
[39] *68th Council Journal,* vol. 2, pp. 573–75.

congressional suzerainty in the District of Columbia, however, these caveats were not implemented, and objections went unheeded. The politically and socially conservative forces that were to coalesce into later, more determined opposition to Shepherd and his improvements program were initially cautious about the legislation creating the territorial government. The *Daily Patriot*, representing the city's most conservative citizens, observed that the taxpayers were behind the new form of government and urged that it be given a fair trial, "trusting that the defects . . . will hereafter so manifest themselves as to work their own cure under a more discreet Congress, and after a practical experiment."[40]

By coincidence, Senate passage of the territorial government bill occurred the same day—February 21—as a carnival under Shepherd's leadership to celebrate new wooden paving on Pennsylvania Avenue NW. Street paving in the United States was in its infancy, and Shepherd and his Board of Public Works colleagues were to make numerous trips during the next two years to Philadelphia, New York, and Boston to study other cities' experiences with new paving techniques. Wooden paving, using blocks impregnated with creosote or other water- and insect-resistant materials, was on trial in more than one city, and in fall 1870 Mayor Emery's administration opened bids for four different types of wooden paving to replace the Pennsylvania Avenue cobblestones, which were noisy, hard on horses' hoofs, and uncomfortable for carriages.[41] Installation of wooden paving was underway by November, and a number of local dignitaries attended a demonstration, complete with a buffet and drinks, for a section contracted to Lewis Clephane, Shepherd's friend and collaborator, who was president of the Metropolitan Paving Company.[42]

The carnival was a success, helped by a $40,000 contribution from the local business community. The avenue from the Capitol to the Treasury Building at Fifteenth Street was decorated with flags and bunting, railroads offered half-price tickets to out-of-town visitors, and the schools were let out. More than ten thousand tourists attended. The Marine Band played all day, the parade was led by Mayor Emery and Shepherd, and a gala ball that

---

[40]Testimony of former D.C. mayor J. G. Berret, *1872 Investigation*, p. 320; *Daily Patriot*, (Washington, D.C.), Jan. 28, 1871; Whyte, *Uncivil War*, p. 98.

[41]*Evening Star*, Oct. 5, 1870.

[42]Ibid., Nov. 2, 1870. Shepherd, a director of the firm, resigned soon after being appointed to the Board of Public Works by President Grant.

evening at the Corcoran Art Gallery (Seventeenth Street and Pennsylvania Avenue NW) to raise money for the long-stalled Washington Monument was pronounced "the most magnificent . . . ever given in the capital."[43]

Who Will be Governor?

Once the territorial government legislation was passed, speculation turned to the impending presidential appointments, especially for governor of the new territory. Not only would the governor wield great authority over the District of Columbia; he would also be the president's personal representative. Blacks and Radical Republicans favored former mayor Bowen and sent a delegation from the City Council and others to visit President Grant February 23 on Bowen's behalf. Grant refused to commit himself, saying only that "a good man" would be appointed.[44]

Trying to derail a major role for Shepherd, Bowen wrote letters to General O. O. Howard, president of Howard University, bitterly protesting Howard's public support for Shepherd's candidacy. In addition, Bowen complained that he had been disparaged by Howard to President Grant in favor of Shepherd.[45] Having long been a champion of equal rights for Washington blacks, Bowen reminded Howard of his record and that Shepherd, in contrast, had been an "unrelenting and outspoken opponent of the education of colored children and has opposed the regular Republican Party in Washington."[46] Howard invited Shepherd's comments on allegations by Washington's black elite that Shepherd was "uniformly opposed to their interests" and to integrated public schools. Shepherd, who was hoping to become governor, knew that his response to Howard would be publicized. In order to obtain the nomination from President Grant, Shepherd also knew that he needed the general's support. Citing his support for the Republican Party and for the "elevation" of blacks, Shepherd replied that he

---

[43]Whyte, *Uncivil War*, pp. 105–6.

[44]*Evening Star*, Feb. 23, 1871.

[45]Bowen to Howard, Feb. 24 and 25, 1871, in O. O. Howard Papers, Bowdoin College Library, Brunswick, Me. (hereafter BCL).

[46]Sayles J. Bowen to General O. O. Howard, Feb. 25 and Mar. 1, 1871, in O. O. Howard Papers, BCL. The Bowen Papers in the Library of Congress, while fragmentary, reveal a judgmental and unforgiving personality.

was a friend of the black race and concluded with the statement that he supported a "unified" school system and opposed any discrimination in the form of race or color in the schools or elsewhere.[47] Shepherd had previously endorsed a resolution for a unified Board of Trustees for black and white schools, but he never supported integrated classes.

A Philadelphia paper with access to inside information in Washington identified "the most prominent candidates at present" as former mayors Matthew G. Emery and Sayles J. Bowen, Collector of the Port of Georgetown J. A. Magruder, and Shepherd.[48] The *Evening Star* kept a low profile, urging only that the governor be from Washington.[49] Shepherd took the high road, saying in a letter to banker Henry Cooke, "I understand that the President is embarrassed as to the appointment of Governor under the new bill. Will you do me the favor to say to Genl. Grant that if his choice is between Mr. Emery and myself I shall withdraw in favor of Mr. E., recognizing his magnanimity in supporting the bill which has virtually legislated him out of office."[50]

It was a surprise to most Washingtonians when President Grant announced the appointment of Henry D. Cooke as governor on February 27. Cooke was a compromise candidate who had an inside track due to the friendship between Grant and Henry's older brother Jay Cooke, the banking impresario who had marketed many of the bonds that financed the Civil War.[51] Henry Cooke, a resident of Georgetown, was best known as Washington representative for his brother's banking interests. He had also sold U.S. government bonds in Europe to support the Union cause in the Civil War. He was personable and generous and had a wide circle of friends, including Shepherd.[52] As far as Jay Cooke was concerned, Henry's principal job in Washington was to look after the family business rather than to direct the

[47]O. O. Howard to Shepherd, Feb. 24, 1871, and response Feb. 25, 1871, in O. O. Howard Papers, BCL.

[48]*Philadelphia Public Ledger*, Feb. 24, 1871, cited in *The Papers of Ulysses S. Grant*, ed. John Y. Simon, 32 vols. (Carbondale, Ill., 1967–2012), 21:193.

[49]*Evening Star*, Feb. 14, 1871.

[50]Letters of Application and Recommendation, Nov. 1, 1870–May 31, 1871, Record Group 59, National Archives and Records Administration, Washington, D.C., cited in *Papers of Ulysses S. Grant*, 21:193.

[51]Tindall, "Sketch of Alexander Robey Shepherd," p. 54.

[52]Tindall, *Standard History of the City of Washington*, pp. 249–50.

affairs of the territorial government. A letter from Jay to Henry in spring 1873 scolded Henry for having allowed himself to become too involved and urged him to resign as quickly as possible.[53]

Board of Public Works Named

It is unknown if a prior understanding existed between Grant and Shepherd regarding Cooke's appointment. Shepherd may have been satisfied with his expected position as one of four presidential appointees to the Board of Public Works, which had already been defined in the territorial government legislation as the likely powerhouse in the new government. As governor, Cooke was ex officio president of the Board of Public Works, and he knew, liked, and trusted Shepherd, so Shepherd's subsequent board ascendancy, first to vice president and then to executive vice president, would not have been unwelcome. Shepherd's elevation appears to have resulted from decisions within the five-man membership of the board and was, no doubt, steered by him in order to put the reins in his own hands. In any event, Henry Cooke appeared happy to let Shepherd take the lead in the Board of Public Works.

Henry Cooke was a conservative Republican unlikely to disappoint the president, and Grant's nomination of the four appointed members of the Board of Public Works on March 2—which included no Radical Republicans or Democrats—confirmed his intention to keep leadership of the territorial government in "reliable" hands.[54] In addition to Shepherd, the nominees were Alfred B. Mullett, the English-born supervising architect of the Treasury and Shepherd's business partner; S. P. Brown, a former colleague of Shepherd's on the Levy Court and developer of the Mount Pleasant area north of Boundary Street (Florida Avenue); and James A. Magruder, a former army engineer and customs agent.[55] Restriction of appointments to the Board of Public Works to the conservative, business-oriented

---

[53]Jay Cooke to Henry Cooke, Apr. 1, 1873, in Ellis Paxton Oberholtzer, *Jay Cooke: Financier of the Civil War*, 2 vols. (New York, 1968), 2:417.

[54]*Senate Executive Journal*, 41st Cong., 3rd sess., Mar. 2 and 3, 1871, pp. 681–82, 685.

[55]Antoinette J. Lee, *Architects to the Nation: The Rise and Decline of the Supervising Architect's Office* (New York, 2002), pp. 73–110; Alan Lessoff, *The Nation and Its City: Politics, "Corruption," and Progress in Washington, D.C., 1861–1902* (Baltimore, 1994), p. 59.

side of the Republican Party sent an unmistakable message to Radical Republicans as well as to Democrats that their views would not be represented on the all-important planning body.

After Shepherd's appointment to the Board of Public Works, he and his wife took a long-overdue vacation along St. John's River in northern Florida, returning to Washington on March 20 ready to do battle in shaping the political environment in which the Board of Public Works would maneuver. Despite many public statements attributed to him during his time in the limelight in Washington, Shepherd left only one personal letter in which he speaks candidly about political strategy.[56] This letter was written while on this vacation to his close friend and political associate George Gideon, whom he addressed as "Uncle George." The subject was organizing for upcoming elections for the territorial legislature and the elected District delegate to Congress. Shepherd's comments in this letter reflect his political acumen and the confidence that he had the ability to bring about intended results:

> You ask who shall we run for Congress. I am not certain in this point yet and do not think we need to be in a hurry in determining. There are a great many considerations to be taken into account when we make up a ticket. I hope Cooke will not issue his proclamation or announce the [twenty-two voting] districts before the 1st prox. [April 1] as it will keep things all in a muddle for nearly 60 days when a short quick canvass will be to our advantage and be far less costly. Cooke I hope realizes that the formation of a proper assembly is vital to the success of his administration as the Board of Public Works needs a wide margin in making such a showing of improvements as will secure the confidence of Congress and the people. . . . I do hope you will perfect your organization silently putting a good worker or more in each district and making a sure thing of it. We must carry the city at all hazards for the Republican Party and see that we put in a clean working majority for the new Govt.[57]

Political opposition to the new government and to the Board of Public Works picked up steam once the major appointments (governor, Board of

---

[56]The Shepherd Papers in the Library of Congress, in which the above letter appears, seem to have been edited by family members sensitive about Shepherd's reputation and determined to put his best foot forward. The family's move to Mexico in 1880 and the Mexican Revolution no doubt resulted in the loss of additional documents.

[57]Shepherd to George S. Gideon, Mar. 11, 1871, Shepherd Papers, box 5, Manuscript Division, Library of Congress, Washington, D.C.

Public Works, and Legislative Council) were made. Although not working closely together, an informal coalition of Democrats, conservative landowners, and blacks from that divided community made its views heard immediately. Opponents favored repeal of the territorial government bill as something "forced upon us without our consent."[58] An early manifestation of this opposition was a public meeting held on March 9 led by Water Commissioner John H. Crane, who was to write pamphlets bitterly critical of Shepherd and would serve as a counsel to the "memorialists" who brought about the 1872 congressional investigation of District affairs. Much of the criticism of Shepherd reflected concern over his real estate investments as well as his intention to use public debt to obtain improvement results not achievable by real estate taxes alone. Crane spoke derisively of the "potent arguments of champagne and oysters" made by Shepherd and his allies at well-known restaurants such as Welker's and Wormley's to woo members of both congressional District committees. Crane noted that the Board of Public Works members were from the northwestern section of the District of Columbia, including Georgetown.[59] Shepherd's reported influence over Governor Cooke was captured in a riddle appearing in William Corcoran's newspaper, the *Daily Patriot*: "Why is the new governor like a gentle lamb? Because he is led by A. Shepherd."[60]

The citywide elections April 20 brought no surprises. Republican candidate and Shepherd ally Norton Chipman, a Union officer who had prosecuted Henry Wirz, commander of the notorious Andersonville Civil War prison camp, easily defeated his Democratic opponent, Richard Merrick, for District delegate to Congress. The elected House of Delegates contained fifteen Republicans, including two blacks, and seven Democrats. Three blacks were appointed by President Grant to the Legislative Council, including Frederick Douglass.[61]

The building blocks for action were now in place, and Shepherd wasted no time getting started. The D.C. Supreme Court ruled in favor of the Board of Public Works by cancelling paving contracts signed by Mayor Emery in

---

[58] *Evening Star*, Mar. 9, 1871.

[59] Ibid., Mar. 10, 1871.

[60] *Daily Patriot*, May 9, 1871.

[61] Tindall, *Standard History of the City of Washington*, p. 251; *Evening Star*, Apr. 20, 1871; Ada G. Piper, "Blacks in the Territorial Government," M.A. thesis, Howard University, 1944, p. 102, Moorland-Spingarn Collection, Howard University Library.

the waning weeks of his administration. The new governor and the board moved into offices at the northwest corner of Seventeenth Street and Pennsylvania Avenue NW, and, at an early meeting, Shepherd was chosen vice president of the Board of Public Works.[62] Shepherd had been thinking about public improvements to the District of Columbia since at least 1863. Now the deck was clear for setting the plan in motion.

[62]Tindall, *Standard History of the City of Washington*, p. 251; *Daily Patriot*, May 15, 1871.

Chapter Six

"Improvements Must Go On"

The Board of Public Works, 1871

J UNE 1, 1871, WAS the long-awaited—and to some the dreaded—day
when the territorial government officially came into existence. The
change in governance was the most dramatic since the establishment of
the nation's capital, and no one knew quite what to expect. Alexander
Shepherd did know, however, and he set about to show what he had in
mind.

The Board of Public Works was fast off the mark. It forwarded a preliminary report on its intentions to the territorial legislature on May 13, two
days before the legislature's first meeting, and followed up on June 20 with
a more detailed version that included specifics on how the board proposed
to fund public improvements. In the preliminary report the board acknowledged having been only recently organized but explained that it was
obliged to advise the lawmakers on legislation required to carry out improvements. The board identified a general and comprehensive system of sewerage as an immediate priority, coupled with a consistent system of street
grades. In addition, the board stressed the importance of integrating Washington City with Washington County, which meant attention to north-
south streets intersecting principal county roads. On the all-important
question of funding improvements, the board report stated its intention to
seek a twenty-to-thirty-year loan and to establish a "sinking fund" to retire
the loan principal. Among its many optimistic statements, the report assured

real estate owners that the enhanced value of their property would more than offset their taxes.[1]

Initial territorial government momentum received a shock when, on June 1, black laborers working for the Columbia Street Railway went on strike for higher wages. The strike lasted a week and had mixed results. The timing and arguments suggested that the strike's purpose was to call attention to curtailed political representation by blacks (and all other voters) under the territorial government. The workers, who had previously made their voices heard via elections and ward politics, regarded the consolidation movement and the territorial government as threats to their influence and hard-won gains.[2]

The laborers demanded a two-dollar wage for an eight-hour workday, a sizeable increase from the previous $1.25 daily rate. Leaders George Hatton and Henry Himber achieved a fleeting victory when, in a meeting two days later, several contractors agreed to pay two dollars a day, provided that the others would do so as well. The contractors eventually backpedaled, however, and none made good on the offer. The race issue was highlighted when many Irish workers went back to work for $1.50 a day. The board became involved, realizing the harm that would be done to its public improvements initiative if it appeared to be oppressing black workers. Responding to a letter from the laborers complaining that $1.25 a day was too little to live on, Governor Henry Cooke sent a letter to one contractor—cosigned by board members Shepherd and Brown—stating that $1.50 a day was the highest wage the territorial government could afford; a letter to another contractor asked him to stop work on Seventh Street improvements until wage accommodation could be reached in order to preserve the peace of the city.[3]

After a week the strike petered out; work was available at $1.50 a day, and the two-dollar-a-day holdouts were not employed. William Wilson (W. W.) Corcoran's *Daily Patriot* accused the government of bowing to mob

---

[1] Text of preliminary Board of Public Works report, in *National Republican* (Washington, D.C.), May 16, 1871; William Tindall, *Standard History of the City of Washington* (Knoxville, Tenn., 1914), p. 253.

[2] Kate Masur, *An Example for All the Land: Emancipation and the Struggle over Equality in Washington, D.C.* (Chapel Hill, 2010), pp. 211–12.

[3] *Evening Star* (Washington, D.C.), June 2, 3, 5, 6, and 7, 1871.

rule, as did the *Evening Star*. However, Frederick Douglass's *New National Era* backed the establishment by applauding the end of the strike and arguing that excessive wages would curtail work and therefore employment.[4] The strike left a bad taste in people's mouths, sending a strong message that the new District government had critics from both conservative and liberal elements that would not hesitate to oppose its policies.

One day after publication of the board's initial report, the *Daily Patriot* editorialized,

> While we are disposed to favor a proper, and even a liberal system of improvements, the public sentiment demands, after the waste, extravagance and corruption of the last five years, that it should be carefully and judiciously devised. . . . The Board of Public Works seems to have marked out on a grand scale various projects which involve great cost and cannot be undertaken without command of large means. . . . Our policy is not to borrow a dollar until the finances are put in order and a sinking fund established for the extinction of the existing debt. But to start with loans is to end with loans, and to make corruption and dissatisfaction inevitable.[5]

The paper followed up with two additional criticisms: the board's intention to introduce new street grades was in violation of its limited mandate to repair and maintain District of Columbia streets, and the board was required to obtain prior legislative approval and appropriation of funds for all board activities.[6] Conservative opinion continued to shift away from tentative support of Shepherd's improvement plans to insisting, in increasingly strident language, on limitations and controls on his plan and methods.

Identifying the Challenges

A retrospective report issued by the board of its plans and the circumstances it faced when launching the public improvements focused on the

---

[4]*Daily Patriot* (Washington, D.C.), June 10, 1871; *Evening Star,* June 7, 1871; *New National Era* (Washington, D.C.), June 15, 1871.

[5]*Daily Patriot*, May 17, 1871. It is puzzling that the paper used 1866 as the starting point for—in its estimation—wasteful local government, since that year saw reelection for the third time of the conservative Richard Wallach. Compared to his successors, Sayles J. Bowen (1868) and Matthew Emery (1870), Wallach would have been more attractive to the *Patriot*'s conservative backers.

[6]Ibid., May 24 and 26, 1871.

preliminary document given to the legislature in 1871, which identified the L'Enfant plan itself as the greatest challenge: "The plan of Washington, as laid out by its founder, evidently contemplated a capital to contain millions of people. The streets and avenues are of greater width than those of any other city in the world and, with the alleys, comprise an area equal to about one-half of that contained within the entire city limits."[7] The report pointed out that Congress had appropriated only meager amounts for maintenance of the streets and squares adjacent to government property (e.g., the Capitol, the White House) and had paid nothing for any other roadway, leaving the residents to bear the full burden. The board called upon the federal government to make an appropriation "to reimburse to the city the amount of money which it has expended for the government."[8]

Another major issue confronting the board was the lack of a consistent and thorough system of Washington street grades. The capital's natural topography was hilly, and such roadwork as had been done followed the natural grades, making road-building and maintenance difficult. "The policy of accommodating grades to particular streets or localities, in compliance with the peculiar ideas of individual property-owners, had prevailed to such an extent that the grade books in possession of the old corporations were, in many instances, utterly inconsistent and worthless," the board reported, "and to this may be attributed many of the changes and apparent errors which have occurred in the prosecution of improvements."[9]

The absence of a comprehensive sewage system proved to be another of the board's principal challenges, since "a large proportion of the drainage emptied into an open ditch known as the canal, which separated the northern part of the city from the government parks and reservations, as well as from south Washington. The current of water, depending on the ebb and flow of the river tides, was insufficient to carry off the deposits made at the outlets of the various sewers, and the canal thus became so offensive as to threaten pestilence, and so unsightly as to disgust every beholder."[10]

The report closed with the trenchant observation that the District of Columbia had been created solely for the national government's own

---

[7] *Report of the Board of Public Works of the District of Columbia from Its Organization until November 1, 1872* (Washington, D.C., 1872), p. 4 (hereafter *1872 Board of Public Works Report*).

[8] Ibid., p. 30.

[9] Ibid., pp. 4–5.

[10] Ibid., p. 6.

purposes and remained controlled by it while withholding funds for the maintenance and improvement of the District. The upshot of this arrangement was that the government "undertook the guardianship of the District, deprived its inhabitants of the right of self-government and of the elective franchise, and made them dependent on the will of the representatives of the States, to whom alone they can look for relief."[11]

One early step Shepherd and the board undertook was to reduce the width of L'Enfant's expansive streets and avenues to a more practical size, but the challenge was how to accomplish this "without bankrupting the people."[12] To that end the board adopted a solution previously proposed by Sayles Bowen and others "to narrow the carriageways as to render the use of improved pavements practicable. This would place the surplus width inside the foot-walks, where it could be parked [i.e., planted] and otherwise beautified at slight expense to the public."[13] Although the board favored "parking" both sides of reduced-width roadways, it adhered to an 1870 act of Congress calling for parking in the middle of selected streets, including Pennsylvania Avenue E., New York Avenue, and Indiana Avenue.[14] William Smith, chairman of the board-created Parking Commission, traced the origin of the parking concept to former Washington mayor Richard Wallach, who suggested it to Shepherd, although Mayor Bowen had also favored it.[15] While credit for implementation of parking as a feature of street improvement unquestionably belonged to the board, the law that approved this arrangement had been enacted in 1870, before the board was created.[16]

Trees were an essential element in Shepherd's plan to implement a parking system for the city, and in 1871 the board established a Parking Commission consisting of William Saunders, superintendent of the Botanical Gardens; William R. Smith, superintendent of the Department of Agriculture Grounds; and John Saul, a local nurseryman. Smith told of visiting Shepherd one day while the latter was being shaved by his barber.

---

[11] Ibid., p. 38.

[12] Ibid., p. 4

[13] Ibid., p. 4.

[14] William Tindall, "The Origin of the Parking System of This City," *Records of the Columbia Historical Society* 4 (1901):84.

[15] Typewritten copy of comments made by William Smith at the 1908 Washington's Birthday banquet hosted by the Association of Oldest Inhabitants of Washington, D.C., and sent to Mrs. Shepherd; courtesy of W. Sinkler Manning Jr.

[16] Tindall, "Origin of the Parking System," p. 78.

Shepherd wiped the lather from his face and emphatically directed Smith to carry out his instructions. A Shepherd family version of the story records Shepherd saying, "Now, Smith, you know I know nothing of tree planting, but I suggest oak trees if possible on some streets . . . put a tree wherever there is damned room."[17] Protecting the trees remained a challenge, however. Senator George Edmunds of Vermont complained to Congress that "whenever we appropriate money to set up a shade tree, there comes along a cow or a horse or a goat, and tears it down the next day. . . . There are not two trees in a hundred in this city . . . which do not show the marks of ill-treatment by horned animals or by pigs or by some animals that are running at large."[18]

Shepherd's intention to build "largely" was made clear in his explanation during an 1872 House investigation into District affairs: "The Board of Public Works, when they entered their duties, concluded that they had been created for something or nothing and that, if for anything, it was to devise and carry out as rapidly as possible, some system of improvements, in order that in this respect the capital of the nation might not remain a quarter of a century behind the times."[19]

Conflict of Interest?

One of the earliest actions taken by Shepherd concerning public improvements in the District of Columbia highlighted the complex mix of public-spirited versus personal-gain motives that has made him grist for the mills of friend and foe alike. The issue was grading F Street, between Seventeenth and Twentieth Streets NW, later anchored on the east by Alfred B. Mullett's massive, "wedding cake" design for the new State, War, and Navy Building. The crux of the controversy was that a legitimate public good involved apparent sleight of hand by Shepherd to his financial benefit, since he had constructed fourteen houses on the north side of the block between

---

[17]Handwritten note by Mary Grice Shepherd at the bottom of William Smith's notes (see n. 15 above), courtesy of W. Sinkler Manning Jr.

[18]*Congressional Globe*, 41st Cong., 3rd sess., Jan. 24, 1871, p. 687, quoted in Constance McLaughlin Green, *Washington*, vol. 1, *Village and Capital, 1800–1878* (Princeton, N.J., 1962), p. 316.

[19]House Committee for the District of Columbia, *Affairs in the District of Columbia*, 42nd Cong., 2nd sess., 1872, H. Rep. 72, p. 735 (hereafter 1872 Investigation).

Seventeenth and Eighteenth Streets.[20] As recounted by Mayor Emery, Shepherd came to him in late April 1871 with an urgent request for authority for grading and "trimming" F Street west of the site of the new federal building. Emery approved the request on the assurance that existing gutters and sidewalks would not be disturbed; the contract was not to exceed $600, although it appears that it was never signed. (This exchange occurred a month after Shepherd and the board obtained an injunction prohibiting the Emery administration from authorizing new improvement contracts.[21])

At this point matters appeared fairly straightforward. The problem, however, came from the fact that the eventual cost of grading and trimming F Street between Seventeenth and Twentieth Streets NW was $54,875 and included cutting down the street from an average two feet at Seventeenth Street to approximately nine feet at Twentieth Street, as attested by outraged letters and testimony of injured homeowners.[22] Needless to say, gutters and sidewalks were massively impacted. The same homeowners also alleged that Shepherd's houses—completed shortly before the roadwork began—appeared to have been built low, so that the grading had the aesthetic effect of raising basement windows higher from the ground. The implication was clear: Shepherd had anticipated the necessity for grading F Street and built his houses to benefit from eventual grading.

A different perspective, however, came from later testimony by Mullett, the board engineer, before the congressional investigating committee, as well as Shepherd's own explanation. Mullett maintained that not only was he the source of the F Street grading proposal but also that Shepherd initially opposed it on grounds of personal cost. Mullett explained that the grading was inevitable because "it was impossible to make a decent finish to the State Department without reducing the proposed grade changes. One object in lowering F Street was to achieve a better system of drainage; the other was to obtain dirt to raise the grades and eliminate that swamp below."[23] Shepherd told the committee that although the other members of the board favored the grading, he was unhappy that it would cost him "ten or fifteen

---

[20]Mayor Matthew Emery to Hon. Charles L. Hulse, Speaker of the House of Delegates, May 24, 1871, in 1872 Investigation, p. 12.

[21]Franklin Howe, "Board of Public Works," *Records of the Columbia Historical Society* 3 (1900):260.

[22]1872 Investigation, pp. 12–47. The final cost was cited in a letter from the Board of Public Works Assistant Engineer dated Feb. 2, 1872 (pp. 43–44).

[23]Ibid., pp. 575–76.

thousand dollars" on his property, but "as we all agreed it would be a great improvement to that section of the city, I yielded, and the grade was established."[24] Shepherd pointed out in subsequent testimony that he paid every penny for the improvements in front of his properties, which were about finished when the cutting began. "As a consequence, I was deprived of the rents of them for six or eight months, and besides had to pay the whole expense from my own pocket."[25]

The F Street controversy not only angered potential opponents of Shepherd and his grand plan of improvements but also raised questions in people's minds about his willingness to use public improvements to strengthen his personal financial position. Although subsequent congressional probes into the latter issue absolved Shepherd of personal corruption, several factors require consideration. City planning in the United States during the last third of the nineteenth century was in its infancy, and public standards governing personal benefits derived from public works had not been clearly articulated or uniformly enforced. In addition, territorial officials and businessmen did not grasp why the public would object to such conflicts of interest, which pervaded the District government but at the same time reinforced the active support of local entrepreneurs that was necessary for growth and development. Today, even the appearance of conflict of interest is thought to undermine government integrity, yet District "improvers" in the 1870s, believing the entrepreneur to be an instrument of progress, felt their activities demonstrated business sense and public spirit. How could there be anything wrong with making money from the progress they had instigated?[26]

Paying for the Plan

At this point, the most important objective for Shepherd and the board was obtaining funding authorization from the legislature for the proposed public

[24]Ibid., p. 401.

[25]Ibid., p. 582.

[26]Alan Lessoff, *The Nation and Its City: Politics, "Corruption," and Progress in Washington, D.C., 1861–1902* (Baltimore, 1994), pp. 66–68. Lessoff uses the term *improvers* to characterize those who favored physical and economic progress at the expense of political and ethical considerations.

improvements program. In mid-May the board sent the legislature a report previewing the intended improvements but lacking the detail required to justify legislation authorizing funding. On June 16, no doubt choreographed in advance, the House of Delegates made a formal request to the board to submit a detailed improvements plan, which was provided four days later.[27] The board's report to the legislature in May had omitted any mention of anticipated costs of improvements, saying only that it would seek loans maturing over a twenty-to-thirty-year period, but the report of June 20 elaborated on the earlier one and put in writing its estimate of the total cost of the improvements at $6,578,397.[28] The portion to be borne "by the treasury of the District" was given as $4,358,698. The report emphasized that the property owners' share of the cost, $2,219,699, limited to one-third of the total, would be less than under the previous tax code. The introductory portion of this vital planning tool emphasized that public improvements would include every portion of the newly consolidated District of Columbia. It would also mean reducing the width of the avenues in the central part of Washington and paving and installing sewers, as well as building a main sewer from Eighth Street NW to Rock Creek.[29]

No one would have imagined at the outset that the eventual cost of building the District of Columbia's infrastructure would be in the vicinity of $20 million. Considering that previous practice had consisted of ad hoc funding scratched together for sketchy and irregular improvements, the Shepherd proposal went far beyond anything previously known to the residents of the nation's capital, both in terms of scope and cost. Shepherd had never been shy about his willingness to use borrowed money to make money: his personal wealth was heavily dependent on building loans. When he joined the new territorial government, his real estate holdings were valued at some $200,000, only 5 percent of which was unencumbered by debt.[30] While other builders erected perhaps a few houses or even a row, Shepherd routinely built rows of houses, all heavily leveraged.[31] He had also been candid about his

[27]*Daily Patriot,* June 16, 1871.

[28]*Report of the Joint Select Committee of Congress Appointed to Inquire into the Affairs of the District of Columbia,* 43rd Cong., 1st sess., H. Rep. 453, 1874, (hereafter 1874 Investigation), Part 1, pp. vi–vii.

[29]Ibid.

[30]1872 Investigation, p. 425.

[31]Wilhelmus Bogart Bryan, *A History of the National Capital from Its Foundation through the Period of the Adoption of the Organic Act,* 2 vols. (New York, 1916), 2:595–96.

intention to use public debt to finance improvements in Washington, but no one expected that the $6,578,397 figure would be just the down payment on Shepherd's grand plan.

Shepherd deferred to Governor Cooke, experienced in these matters, to formulate the loan package and present it to the legislature. The package that Cooke presented called for issuing twenty-year bonds at 7 percent annual interest. In addition, the governor himself would be responsible both for selling the bonds and for creating a mechanism through assessments against taxable property in the District to generate sufficient funds to pay the annual interest on the bonds and gradually to repay the principal.[32] The House of Delegates approved the measure in one week. The only changes made by the Legislative Council before passage of the final bill in early July were to reduce the total amount of loans from $4.6 million to $4 million, with a maximum disbursal of $1.5 million in 1871 and $2.5 million in 1872. The following restrictions were also made on board actions: only contracts 20 percent or more below estimates would be accepted by the board; all disbursements would be made by board vouchers upon the District Treasury; and the amount of work done must exceed the voucher by at least 10 percent before payment.[33]

Although Shepherd had directed his confidant George Gideon to make sure that the initial territorial elections in 1871 would guarantee support for the territorial government and public improvements, there is little evidence of fraud in the process. Other than the usual complaints that blacks from nearby Virginia and Maryland were brought in to vote, there were residual allegations of the manipulation of voting tickets (i.e., ballots). Separate tickets were issued to designate support for or against the $4 million loan. During the 1872 congressional investigation of District affairs, some twenty pages of testimony were devoted to attempts by Shepherd's opponents to prove that, at least in the Fifteenth District, there were attempts to suppress access to "against" loan tickets, but anecdotal evidence was not conclusive.[34] There was no indication of citywide fraud.

---

[32]Records of the Government of the District of Columbia: Laws of the Legislative Assembly, June 22, 1871–June 20, 1874, vol. 1, July 10, 1871 (hereafter Laws of the Legislative Assembly), Record Group 351, National Archives and Records Administration, Washington, D.C. (hereafter NARA).

[33]*Evening Star*, July 7, 1871.

[34]1872 Investigation, pp. 280–99.

Criticism of Shepherd and the board in the *Daily Patriot* grew with approval of the loan bill and identification of which neighborhoods were marked for improvements. Shepherd's intention to focus on the northwest portion of the city brought howls from residents of Capitol Hill, led by former Shepherd ally and developer Albert Grant. At a public meeting to protest apparent downgrading of attention to Capitol Hill, Grant alleged that the men composing the board were either from Georgetown or Washington County and that none of them owned land east of Ninth Street. He maintained—correctly—that it had been originally intended for Capitol Hill to become the finest portion of the city.[35] Conservative, land-owning, tax-paying residents, many of them "old citizens," signed a letter to the legislature protesting passage of the loan bill. The *Daily Patriot* described the group as primarily men who had long been identified with the District, engaged in business there, recognized for enterprise and integrity, and had high standing in the community.[36] Among the signers were bankers W. W. Corcoran, George Washington Riggs, and John B. Blake; jeweler M. W. Galt, investors J. Van Riswick and W. G. Metzerott; wealthy residents Enoch Totten, J. C. McKelden, William H. Philip, and P. G. Shedd; former mayor James G. Berret; and widely respected General Montgomery C. Meigs. A major theme of the group was paying for improvements, with all but one strongly preferring to rely on annual appropriations "after the system of the General Government."[37] Old-line conservatives like Corcoran and Riggs, who had supported Shepherd and Emery against Mayor Bowen, were now de facto aligned with Radical Republicans ostensibly in league with the black laboring class in opposing board domination of the D.C. government.[38] Nevertheless, Shepherd's opponents always maintained a pro forma commitment to beautifying the nation's capital even as they dug in their heels and put every possible obstacle in the way of the board improvements plan.

Governor Cooke began selling the bonds as soon as the authorizing legislation was passed by the Legislative Council in early July. Supporters of the board and the new government were encouraged by his success in having sold $1.5 million of the new D.C. bonds in New York City at 97.5 cents on

[35]*Daily Patriot*, July 7, 1871. Grant's statement was partially incorrect, since Shepherd had built a number of elegant residences east of the Capitol.

[36]Ibid., July 20, 1871.

[37]Ibid., July 7, 1871.

[38]Masur, *Example to All the Land*, p. 221.

the dollar, with proceeds to be delivered in batches of $500,000.[39] Yet even as this good news for public improvements came in, opponents of the loan bill took their challenge to the next level in a demand before Judge Andrew Wylie of the D.C. Supreme Court for an injunction to block issuance of the bonds; Shepherd's response was to halt all street work in anticipation of a negative decision.[40] The complexity of the issue, as well as its high stakes, became clear when Governor Cooke responded to the injunction request by saying that he had already signed bonds totaling $500,000 and had made "conditional negotiations" for further sale in Europe, provided no blocking injunction was issued, with a promise of $1 million more on the same terms.[41]

First Legal Roadblock

For three days in August Judge Wylie heard arguments for and against the injunction, with the board providing a rebuttal affirming that all board actions would be controlled by the organic law of the District and assuring the judge that "our only purpose in desiring the use of funds is to advance the interest of the District and of the people thereof." The board also cited its intention to clear everything with a newly created Advisory Board of Engineers, which included General Meigs.[42] On August 4 the judge granted the Citizens Association the requested injunction against the $4 million public works loan, saying that the District's inherited debt must be considered part of total D.C. debt, per the organic act. Wylie noted that "responsibility rested with those who had acted with too much haste."[43] The determination of the Board of Public Works to forge ahead despite this setback was captured in an observation by D.C. Counsel William Cook: "improvements must go on; *by* the taxpayers, *through* the taxpayers, or *over* the taxpayers, if necessary."[44]

Shepherd and his supporters quickly convened a mass meeting at Lincoln Hall in support of the improvement bonds. Senator William M. Stewart of

---

[39] *Evening Star,* July 22, 1871.
[40] *Daily Patriot,* July 25, 1871.
[41] Ibid., Aug. 1, 1871.
[42] *Evening Star,* Aug. 1, 1871.
[43] Tindall, *Standard History,* p. 253; *Daily Patriot,* Aug. 5, 1871.
[44] *Evening Star,* Aug. 5, 1871 (emphasis in original).

Nevada, Shepherd's ally and builder of the first mansion on Dupont Circle, told the audience, "Congress should lay hold and help and pay taxes on the Government property the same as the citizens are assessed for, and [he] believed that it would be when a little life was shown on the part of the citizens." Endorsing one of Shepherd's main arguments, Stewart added that District residents must be willing to assume debt in exchange for improvements, and Congress would be disposed to help. Invoking the threat of removal of the capital, Shepherd followed by saying that District residents must "prove ourselves worthy of retaining here the capital of the nation, or failing in this . . . we are to relapse into a mere provincial city." Justifying the need for loans, Shepherd said that the board insisted on an appropriation adequate to insure completion of all the agreed projects, "not wishing to depend upon the contingency of yearly appropriations." He then brought forward the argument for improvements that perhaps underlay much of his political calculation: improvements would attract out-of-town investors, "wealthy, refined, and influential persons who now shun our city in consequence of the barbarous condition of its streets and roads."[45]

Because Washington had never been able to develop significant industry or commerce, entrepreneurial energies were channeled into real estate and development. Shepherd and the "improvers" saw development as a way to make the District attractive not only to local investors but also to outsiders, raising the demand for real estate. Rising property values would be both a sign of increased demand and an inducement to further investment.[46] L'Enfant's and George Washington's plans for Washington had envisioned the city functioning as both a political and commercial capital, but the canal through the city had turned into an open sewer of little business value other than to bring in lumber and coal for local merchants. The canal had become a *de facto* barrier between the developing city north of the canal and the "island," below, including the Mall and the Smithsonian Institution. Shepherd knew that the future of the city would have to be based on its political role and, ideally, on its attractiveness as an investment destination for out-of-towners.

To increase public confidence in its plans, the board created an advisory board of engineers composed of well-known and respected names in

---

[45]Ibid., Aug. 8, 1871.
[46]Lessoff, *The Nation and Its City*, p. 65.

engineering and urban design: in addition to Meigs, quartermaster-general of the U.S. Army, who supervised construction of the Washington Aqueduct and the extensions on the Capitol, the group included Frederick Law Olmsted, designer of New York's Central Park and the U.S. Capitol grounds; General Orville Babcock, commissioner of Public Buildings and Grounds; General A. A. Humphreys, chief of the Engineer Corps, U.S. Army; and Major General Joseph K. Barnes, surgeon general of the United States. The Board of Public Works promised it would submit its plan of improvements to the advisory board, and no work would be initiated until approved by them.[47] The *Daily Patriot* caustically attacked this "flank movement" by the board, which it pointed out was not authorized by law, had no defined duties or sphere of action, and therefore had no binding authority on board actions. The paper's position seemed to be confirmed in a report on a meeting of the advisory board at a lunch in August, when the paper observed that "there seemed to be no real business before the meeting."[48]

The Legislature Agrees

Judge Wylie's injunction blocking sale of the improvement bonds was not enough to slow Shepherd's determination to forge ahead with street work. He quickly obtained approval from the legislature for an additional $500,000 to avoid technical objections raised by the plaintiffs, and work recommenced.[49] The bridge loan was followed by two additional, dramatic steps: legislative approval of a plebiscite on November 22 to demonstrate popular support for the $4 million loan, and a bill authorizing a second improvements loan of $4 million, with the proviso that it was to be submitted to a popular vote in the next general election, now set for November 22.[50] The second $4 million loan was not intended to double the funds available to the board for improvements but rather to be available in the event that Judge Wylie's injunction was not overturned.

---

[47]*Evening Star,* July 11, 1871.
[48]*Daily Patriot,* July 12 and Aug. 19, 1871.
[49]Tindall, *Standard History,* p. 252.
[50]Laws of the Legislative Assembly, vol. 1, Aug. 19, 1871, RG 351, NARA; Tindall, *Standard History,* p. 253.

There was little doubt by this point that the House of Delegates was the willing tool of Shepherd and the board. Shepherd's instructions to his political ally George Gideon the previous spring made clear his determination to insure that the delegates supported the board and the public improvements program. The appointed Legislative Council was not a threat because it owed its existence to President Grant, with its composition no doubt guided by Shepherd and other supporters of improving the nation's capital. It took the House of Delegates only one week and two legislative sessions to approve the largest funding bill ever approved in the District of Columbia; it was approved by the upper house and signed by Governor Cooke nineteen days after being first presented.[51]

Conflicting testimony about the board's pressure tactics was given to the 1872 congressional investigation, with one former council member saying, "any resolution or bill which [the Board of Public Works] took an interest in having passed did pass, and frequently passed immediately; and . . . such bills as they did not express any interest in or approve of never did pass. . . . My observation and information satisfied me that the council and house of delegates . . . were wholly and completely subservient to the Board of Public Works." He added that some of the board had repeatedly used "the strongest personal solicitations" to induce him to vote for the bill, noting that the solicitors even invoked "personal honor" in their appeals.[52] D. L. Eaton, a board supporter in the House of Delegates, told the same investigators, however, that no member of the board attempted to exercise "undue" influence, describing the lobbying as a "consultation" that "gentlemen would have with one another as to the best interests of the public."[53]

A Shepherd opponent in the House of Delegates, John Harkness, provided a sarcastic riposte in the form of a resolution: "RESOLVED: That the fifteen members of the Republican side of the House by and with the advice of the Board of Public Works be, and they are hereby authorized to declare all the remaining acts prepared under their auspices as valid and in full force, without form of law." Harkness explained, "Measures were concocted by the majority in caucus and brought in the House and rushed through under the operation of the previous question, without allowing

---

[51]Howe, "Board of Public Works," p. 262; Laws of the Legislative Assembly, vol. 1, July 10, 1871, RG 351, NARA.

[52]1872 Investigation, pp. 364–65, 368.

[53]Ibid., p. 644.

debate or amendment."[54] An embittered Sayles Bowen published a letter excoriating the House of Delegates for "having surrendered every right reserved to the people by the organic act," arguing that the board "are not responsible to, and are entirely independent of, the voters of the District."[55] The opposition *Daily Patriot* scathingly referred to the board's acolytes in the House of Delegates as "partisan pimps."[56]

In the spring of 1871 Governor Cooke signed a lease on the Morrison Buildings to accommodate his office and the board. These structures, two adjoining, run-down wooden buildings on 4½ Street between Pennsylvania Avenue and C Street NW, required extensive renovation. The legislature appropriated $48,000 to cover costs, but when it was revealed that the cost had risen to $84,000—almost twice the appropriation—it created a sensation. Henry Searle, the architect overseeing the project who had designed Shepherd's Bleak House in Washington County, provided testimony before the 1872 investigation confirming that a committee of board members—Shepherd, Mullett, and Magruder—appointed by Governor Cooke oversaw the renovation. Searle defended the expenditure of about $20,000 (not included in the original estimate) to create fireproof vaults, since he considered it "criminal" to jeopardize public records.[57] In later testimony, Shepherd said that the final cost of renovating the buildings was reduced to $58,000 by an internal committee appointed by the board. The territorial government departments moved into their new quarters at the end of August. The Morrison Buildings contretemps was an early indicator of Shepherd's and the board's willingness to interpret financial requirements more as suggestions than as requirements. It was a pattern that became increasingly apparent.

Shepherd's social activities that spring included the opening of the Washington Club at 1409 New York Avenue NW, in a building he purchased from D.C. congressional delegate Norton Chipman, while he simultaneously, but unsuccessfully, tried to maintain a positive relationship with W. W. Corcoran.[58] During the intense, early phase of the territorial government,

[54]*Daily Patriot*, Aug. 21, 1871.

[55]Ibid., Oct. 27, 1871.

[56]Ibid., July 1, 1871.

[57]1872 Investigation, pp. 248–52, 389.

[58]Shepherd was still trying, albeit unsuccessfully, to keep lines open to Corcoran, offering to host a formal dinner for him, which Corcoran declined; backers were mainly Shepherd allies (*Evening Star*, Sept. 9, 1871). Corcoran's friendship became even more elusive after

when Shepherd was launching the public improvements program, he lost no time in using the Washington Club to support his plans. As an expert at lobbying Congress, Shepherd understood the value of a comfortable setting in which to discuss issues informally while playing cards or relaxing in the club rooms. While the forty original investors in the club included Shepherd confidants such as Cooke, Lewis Clephane, Hallet Kilbourn, and William Huntington, it also included District residents of conservative reputation and "prominent democrats" such as former mayor and club president J. G. Berret and Richard T. Merrick. In 1874 Merrick was to play a leading role in the congressional investigation of D.C. affairs as counsel for the memorialists (i.e., signers of the formal complaint against the board). The investigation intensively probed connections between club members and the territorial government, but Shepherd turned questions aside by stating that only six members out of forty were contractors, and only three besides himself had an official connection with the government.[59] As noted by historian William Maury, however, "only two members of the leadership of the club did not either hold, at some time or another, an official position with the territory, or act as a major contractor for it."[60] The Union Club, another, smaller club organized by Shepherd, also served as a vehicle for personal influence within the territorial government.

Although they could not stop the seemingly invincible march of the board, Shepherd's opponents found other ways to express dissatisfaction. In the 1860s Shepherd had been a member of the Metropolitan Club, already a prestigious social club, but he was not invited to join when the club was reorganized in December 1872. The new officers included Shepherd's opponents Corcoran and Riggs, along with Shepherd admirers General William T. Sherman and Admiral George Porter.[61] Having established the Washington and Union Clubs, Shepherd may have felt that he didn't need more social access, but the Metropolitan Club attracted the most socially

---

sewerage from Board of Public Works projects backed up into the Corcoran Art Gallery and the Louise Home, a residence Corcoran had endowed for aging Southern ladies (*Daily Patriot*, Feb. 19, 1872).

[59] 1872 Investigation, pp. 157–59; *Daily Patriot*, Mar. 4, 1872.

[60] William M. Maury, "The Territorial Period in Washington, 1871–1874, with Special Emphasis on Alexander Shepherd and the Board of Public Works," PhD diss., George Washington University, 1974, pp. 96–97.

[61] John-Manuel Andriote, *The Metropolitan Club of the City of Washington* (Washington, D.C., 1997), pp. 21–26.

respectable Washingtonians and national officials resident in the city, and it is inconceivable that Shepherd did not notice the snub for what it was.

The early months of board activity were publicized in a flurry of reports and announcements in fifteen local newspapers that constituted a nonstop board progress report as well as an effort to co-opt the local press into supporting the board program. The cost of press announcements became an issue in the 1872 investigation, in which the memorialists alleged "unparalleled profligacy" for board printing and advertising that totaled more than $100,000. Governor Cooke, in a letter no doubt drafted by Shepherd, acknowledged that the "bitterly hostile" efforts of antiboard forces and loan opponents had required a massive counterthrust.[62] The investigation report agreed that much of the advertising was "unnecessary," since focusing on three or four of the papers with the widest circulation would have met publicity needs.[63] Shepherd, however, knew that paid ads in all the papers would support friends and possibly mitigate the wrath of opponents.

A Contractor Bonanza

Shepherd's intention to build "largely," with unprecedented levels of city bonds, would create a bonanza for contractors, a number of whom had already been involved with him as a result of his own home-building projects in the years preceding establishment of the territorial government. It was also evident that Shepherd was creating this new structure based on his personal experience and boundless self-confidence rather than on theoretical models, which did not yet exist in the field of city planning. The scale of proposed improvements vastly exceeded anything that board members had undertaken previously, and they created multiple new board departments, as well as mobilizing resources in the customary way by offering lucrative contracts to friends and acquaintances.[64]

Shepherd's original strategy in negotiating for road, sewer, and other contracts was twofold: pay cash and establish set prices for work. From his experience in the plumbing and gas fitting business over a decade, Shepherd

---

[62] 1872 Investigation, pp. 191–92.

[63] Ibid., p. v.

[64] Alan Lessoff, "Political Economy in Gilded Age Washington," unpublished paper, pp. 11–12.

knew that contractors routinely inflated bids because they feared being required to accept certificates (in lieu of cash) that they would have to sell at a discount to banks or other buyers. As a matter of policy, Shepherd imposed a 15 percent reduction of all bids, calculating that contractors would accept a slightly lower-priced contract if secure in the knowledge that they would be paid quickly and in cash.[65]

Shepherd's second contracting innovation was to establish a set price for each kind of improvement project rather than being obligated to accept the lowest bid. His argument was that his policy would place all bidders on the same basis and allow him to select the most qualified for the job. While the system worked well enough at the outset, it soon became apparent that, with the scope of work involved and the number of contractors submitting bids, including many from firms outside Washington and previously unknown to the board, the system became unwieldy. Contractors sold and resold their contracts to the highest bidder, often to individuals with little or no experience or ability to complete the work in a satisfactory manner. The system also became a source of favoritism, since flat prices permitted the board to select whomever they wished from among the bidders. The 1874 congressional investigation into District affairs turned up extensive evidence of the corruption and inefficiency resulting from what Shepherd had thought would be an innovative approach.[66]

For their part, contractors from near and far smelled a feast in the making in Shepherd's Washington, and they positioned themselves to partake. The board had advertised widely for bids on street paving, to be opened September 1, and would-be contractors with ties to Shepherd intended to be ready. In an August 25 letter made public three years later, real estate investor Hallet Kilbourn revealed his strategy to William S. Huntington, cashier of Henry Cooke's First Metropolitan Bank, detailing a trip to Philadelphia and New York to "gobble up" contracts for all the asphalt or concrete pavement they could, along with associated equipment. Kilbourn said that when the board opened the street paving bids September 1, "We propose to be ready for them," making "a small ring of about seven persons," with himself, contractor John O. Evans, Clephane, builder Moses

---

[65]1874 Investigation, Part 3, p. 1409.

[66]Ibid., Part 1, pp. 3–7, 7–8, 42–44. The records start with fresh numbering at numerous points within a section, making ready location of citations difficult.

Kelly, John Kidwell, and Huntington as six of the seven; the group had long-standing personal and professional ties to Shepherd. "We shall try and control the entire lot of asphalt pavements." While Kilbourn, long involved in real estate transactions in Washington, may have seen the term *ring* as descriptive or even optimistic in terms of results, it set off howls of indignation and reproach when made public, because to those without access to the personal relationships on which Shepherd built so much of his successful business and political career, it symbolized corruption and cronyism.[67]

During the early months of the territorial government, most of the fault lines within the Shepherd public improvements program were exposed. Henceforth, the program would need to race against the weather, political opposition, and spiraling management confusion to determine whether the capital's bold experiment in governance and development would prove to be a success, a failure, or a combination of the two.

---

[67]Ibid., Part 2, pp. 254–59.

Chapter Seven

"More Work of Improvement Was Undertaken at Once Than Was Wise"

Meeting Opposition to the Board of Public Works, 1872

THE FAST PACE of the Board of Public Works' projects in the winter of 1871–72 and the disruption they brought contributed fodder for the opposition, culminating in the January to May 1872 congressional investigation into Shepherd's and the board's activities. The year 1872 proved to be the high-water mark for the territorial government and the Board of Public Works.

The original streets of the District had followed its natural topography of hills and valleys, interlaced with streams and marshy areas, resulting in an up-and-down road system that defied installation of public services such as water mains and sewers. Consequently, road crews had to rationalize street grades to meet engineers' specifications before road surfacing—or any other improvements—could proceed. Unfortunately, this situation created problems reported in the opposition press in early December 1871:

> The property-owners on streets where the grade is altered are not consulted, and their unanimous objection is to no avail. Their homes are left for months, high up on the brink of red-clay precipices, accessible only by ladders. So much work was undertaken at once that nothing has been completed; and the hard winter weather that has set in makes the condition of the streets that have been torn up for regrading and paving wretched and dangerous. They are full of muddy sloughs and pools of

water, and are cut up with deep ditches, where sewers are in process of construction.[1]

This was not the best way to develop public support for a massive public utilities program.

As the press description above indicates, the fall of 1871 saw growing criticism from Shepherd's opponents, who were uncertain how aggressively to respond. A short-lived press voice of the opposition, *The Citizen*, was in danger of collapsing for lack of funds, and the decision by the D.C. Supreme Court in November to overturn Judge Wylie's August injunction against the $4 million loan for improvements struck another blow to Shepherd's opposition. Despite the court's ruling in their favor on the bonds issue, the territorial government, leaving nothing to chance, went ahead with a November 22 plebiscite on the loan, which carried overwhelmingly: 14,748 in favor and only 1,202 against.[2] Nevertheless, a smear campaign persisted against Governor Henry Cooke's efforts to market the District's bonds in Europe. Cooke received evidence that potential German bond purchasers were being told by loan opponents in Washington that the injunction against the loan remained in place and that the bonds were not considered a first-class security. A letter to Cooke from Seligman and Company (New York), which was marketing the District's bonds in Germany, was intended "to put you and all good people of the District on their guard against the malevolent actions of some of your citizens." Cooke noted, "The object of these malicious and unfounded statements is to embarrass and retard the work of improvement."[3]

The plebiscite results and the removal of the antiloan injunction were given a strong vote of support by President Ulysses S. Grant in his annual message to Congress in December. Grant, an admirer of Shepherd's way of doing things—not unlike his own bulldog tenacity during the Civil War—noted that

> the results [of the territorial government] have thus far fully realized the expectations of its advocates. Under the direction of the Territorial officers, a

---

[1] *Daily Patriot* (Washington, D.C.), Dec. 4, 1871.

[2] *Evening Star* (Washington, D.C.), Nov. 23, 1871.

[3] Territorial Government, Letters Sent, Gov. Cooke to George F. Baker, vol. 1, p. 483; Letters Sent, vol. 2, Feb. 1, 1872, Record Group 351, National Archives and Records Administration, Washington, D.C. (hereafter NARA).

system of improvements has been inaugurated by means of which Washington is rapidly becoming a city worthy of the nation's capital. The citizens of the District having voluntary taxed themselves to a large amount for the purpose of contributing to the adornment of the seat of government, I recommend liberal appropriations on the part of Congress, in order that the Government may bear its just share of the expense of carrying out a judicious system of improvements.[4]

Public opinion on how much progress was achieved in the public works program during the early surge of road-building activity varied. Pro-Shepherd opinion was expressed in early January 1872 by the *Evening Star,* which reported that sufficient progress had been made that Washington was becoming "a first class winter residence . . . for the first time in the history of Washington the city has streets sufficiently well paved to allow of pleasure-driving every day through the winter, and the brilliant spectacle of Pennsylvania Avenue of an afternoon is a foretaste of what the future will show when the wealth of the country shall congregate here, as it is beginning to do for its winter Newport or Saratoga."[5] Real estate analyst-investor and Shepherd colleague James Latta underscored the positive impact of the improvements on real estate in later testimony confirming a correlation between improvements and rising real estate prices: "I know of no single locality in Washington City in which real estate has not been advanced in consequence of improvements. Take it in South Washington, or in the extreme eastern part, or in the northern or western or central part, all unimproved property has increased in value; improved property less than unimproved." He quoted from a published report as of March 1, 1872: "The increase in the value of the property conveyed is owing largely to the fact that persons of wealth from all sections of our country are purchasing residence sites, and making investments here, with a view of making Washington their winter homes and enjoying the many and rapidly increasing attractions of the nation's capital."[6]

The harsh winter, however, strengthened the case for an organized attack by Shepherd's opponents. Press accounts during the winter made

---

[4]Ulysses S. Grant, "Third Annual Message," in *A Compilation of Messages and Papers of the Presidents, 1789–1908,* ed. James A. Richardson, 10 vols. (New York, 1909), 7:154.

[5]*Evening Star,* Jan. 6, 1872.

[6]House Committee for the District of Columbia, *Affairs in the District of Columbia,* 42nd Cong., 2nd sess., 1872, H. Rep. 72, pp. 624–25 (hereafter 1872 Investigation).

frequent reference to the ghastly weather conditions, and anguished reports of citizen frustration surfaced regularly about the havoc wrought by Shepherd's program on people's daily lives due to the torn-up condition of most of the streets in the downtown area of Washington. In testimony before the 1872 congressional investigation into D.C. affairs, Shepherd justified his aggressive strategy in part as a way of getting back at opponents: "Because certain people in this District have fought us ever since the new government was organized; they enjoined us, and succeeded substantially in preventing us from proceeding with the work during most of the season."[7] Commenting on the negative effect of the weather on roadwork, Shepherd later told the investigation that "if we had had thirty days more, we would have had the thing very nearly finished up." Shepherd estimated that the winter of 1871–72 had started a month earlier and ended a month later than usual, significantly shortening the time available for roadwork.[8] Evidence was mounting that Shepherd was prepared to forge boldly ahead with the road construction program and did not attempt to win over the growing numbers of his critics.

Congressional Investigation of the Board of Public Works

Shepherd's opponents were, however, determined to stop him, and more than one thousand local residents and taxpayers delivered a signed "memorial" (petition) to the House of Representatives on January 22, 1872, charging the board and other officers with "extravagance and mismanagement."[9] Petitioners, including a number of prosperous Washingtonians, made a point of associating themselves with "good government, promoting the general prosperity, and securing an economical administration of the municipal affairs of the said District," themes that would recur regularly in attacks on Shepherd.[10] The fifteen charges detailed in the memorial were a mixture of

---

[7]Ibid., p. 404.

[8]Ibid., p. 588.

[9]Ibid., p. xxi.

[10]Ibid., pp. 2–8. Wealthy petitioners included Joseph H. Wilson, John Purdy, J. J. Coombs, John C. Harkness, and George Mattingly. Purdy and Harkness, with Charles County roots, had known and worked with Shepherd's father, suggesting that family ties did not transfer to the younger generation.

the serious (making improvements not authorized by law on "a scale of recklessness" so burdensome that it amounted to "confiscation") and the marginal (creating "many new bureaus" requiring more employees and salaries).[11]

The memorial prompted creation of an investigating committee consisting of eight members of the House of Representatives headed by Representative H. H. Starkweather (R-Conn.), known to be sympathetic to Shepherd's public works objectives, supported by four other Republicans and one Democrat. Shepherd opponents were two Democrats, Robert B. Roosevelt of New York, an uncle of future president Theodore Roosevelt; and John M. Crebs of Illinois.[12] The investigation lasted from the day the petition was delivered until presentation of the committee's report on May 13.

Early testimony was intended to impugn Shepherd's integrity and set the stage for broader charges. Witnesses were queried about grading in front of Shepherd's own houses on F Street NW and also about the improvements made to Seventh Street Road (later Georgia Avenue NW), which provided access to Bleak House.[13] When asked whether the location of Bleak House had influenced his decision to improve Seventh Street Road, Shepherd was categorical: "None whatever. I use the Fourteenth St. Road in the summer. The Seventh St. road is simply for the supply of the city from the country, for the bringing in of produce such as is needed. It is a road that I never use, and I do not drive on it twice a year."[14] He added, "Nothing has more retarded [Washington], and kept the price of provisions so high, as the bad roads leading to the city."[15] As proved to be the case with most of the challenges to Shepherd's activities, hostile testimony was either deflected or countered with supportive witnesses.

Shepherd testified before the committee on six occasions as well as providing additional comments on points of detail. His tone throughout was positive and focused on the future. He was proud of his accomplishments and confident that the results of board improvements would be met with general acclaim, despite problems. Shepherd's testimony on March 16,

---

[11]Ibid., pp. i–ii.
[12]Ibid., p. xiii.
[13]Ibid., pp. 36, 88–91.
[14]Ibid., p. 601.
[15]Ibid.

responding to questions from one of the memorialists' counsel, summed up his approach. Asked whether he thought the District of Columbia could bear "without great oppression" the expenses that would be incurred in carrying out board plans, Shepherd responded, "I do. I look upon it just as I look upon a valuable house which is out of repair and which I could make available to bring me an income by putting it in repair. I should think it policy on my part to borrow the money, and spend 5 or 10 per cent on it to accomplish that result. It would benefit the neighborhood, it would benefit me, and it would be a good investment."[16] Pressed on whether expenditures in excess of the stated value of the "house" would be a sound investment, Shepherd responded, "I certainly would [invest] if I could get a proportionate increase in consequence. I think it would be very good policy. It is the way the country has been built up."[17] Responding to a question about his personal worth, Shepherd emphasized the personal sacrifices he made as a public official. He estimated his real estate holdings in Washington at "about a half a million dollars," although assessed at about $300,000, adding, "I should like to say . . . that I am worth a great deal less than I would have been if I had not touched the Board of Public Works. I mean that my time would have been worth a good deal to me if it had been devoted to my own business."[18]

Shepherd deflected attention from himself in testifying before Congress, taking the opportunity to make a strong statement for federal assistance in maintaining and improving the capital's infrastructure:

> If the United States Government will appropriate annually its proportion of taxes on its property, all the improvements—not included in this four million dollar loan—can be carried out without increasing the burden on the taxpayers one dollar. I have been kicking my heels at the doors of Congress for the past five years to obtain appropriations for this District, and have been invariably met with the response: "Why not do something for yourselves? Why are you paupers? Why do you not show some disposition to make a start in this matter?" This movement is based on that suggestion. After we make a start and try to improve the city, Congress should do its part. It cannot rid itself of responsibility in that response.[19]

---

[16]Ibid., p. 396.
[17]Ibid.
[18]Ibid., p. 400.
[19]Ibid., p. 586.

The committee later endorsed Shepherd's call for federal support by acknowledging that L'Enfant's wide streets and avenues, along with the intersecting squares intended for public use,

> "demonstrate the propriety and original intention of the General [i.e., federal] Government bearing a proportion of the cost of improving and keeping them in repair. . . . This single suggestion, together with the fact that the United States has reserved to itself and still holds so large a proportion of the real estate of the District, shows beyond the necessity of argument the manifest injustice of devolving the whole expense of such improvements upon the citizens or upon those who may happen to own some of the lots in Washington."[20]

A Tweed Connection?

Shepherd's opponents —Democrats as well as anti-Grant Republicans— made continuous attempts to associate him with the atmosphere of corruption that was beginning to seep out from President Grant's inner circle. New York papers, the *Sun* and the *Herald* in particular, launched a campaign to link Shepherd with "Boss" William Marcy Tweed, New York's Tammany Hall Democratic chieftain, who had recently been indicted on charges of defrauding the people of New York of millions of dollars in a systematic assault on public monies. The most damaging consequence was to hang the label of "boss" on Shepherd in order to equate him with Tweed and also damage President Grant, known as an admirer of Shepherd and a supporter of his public works campaign in the District of Columbia. The anti-Shepherd campaign suffered a setback when James G. Berret, former mayor of Washington and former business manager of the *Daily Patriot*, the principal newspaper voice of Shepherd's enemies, testified before the investigating committee that the principal stockholder in the paper was none other than Boss Tweed himself.[21] The issue of a Shepherd-Tweed connection had become blurred because of Shepherd's trips to New York and Philadelphia to study street paving techniques with city officials. Shepherd denied ever having met Tweed, only to be confronted with a letter from Tweed saying

---

[20]Ibid., p. xii.

[21]Ibid., p. 320. Berret was not a personal opponent of Shepherd and served as president of the Washington Club.

that Tweed had met him briefly, although Tweed did not remember him. Furthermore, Tweed had instructed a New York public works official to show Shepherd's group the forms used for New York City contracts. Nevertheless, Shepherd insisted that he had not met Tweed in the course of an acknowledged visit to the New York engineer's office on Broadway and had never corresponded with him.[22]

Although numerous other topics were included in the 750-page proceedings of the investigation, the memorialists were unable to achieve their objective of forcing Shepherd and the board to alter their plans or even submit their activities to closer scrutiny. The committee majority report of May 13, 1872, signed by Chairman Starkweather, four other Republicans, and one Democrat, noted that the investigation, which lasted more than ninety days and heard more than two hundred witnesses, saw both sides represented by counsel and was open to the public. Taken all together, the report was a vote of confidence in Shepherd, even though caveats about his qualifications and methods foreshadowed future problems. On the critical issue of corruption, the majority noted the memorialists' attempt to show that the board had, "in their official capacity, acted corruptly, and been influenced by motives of personal gain." This charge, however, had been abandoned by opposition counsel at the close of the investigation.[23] The majority did, however, slap the hands of the improvers, emphasizing their inexperience and excessive zeal:

> There was inexperience on the part of many; there was the lack of careful and cool legislation. In the anxiety to redeem the city from the charge of being behind, in its streets and public institutions, other cities of the country, the new authorities became somewhat intoxicated with the spirit of improvement. . . . The committee are disposed to think that more work of improvement was undertaken at once than was wise, though the delays caused by the injunction [against the loan], and the suspension of work by the unusually early winter, make it impossible to say whether all the work begun could have been completed if these drawbacks had not existed. The result that many of the public streets were left in a broken-up condition through the winter doubtless caused much of the disaffection among the citizens.[24]

---

[22]Ibid., pp. 404, 423.
[23]Ibid., p. ii.
[24]Ibid., p. iv.

The majority report's final assessment vindicated Shepherd and echoed his call for congressional support for District improvements: "The governor and members of the Board are, on the whole, entitled to the favorable judgment of Congress, and are to be commended for the zeal, energy, and wisdom with which they have started the District upon a new career of improvement and prosperity; and the District itself is entitled to fair and generous appropriations from Congress, in some manner corresponding to the valuation of the property owned by the United States."[25]

However, the committee's minority report, signed by Democrats Robert B. Roosevelt and John M. Crebs, came to virtually opposite conclusions. Speaking of the "reckless extravagance" and assumption of powers by the board, the report stopped short of calling for a drastic change in the government of the District but insisted that all officers of the government should be made directly responsible to the people for their acts through election of all but the governor.[26]

Shepherd's mantra for justifying his actions—that they followed the "law of necessity"—had survived an assault by his opponents, funding was still available, and the return of decent weather meant that work on the capital's streets, sewers, trees, water mains, and gas lights could continue without legal challenge. Later events in the year, including President Grant's reelection in November and his official endorsement of the board' projects, would strengthen Shepherd's hand. Nevertheless, all was not well. The court challenge to the $4 million loan the previous summer and the ability of Shepherd's opponents to trigger a major congressional investigation showed that the opposition was well organized and determined to challenge and slow, if not stop, the board.

The Social Shepherds

Through the years of the territorial government Alexander and Mary Shepherd maintained an active social life, often hosting elaborate receptions and dinners at their residence on Tenth Street and at Bleak House

---

[25]Ibid., p. xiii.
[26]Ibid., p. xx.

at which invited guests often included members of Congress and other potentially useful political figures. One week in January 1872 gives the feel of the social pace. The Shepherds attended two large parties, one at board member Brown's residence in Mount Pleasant and the other a large dinner reception at the home of Attorney General George H. Williams; Shepherd also attended a stag dinner at the Farragut Square residence of journalist and publisher George Alfred Townsend. The week was crowned by an elegant dancing party at the Shepherd residence to celebrate their tenth wedding anniversary. The *Evening Star* gushed over "the party of the week" at the elegant home so well suited for hospitality, which was thrown open from basement to attic, plus a temporary building with spacious ball and supper rooms lighted and heated as comfortably as the remainder of the house.[27]

Just one week later, the Shepherds were back in the social columns when they hosted "the sensation of the season," a masked ball at their home promised by the enthusiastic press to be one of the most brilliant and beautiful of its kind. The party started with dinner at 11:00 p.m. and ended at 4:00 a.m. after the dancing concluded. Five first-floor rooms were opened up for the party and displayed statues and floral pyramids. In the foyer were stuffed figures of Alexander and Mary Shepherd. Two knights in full armor gave directions; there were also two suits of Japanese armor at the front entrance. Shepherd was dressed as one of Alexandre Dumas's three musketeers, and Mary Shepherd came dressed as Rebecca from Sir Walter Scott's *Ivanhoe*.[28] Shepherd's guests typically included members of congressional committees dealing with District of Columbia affairs as well as other federal officials and area business leaders.

During this time Shepherd made sure to maintain strong ties with President Grant's White House and with the national Republican Party. He was selected as a District of Columbia delegate to the Republican presidential nominating convention in June and journeyed to Philadelphia with John F. Cook, a prominent local black Republican, to nominate Grant for a second term. Shepherd was a member of the Resolutions Committee, the equivalent of today's platform committees, and lent his name to a progressive party

---

[27]*Evening Star,* Jan. 25, 27, 29, and 30, 1872.
[28]Ibid., Feb. 1 and 9, 1872.

platform that reconfirmed support for the landmark constitutional amendments on black citizenship and voting rights. The platform also called for "complete liberty and exact equality" in the enjoyment of "all civil, political, and public rights" and affirmed the Republican pillars of free labor and the formation of capital, "these two great servants of civilization."[29]

Supervision of the board's building program was not without personal cost to Shepherd. Management of his personal business affairs—in which he had excelled—fell victim to the press of public business. Up to a short time after taking on his public responsibilities, Shepherd had been one of the most active Washingtonians in recorded real estate transactions, but from early 1872 on, Shepherd's name appears less frequently in real estate activity records. The public record confirms what Shepherd himself said—that he would have been much better off financially had he been able to devote his time to personal wealth management than to public works for the nation's capital.[30] However, his plumbing company, Shepherd and Brothers, remained an active and successful bidder on many projects during the territorial government period, and Shepherd maintained his principal office on the second floor of his new building at Twelfth Street and Pennsylvania Avenue NW, where he conducted personal as well as the people's business. Shepherd made a nominal distinction between work done on each of the two building floors, but it was in reality a distinction without a difference.

Responding to pressure from residents' complaints about high taxes and damage to their property as a result of the board's road-building activity, Governor Cooke wrote a letter to the Legislative Assembly in May requesting passage of a law to assess benefits and damages to properties abutting streets and avenues under improvement.[31] A month later he signed a law authorizing payment of damages to those hurt by public works improvements, provided that they were approved by the legislature before payment.[32] Citing this law, in early fall the *Evening Star* felt obliged to publish blank forms for residents to use in submitting claims for damage caused by the board.[33]

---

[29]Ibid., June 7, 1872.
[30]The *Evening Star* issues of the fall and winter of 1871–72 constitute the public record.
[31]D.C. Records, Letters Sent, vol. 2, May 2, 1872, RG 351, NARA.
[32]Ibid., vol. 2, June 20, 1872.
[33]*Evening Star*, Sept. 21, 1872.

Formidable Opponents

Shepherd had a polarizing effect on contemporaries: most were either strong supporters or became implacable opponents. Differences were not so much over what kind of city Washington should become as a combination of business rivalry and personal animosity. Opponents included those such as developer Albert Grant, who saw the focus of Shepherd's improvements as a threat to his investment in Capitol Hill development. Despite Shepherd's personal wealth, many of his opponents were also men of great resources that could be applied to the conflict with him. Besides William Wilson (W. W.) Corcoran and banker George Washington Riggs, William B. Todd and W. W. Gunton (president of the Bank of Washington) each owned property assessed at over $450,000. Dr. John B. Blake, president of National Metropolitan Bank, and Henry S. Davis had lived in Washington for over fifty years. Davis, Jesse B. Wilson, and patent attorney Columbus Alexander, lead counsel against Shepherd in the 1874 congressional investigation, all held property in excess of $100,000.[34] Corcoran, however, would become Shepherd's most prominent adversary. A conservative Democrat and Confederate sympathizer whose daughter married former southern congressman George Eustis, Corcoran fled Washington and spent the Civil War in Europe.

It was as though circumstances conspired to enrage Corcoran against Shepherd. In October 1872 sewer construction near the Corcoran Gallery of Art (now the Renwick Museum of the Smithsonian Institution), which had been Corcoran's gift to the nation's capital near the White House, caused damage and elicited a protest to Shepherd from the gallery secretary: "From some unknown cause the water is backed into the basement of the . . . building, doing much damage, and rendering the place, at times, unfit for use. Please let it have your early care and oblige."[35] Another of Corcoran's favorite projects to suffer from nearby road work was the Louise Home, a handsome building at Fifteenth Street and Massachusetts Avenue NW that he built and endowed for genteel ladies of southern sympathies who had fallen on difficult times. In August 1872 Corcoran's personal assistant wrote

---

[34] Alan Lessoff, *The Nation and Its City: Politics, "Corruption," and Progress in Washington, D.C., 1861–1902* (Baltimore, 1994), p. 59.

[35] A. Hyde to Board of Public Works, Oct. 3, 1871, Box 60, p. 471, Papers of William W. Corcoran, Library of Congress, Washington, D.C. (hereafter DLC).

to Shepherd alerting him to the possibility that roadwork would cut off the Louise Home sewer, creating a need for an immediate hookup with another sewer to forestall problems.[36] Only days later, the assistant again wrote to Shepherd, saying that because of Sixteenth Street having been filled in before installing a sewer into which the lots could drain, the Louise home was flooded: "Some 2 feet of muddy water [gathered] on the parlor floor," forcing the residents to move out and damaging the furniture. The letter went on to say that the building itself was damaged and would be uninhabitable until repairs were made. The letter added, in a tone of resignation, "The 16th St. sewer is . . . blocked up at L Street, and will probably have to come out, and hence is useless."[37]

Feeling pressure, Shepherd lashed out at Corcoran in a series of published exchanges with the owners of the *Daily Patriot* over what Shepherd considered a libelous article charging the board and "the Washington Ring" with having sent hundreds of local blacks to North Carolina to vote illegally; the article also alleged that "the ring" had used D.C. tax funds to elect Senator John Patterson of South Carolina, whom it "owned." Shepherd denounced the charge as an unqualified lie and demanded proof or a retraction. What made the letter more incendiary was that Shepherd addressed it to "W.W. Corcoran, Principal Stockholder" and two trustees of the paper.[38] Nothing came of these exchanges, but they added to the increasingly poisonous atmosphere between Corcoran and Shepherd, two of Washington's most powerful men.

Filling the Canal

One of the most dramatic changes made by Shepherd and the board was to fill in the Washington Canal, a process begun in 1872 and completed in 1873. The Washington Canal was evidence that the Father of the Nation did not always get it right. George Washington had intended the new city to serve as both a political and commercial center for the nation, and the

---

[36]A. Hyde to Board of Public Works, Aug. 2, 1872, Box 62, p. 265, Papers of William W. Corcoran, DLC.

[37]A. Hyde to Board of Public Works, Aug. 5, 1872, Box 62, p. 275, Papers of William W. Corcoran, DLC.

[38]Text reprinted in *Evening Star*, Aug. 17, 1872.

Washington Canal was to allow goods to be transported from the navigable Eastern Branch/Anacostia River to Georgetown faster than by the silting-in, tidal Potomac River. By the time President John Quincy Adams turned the first shovelful of dirt for the Chesapeake and Ohio Canal in 1828—intended to provide water transport to the Piedmont region to the west—Washington Canal was already turning into a virtual cesspool because it received most of the city's sewage not hauled away nightly by wagon.[39] The normal water level of the canal was close to that of the Potomac River, and the river tides resulted in the sewage moving first one way and then the other, never flushing into the river as intended.

Dr. Joseph Henry, longtime secretary of the Smithsonian Institution and a canal neighbor, told anyone who would listen about the importance of closing the canal, principally from a public health perspective. In this effort he was joined by the Washington Board of Health, a body established by the same legislation that created the territorial government and the board. The portion of the city on the south side of the canal, despite the presence of the Smithsonian Institution and Andrew Jackson Downing's plantings on the Mall, suffered from isolation and grew into an urban slum requiring constant attention from the Metropolitan Police Force.

The canal was a topic of inquiry during the 1872 investigation into District affairs, and professional opinion was divided on whether to dredge and narrow it or close it altogether. Civil War veteran General Nathaniel Micheler, the engineer in charge of Washington public buildings and grounds, took a hard line: "I should look upon it as most unwise to attempt to close any portion of the canal, or to convert it into a covered sewer. . . . First. If it were converted into a sewer it would have to be dredged. Second. If filled, provision would have to be made for sewerage at an expense of not less than $1,000,000. Besides, the expense of filling would be three times that of dredging."[40] General Montgomery C. Meigs, who served on Shepherd's Advisory Board, also weighed in against canal closure. An investigation opposition witness, landowner William H. Philip, described his own and Meigs's shock at learning after the fact of the decision to close the canal,

---

[39]Even more damaging to the canal's commercial prospects was the fact that the C&O Canal was launched the same year as the Baltimore & Ohio Railroad received a charter to lay tracks into Washington, dooming the canal system to obsolescence before it was ever built.

[40]*1872 Investigation*, p. 205.

which in Meigs's case violated Shepherd's promise to have the Advisory Board approve all improvement projects before proceeding.[41]

Board Treasurer James Magruder acknowledged that the board had never "formally" consulted the Advisory Board about canal closure. Pressed, Magruder explained, "We have appointed meetings for these gentlemen several times, but we never got a majority of them together after the first meeting." Magruder confirmed having personal, "informal" meetings with General Babcock and added that he had talked with General Meigs, "but he did not agree with me."[42] There is no evidence that Meigs personally bore Shepherd any ill will, but there was a growing body of evidence that Shepherd was determined to carry out his improvements plan as he saw fit, with decreasing reference to his own promises as well as legislative guidelines.

The board's chief engineer, Alfred B. Mullett, counterproposed that the canal should be closed from Seventh Street to Seventeenth Street NW:

> It has been and always will be, until an intercepting sewer is constructed, nothing more than an enormous cess-pool [*sic*]. Its value for commercial purposes is a myth; and it has been of no benefit . . . to anyone save a few petty officials connected with its management. . . . It appears to me, further, the height of insanity to expend a large sum of money to perpetuate in the heart of the capital of the nation an open ditch, for no other ostensible reason than for a landing place for wood, coal, oysters, and other similar articles, when the magnificent river front is almost entirely unoccupied.[43]

Besides joining the separated portions of the city, canal closure would also make possible laying a parallel sewer and creating "B" Street, later known as Constitution Avenue. While not advertised as such, closure of the canal signaled, once and for all, that Washington's future would be as a political capital only; hopes for river- and canal-borne commerce had failed, and industry would have to look elsewhere. While most of Shepherd's public improvements projects in the District of Columbia followed L'Enfant's original plan for the city, removal of the canal was Shepherd's most prominent deviation from the plan and reunited the neighborhoods on both sides of the canal, previously linked by nine small bridges.

---

[41] Ibid., pp. 199–200, p. 224.
[42] Ibid., p. 349.
[43] Ibid., pp. 147–48.

Carpe Diem

In the fall of 1872 Shepherd made two of his most dramatic moves to over-come obstacles to his plans to beautify Washington, D.C. The first was de-struction of the Northern Liberties Market, a haphazard collection of sheds on a square at the intersection of Massachusetts and New York Avenues and Eighth St. NW, whose removal Shepherd had been planning as precursor to relocating the market to a new, more desirable location. Shepherd was well aware of stallholder opposition to a move, and anti-Shepherd attorneys were scheduled to present their petition for an injunction in court on Sep-tember 4. The previous evening Shepherd signed a board order to remove the Northern Liberties Market "tonight." According to a story circulated by Shepherd, he arranged for the judge expected to hear the case to be taken on a carriage ride by a friend, with instructions to return late.[44] During the judge's absence from the city, a gang of two hundred laborers set to work destroying the market while fifty policemen directed by Police Chief A. C. Richards looked on. Within five hours the work was done, although, tragi-cally, a lingering stallholder and a boy hunting rats with his dog were killed as the structure came down.[45] The deaths were a reminder to the impetu-ous Shepherd that precipitate action could carry costs.

Shepherd's second and more dramatic assertion of power occurred in mid-November and involved a confrontation with the powerful Baltimore & Ohio Railroad company, which had a monopoly on providing rail ser-vice into the District of Columbia. Tracks of a B&O subsidiary, the Balti-more and Potomac railway used by the Washington and Alexandria Railroad, ran across the mall at the foot of Capitol Hill, creating a differ-ence in grade, a physical obstruction, and an eyesore. At the beginning of October Shepherd wrote to General Orville Babcock, superintendent of public buildings, explaining his intention to remove the tracks and asking Babcock, who was also responsible for the Capitol grounds, for authoriza-tion, which was granted.[46] The evening of November 18–19 Shepherd as-sembled four gangs of fifty men each that went to work on the rails after the last engine had left the nearby B&O depot. Tackling different sections of

---

[44]*New York World,* Jan. 21, 1876, reprinted in *Evening Star,* Jan. 29, 1876.
[45]*Evening Star,* Sept. 4, 1872; William M. Maury, *Alexander "Boss" Shepherd and the Board of Public Works,* GW Washington Studies, No. 3 (Washington, D.C., 1975), p. 41.
[46]*Evening Star,* Nov. 19, 1872.

track, the teams completed the job in five hours; in the morning a B&O engine showed up with a crew, collected the rails, and hauled them away.[47] Shepherd confidant and legal advisor William Mattingly told the rest of the story years afterward: "a few days later [there was] an interview between [Shepherd] and John W. Garrett, the then president of the railroad company, at Wormley's Hotel, at the corner of Fifteenth and H Streets. At the conclusion of the interview, Mr. Garrett said to Shepherd, 'Any time you are willing to accept the position of Vice-President of the B&O, I will gladly see that you get it. You are just the man the company needs and wants.'"[48]

Board of Public Works First Progress Report

The 1872 Report of the Board of Public Works to the President was a bound volume of over two hundred pages summarizing the board's activity and containing texts of historical documents supporting Shepherd's thesis of federal responsibility for the District of Columbia's infrastructure as well as detailed descriptions of items purchased and work done. The account of the work accomplished by the board from its organization in spring 1871 until November 1, 1872, was impressive by any standard and even more so considering the human and natural obstacles overcome by the board in the process. The report cited the following achievements:[49]

Main Sewers	"About" eight miles
Gas Mains	"About" 42 miles (Washington Gas Light Co.)
Street Pavements	115.36 miles of "improved carriageway pavements"
Sidewalks	93.3 miles
Trees	2,000 planted; 17,200 in reserve nursery

The 1872 report provided not only a massive amount of information about board achievements and the historical context in which they took place; it also said a great deal about how Shepherd saw himself. Considering later

---

[47]Ibid.

[48]William F. Mattingly, Address at Shepherd statue unveiling, May 9, 1909, Washingtoniana Collection, Martin Luther King Jr. Library.

[49]Report of the Board of Public Works of the District of Columbia, from its Organization until November 1, 1872 (n.p., n.d), copy in author's possession.

developments, in the early stages of the territorial government Shepherd considered himself thorough and highly organized, creating a paper trail to drive the point home. The 1872 report may be looked at as Shepherd's way of telling his critics that everything they needed to know about board practices could be found in its pages. While there was much about how Shepherd went about the people's business that remained open to question, he saw himself as a meticulous and accountable recordkeeper. For example, at the end of September a special commission appointed at his initiative completed a compilation of all the statutes in force in the District of Columbia, totaling some one thousand pages. Pending approval by Congress and the Legislative Assembly, the statutes were to be published in one volume.[50] At Shepherd's direction, the board established the first building codes for the District of Columbia. The guidelines, prepared by newly appointed member of the board and Inspector of Public Buildings Adolf Cluss, established comprehensive rules for building construction and safety.[51] As a member of the Board of Aldermen prior to the territorial government, Shepherd had made other contributions to collecting and making available information about the District of Columbia such as maps and photographs for reference purposes. In short, Shepherd demonstrated time and again that he was in favor of making vital statistics available for builders and developers.

What Shepherd could not publish or acknowledge, however, was his inability or unwillingnesss to question his own motives and actions and his tendency always to consider his actions in the public interest, regardless of whether the public was consulted or otherwise made party to the decision. As long as District affairs were more or less under control, and as long as funding was available to pay for the public works program, he would hew to this line. Once things began to spiral out of control, however, the lack of oversight inherent in Shepherd's individualistic management style became a problem that ended up magnifying rather than reducing governance errors.

The fall of 1872 saw reelection of President Grant by a resounding margin as well as a Republican sweep of both Houses of Congress, with two-thirds majorities in both.[52] A 15 percent increase in the value of District of

---

[50]*Evening Star*, Oct. 1, 1872.
[51]"Report of Inspector of Buildings," *1872 Board of Public Works Report*, pp. 91–96.
[52]*Evening Star*, Nov. 6, 1872.

Columbia real estate in the immediate past year provided a strong, albeit implicit, endorsement of the actions of the Board in making Washington a more elegant and livable place. The *Evening Star* attributed the rise to "the confidence of the people in the new order of things" and "vindication" of the board's actions, "whatever minor mistakes may have crept into the details of their vast function."[53] Not even an alarming outbreak of the usually fatal epizootic horse disease could break the positive mood, although the epidemic brought a temporary halt to the use of almost all horse-drawn vehicles and slowed road progress as winter approached.[54]

The board, despite having left much of downtown Washington a mess of uncompleted road projects over the previous winter, had been able nonetheless to provide a glimpse of a better and more appealing future for the city. Even Shepherd's most bitter opponents felt obliged to declare themselves in favor of public improvements, while continuing to criticize his program by varying degrees for such things as excessive haste, confusion, and expense, as well as inadequate planning and dictatorial control. As matters turned out, 1872 had indeed proved to be the zenith of the territorial government, and 1873 would see a steady downturn in the board's fortunes.

---

[53]Ibid., Nov. 8, 1872.
[54]Ibid.

Chapter Eight

"They Must Have a Republican Boss Tweed for Campaign Purposes"

A Troubled Territorial Governor, 1873–1874

In 1873 the fortunes of the territorial government and the Board of Public Works turned irreversibly sour, and Shepherd came under constant attack from a growing number of critics. The bright hopes of the previous two years dimmed, even though public works progress continued. Events beyond Shepherd's control loomed large and seemed to work in concert with local issues to undermine his efforts.

By 1873 Shepherd was forced to deal with the reality that the territorial government was running out of money. This state of affairs compelled him to resort to practices his predecessors used, and which he had derided, including paying contactors in certificates that they had to resell, often at a substantial discount, instead of paying them in cash, a practice that had been a bedrock of board policy for financing development at the start.[1] Shepherd pursued other, desperate solutions to the territory's financial crisis. The story is told that after a meeting with the city auditor at which Shepherd was informed that the city was broke, he met with William A. Cook, the city's lawyer, to seek a solution. After a discouraging meeting, Cook, a religious man, went home and prayed for a solution. Not long thereafter he drafted the legislation with a novel concept: a sewer and drainage system under which the District of Columbia was divided into districts in which

---

[1]Alan Lessoff, *The Nation and Its City: Politics, "Corruption," and Progress in Washington, D.C., 1861–1902* (Baltimore, 1994), p. 76.

adjacent landowners were billed, regardless of whether sewer lines had reached their property. This creative financing measure—quickly enacted by the legislature—called for the issuance of two million dollars' worth of sewer certificates bearing interest at 8 percent. Sewer certificates were followed quickly by water fund certificates, which were intended to pay for water mains and fire hydrants. The sinking fund commissioners were authorized to issue these certificates in amounts not to exceed $165,000 for overdue and future improvements assessments.[2] Another bill allowed Governor Cooke to anticipate tax collection based on certificates for future taxes due, which would be sold to banks and speculators at a discount. This would provide funds called a "temporary loan" to meet board expenses. Property owners could redeem the tax certificates by full payment of taxes due plus fees to the certificate holder.[3]

In January 1873 Congress approved a payment of $1.25 million to the District, the largest single congressional commitment to date, to pay for street improvements adjacent to government properties. The payment was significant on a broader level as recognition by Congress that it must make a proportionate contribution to the expense of running the nation's capital.[4] In March Congress appropriated a further $2 million for street operations bordering federal land. The sum of these two payments equaled more money toward the improvement of the capital than had been appropriated during the preceding seventy years.[5] The two congressional appropriations were a major step forward for Shepherd in his long fight to see Congress accept its financial responsibility toward the District of Columbia.

The second half of 1873 saw noteworthy developments for both the District and Shepherd. For Shepherd there were two such events: completion of an elegant mansion at the northeast corner of Connecticut Avenue and

---

[2]Records of the Government of the District of Columbia: Laws of the Legislative Assembly, June 22, 1871–June 20, 1874 (hereafter Laws of the Legislative Assembly), vol. 2, June 23, 1873, Record Group 351, National Archives and Records Administration, Washington, D.C. (hereafter NARA). A sinking fund is a fund accumulated to pay off a public or corporate debt. The story of Cook's divine inspiration is attributed to longtime Shepherd aide and local historian William Tindall in John Claggett Proctor, *Washington Past and Present: A History*, 2 vols. (New York, 1930), 1:141.

[3]Laws of the Legislative Assembly, vol. 2, June 25, 1873.

[4]James Huntington Whyte, *The Uncivil War: Washington during the Reconstruction, 1865–1878* (New York, 1958), p. 156.

[5]Alan Lessoff, "Politics of Development," unpublished paper, Johns Hopkins University, 1984, p. 41.

K Street NW and his appointment by President Grant as governor of the territory of the District of Columbia, replacing Governor Henry Cooke. Shepherd had commissioned his friend and fellow board member Adolf Cluss to design a new home for him in the block across from the north side of Farragut Square. Cluss designed all three homes on that block: Shepherd's, his own, and one for real estate investor and Shepherd associate Hallet Kilbourn. Shepherd wanted a large, elegant home in a prime spot where he and his wife could live in luxury with their seven children and entertain on a grand scale. Cluss, Washington's most admired architect, was just the man, and the homes for himself and Kilbourn, while elegant, were considerably smaller than Shepherd's.

Construction of the Shepherd mansion took two years, cost Shepherd an estimated $150,000, and covered most of the quarter acre of land on which it sat. The house was designed for entertaining, with a large drawing room, picture gallery, circular reception room, library, dining room with bay window facing Connecticut Avenue, and pantries "large enough for Presidents' bedrooms" on the first floor. The basement contained a billiard room, a suite of offices for Shepherd and associates, and servants' quarters; the upper floors had fourteen bedrooms. Skylights shed tinted light on the interior, walnut balusters were inlaid with bronze, and wainscoting mingled sandalwood, silverwood, laurel, and spotted maple.[6] Shepherd used the mansion to host many social events during his remaining time in power in Washington.

The Panic of 1873

The Panic and depression of 1873 hit Washington in the fall of that year. During the years following the Civil War, investment in the American railroad system had risen dramatically, capped by the driving of the "Golden Spike" in 1869, when the Union and Central Pacific Railroads joined the

---

[6]Ernest F. M. Faehtz and Frederick W. Pratt, *Real Estate Directory of the City of Washington, 1873–1874*, 3 vols. (Washington, D.C., 1873–74), vol. 1; George Townsend, aka "Laertes," National Capital Gossip, Nov. 16, 1875, typescript by ARS daughter Grace S. Merchant in Shepherd Papers, Library of Congress Manuscript Division, Washington, D.C.; James Goode, *Capital Losses: A Cultural History of Washington's Destroyed Buildings*, 2nd ed. (Washington, D.C., 2003), pp. 183–85.

East and West Coasts in Utah Territory. Financier Jay Cooke, brother of D.C. territorial governor Henry Cooke, launched a sale of bonds for a northern version of the transcontinental railway, the Northern Pacific, but became overextended when the bonds did not sell, and his financial empire quickly became distressed.[7] Events moved swiftly as word spread that Jay Cooke & Company was in trouble. The collapse of Cooke's empire sparked a panic that caused a national depression, and the District of Columbia was soon in financial distress from the loss of bank liquidity and access to credit. The *New York Times* reported that the crash removed about $800,000 from circulation in Washington, D.C., alone, and banks called in loans in an effort to shore up their reserves against withdrawals.[8] Commercial activity ground to a halt.

Governor Cooke sent President Grant a letter of resignation on September 10, saying that the combined demands of his private and public duties had become too exacting to continue. The letter singled out for praise Shepherd and the other members of the Board of Public Works "whose energy, courage, and comprehensive judgment have achieved such brilliant results."[9] President Grant's response was to accept the resignation with regret and point out that "the national capital has advanced towards what it should be with a rapidity that astonishes and pleases everyone who has been away from it for a few years and returns."[10] Grant promptly named Alexander Shepherd as the new governor.

Shepherd's appointment as governor on September 13 was a bittersweet promotion. Originally an aspirant for the post, Shepherd had settled for his position on the Board of Public Works, which turned out to be the most influential office in the territorial government. Perhaps reflecting local and national economic distress, the handover of the governorship was a low-key swearing-in at former governor Cooke's Georgetown residence, with only a handful of officials and personal friends on hand. Cooke said that any regrets at leaving were "banished" by knowledge that Shepherd was to be his replacement.[11] The personnel changes at the top of the territorial government

---

[7] This happened in part because of downward market pressures triggered by European banks calling in their U.S. loans after the German government ceased to mint silver *thalers*, resulting in a sharp drop in the international price of silver.

[8] *New York Times*, Oct. 26, 1873.

[9] *Evening Star*, Sept. 13, 1873.

[10] Ibid.

[11] *Evening Star*, Sept. 15, 1873.

generated a shuffle on the board. Shepherd was now board president ex officio but was not replaced as board executive vice president, and Cluss, already alarmed by questionable board practices, resigned as chief engineer, to be replaced by banker John B. Blake. Hotelier Henry A. Willard took the place of S. P. Brown, who also resigned.[12]

Despite anxiety about economic conditions locally and across the nation, Shepherd and the board described another year of achievements in the board's second annual report, published in November. The statistical shorthand listed the following aggregate achievements since the onset of work in spring 1871: "One hundred and twenty-three miles of sewer, varying in size from thirty feet to six inches . . . nearly two hundred and eight miles of sidewalks . . . upward of one hundred and fifty-seven miles of improved roadways . . . more than thirty miles of water mains [plus] nine miles . . . lowered and relaid to suit new grades."[13] The report also listed the following: "Thirty-nine miles of gas mains have been laid, and the number of public lamps increased to 2,954 . . . 6,236 trees have been set out, and 23,240 prepared for the next season."[14]

Seeking to advance long-standing arguments for Congress to accept financial responsibility for the District of Columbia, the report stated that "since 1802, D.C. residents had paid a total of $18,148,445 for street and sewer improvements, while Congress had contributed only $4,476,706. . . . Imbued with patriotic pride, our citizens will at all times cheerfully bear their just proportion of the expenses necessary for the adornment of the National Capital. They petition for no relief from such a burden, heavy though it was; but simply ask that the nation, mindful of its own obligations, will perform its part in the laudable effort to make the metropolis of the American Republic the grandest of the cities of the world."[15]

By the end of 1873 Shepherd was the governor of a territory that was out of money. Although the board report for 1873 contained evidence of progress, Shepherd was forced to spend most of his time fending off attacks on the territorial government and scrambling to keep improvements from

---

[12]Ibid., Sept. 13, 1873; William Tindall, *A Standard History of the City of Washington* (Knoxville, Tenn., 1914), p. 252.

[13]*Report of the Board of Public Works of the District of Columbia, November 1, 1873* (Washington, D.C., 1873), pp. 1–2.

[14]Ibid.

[15]Ibid., p. 4.

grinding to a halt in the face of an empty treasury. As matters turned out, these were to be his principal official activities as long as the territorial government lasted. The Panic of 1873 also caught Shepherd in an awkward personal situation: he was overleveraged through borrowed money for purchase of land and building materials and unable to devote attention to managing his own affairs. Having made his fortune in real estate development and house construction in the District of Columbia, Shepherd's personal wealth was closely tied to the financial markets. In 1872 he was largely unrepresented in real estate transactions because of the press of board business, but in 1873—evidently unaware of the looming financial crisis— Shepherd reentered the real estate market, buying and selling house lots in Washington in a burst of summer activity. An informal calculation based on press announcements showed him purchasing lots between May and August 1873 at a cost of $195,000 and selling lots totaling $114,000, plus purchases of 550 acres of land in Prince Georges County, Maryland, along with sales announcements for at least four large houses in the District that did not list prices.[16] As a result, Shepherd had maximum credit exposure just as the economy collapsed.

The impact of the depression of 1873 on Shepherd's personal finances was devastating, although the full extent of the damage was not immediately apparent. (An indicator of Shepherd's strong financial image among local banks was a ninety-day personal note in early 1874 for $7,600 to the Farmers and Merchants National Bank of Georgetown to guarantee repayment of the bank's loan to the D.C. government.[17]) However, a perhaps more realistic indicator of Shepherd's financial status was reflected in his transferring title to the K Street mansion in June 1874 to brother-in-law Andrew Bradley and attorney William Philip as trustees for collateral for a $35,000 loan from Philadelphia financier George S. Pepper. The mansion was used as collateral for a further $10,000 loan from Pepper a year later. The status of the property was to remain in dispute long after Shepherd's departure for Mexico in 1880 and was not resolved until 1912.[18]

---

[16]See *Evening Star*, May 5, 15, 16, 21; June 17, 20; Aug. 7; Sept. 8, 29, 1873.

[17]Shepherd to Farmers and Merchants National Bank, Letters Sent from the Office of the Governor, Jan. 2–June 20, 1874, RG 351, vol. 3, p. 151, NARA.

[18]Equity Court File no. 6201, June 1, 1874, RG 21, NARA. The property was assessed on June 30, 1878, for $56,674.

Grant and Shepherd

Shepherd's personal relationship with President Grant is the stuff of speculation but only scattered documentary evidence.[19] Grant had lived in Washington for several years before his election as president in 1868, and he
came to know the key players in urban development, including Henry Cooke,
through his friendship with Cooke's older brother Jay, a major contributor
to the Republican Party.[20] As we have seen, well before installation of the
territorial government in spring 1871, Shepherd had been seeking support
for change in the capital's system of governance; thus contact with Grant,
an important figure among the capital's power brokers, would have been
natural. A meeting between Grant and Shepherd occurred in January 1870,
when Shepherd was part of a small group of leading Washington businessmen who met with Grant at the White House. Headed by banker William
Wilson (W. W.) Corcoran, the group made the case that continuing talk of
removal of the capital to the West was having a harmful effect on local business. Grant responded that he wished to see the District of Columbia
"made such as to arouse the pride of the citizens of the Republic" and
pledged to help "to the full extent of [his] power."[21]

There is abundant evidence of Grant's interest in and support for
Shepherd's work to build the infrastructure of Washington, reflected in
strong wording in Grant's annual messages to Congress from 1871 through
1874. In his comments on the board's first months of activity, Grant urged
liberal appropriations on the part of Congress so that the government would
bear its just share of the expense of carrying out a judicious system of improvements.[22] A year later, Grant stayed on message, commending the improvement of the condition of the city of Washington and surroundings and
the increased prosperity of the citizens and restating the federal government's obligations to share the costs, citing the need for congressional

---

[19]For example, the thirty-one-volume series of the papers of President Grant, edited by
the late John Y. Simon, includes only a handful of items related to the relationship
between Grant and Shepherd, and these on seemingly trivial matters.

[20]Whyte, *Uncivil War*, pp. 91–93. Whyte maintained that Shepherd became a member
of Grant's influential "Kitchen Cabinet."

[21]*Evening Star*, Jan. 22, 1870; *New York Times*, Jan. 23, 1870.

[22]Ulysses S. Grant, "Third Annual Message," in *A Compilation of the Messages and Papers
of the Presidents 1789–1908*, ed. James D. Richardson, 11 vols. (Washington, D.C., 1911),
7:154.

reimbursement and liberal appropriations for work already done—as well as planned—in front of federal properties.[23] Grant continued his praise of Shepherd's achievements in his 1873 message to Congress, despite the fact that the District's insolvency and the financial crisis had soured the local and national mood. Grant described the District as "one of the most sightly cities in the country, [which] can boast of being the best paved." No doubt reflecting wording provided by Shepherd, the message went on to note systematic planning of street grades and sewer and water main locations *before* the work had commenced. Grant again called on Congress to pursue a liberal policy toward the District of Columbia and invoked national pride for all citizens visiting Washington, who would know that they, too, were part owners in the investments.[24] Ever loyal, President Grant endorsed Shepherd's long-standing views in his 1874 message (after the revocation of territorial government in June of that year) by urging that the proportion of District expenses borne by the federal government should be "carefully and equitably defined."[25]

There were periodic press reports over the years of social contact between the Shepherds and the Grants, and it would have been customary for a prominent figure such as Shepherd to be invited to White House social events. He was a member of small groups invited by Grant for house visits to Cape May, New Jersey, and City Point, Virginia. Grant also visited Shepherd's luxurious K Street residence, which was only a short distance from the White House.[26] A newspaper interview with Grant in 1873 described him as a friend and advocate of Shepherd and said that the President "has taken particular pains to give the work done under the orders of the board his personal supervision." The account went on, "It is evident that [Grant] endorses fully the course of Governor Shepherd, and those who attempt to fight that gentleman, in or out of Congress, will find that in the President he has a powerful and earnest supporter."[27]

---

[23]Grant, "Fourth Annual Message," in Richardson, *Compilation of the Messages and Papers of the Presidents*, 7:204; *Evening Star*, Dec. 2, 1872.

[24]Grant, "Fifth Annual Message," in Richardson, *Compilation of the Messages and Papers of the Presidents*, 7:255.

[25]Grant, "Sixth Annual Message," in Richardson, *Compilation of the Messages and Papers of the Presidents*, 7:302–3.

[26]*World Graphic* (New York), n.d., 1876; *Evening Star*, Sept. 23, 1873.

[27]*Philadelphia Press*, Oct. 12, 1873, reprinted in *Evening Star*, Oct. 17, 1873.

For his own part, Shepherd was a proud and unabashed admirer of Grant, whose support for public improvements in the nation's capital was critical, particularly after the Republican Party swept both Houses of Congress in 1872. In an 1876 press interview Shepherd spoke warmly of the relationship: "[Grant] was as steadfast a friend as I had. . . . I do like President Grant, because he is every inch a man. I am an admirer of out-and-out manhood. I never knew the President to prevaricate or go back on his word. And I never knew him to forgive a man who was guilty of doing either. He sustained me because he believed I was right. He would have thrown me overboard in an instant if he had had proof to the contrary."[28]

In an interview some years later Shepherd said, "I don't believe I ever went to [President Grant] without getting the full weight of his power and influence in behalf of my undertaking." Shepherd felt confident being direct with Grant, describing one meeting (ca. 1876) in which Shepherd spoke freely, advising Grant to "lop off the heads of some fellows" who were close to him and were even "traitors," or Grant would be sorry. "It was the only occasion I recall that he appeared miffed at what I had to say." Shepherd reported that Grant later told him that "he always regretted that he did not take some of the advice I gave him then."[29] Shepherd, often able to take the long view about political realities, believed that at least part of his own troubles came from his close association with Grant. One of Shepherd's daughters recounted a conversation between her parents: " 'They are persecuting you, Alex,' said my Mama's voice, after Papa read her something from the morning paper propped up on his glass of cream. 'It's a cruel slander!' 'It's all politics, darling,' said Papa. 'They are hitting at the dear old General through me. They must have a Republican Boss Tweed for campaign purposes.' "[30]

Criticism of Grant and Shepherd intensified in late 1873. The nation was disillusioned with President Grant as a result of the growing number of scandals involving his associates. The autumn crash shook the country's financial pillars and brought into sharper relief the growing problem of Grant's associates and relatives being engaged in illegal or at least morally

---

[28]*New York World,* Jan. 21, 1876, reprinted in *Evening Star,* Jan. 29, 1876.

[29]*Evening Star,* Sept. 9, 1887.

[30]Typescript, no doubt by ARS daughter Grace Shepherd, Shepherd Papers, Library of Congress.

questionable conduct. Democrats and Liberal Republicans alike attacked the White House for the appearance of corruption—not all of it attributable to presidential associates—in such actions as an 1869 attempt to corner the market in gold and the 1872 Crédit Mobilier scandal.[31] The operating methods of Shepherd and the board were regarded by critics of the administration as fuel to heap on the anti-Grant fire. The board's practice of awarding contracts to Shepherd's associates and others of questionable competence had become an issue in Washington and was picked up and amplified in New York newspapers in particular.[32] Hamilton Fish, Grant's long-serving secretary of state, was caustic in describing the machinations of Shepherd and trusted confidants of Grant such as Orville Babcock, Grant's personal secretary.[33]

Later in the year, Shepherd [then Governor] asked U.S. Treasury Secretary William Richardson to advance payment of September salaries to local employees in order "to relieve the financial pressure under which the city and people are laboring." Richardson agreed, and Shepherd also obtained agreement from the Navy Department to advance salaries to its local employees.[34]

The District's desperate financial condition provided the backdrop for the most sustained and effective assault on Shepherd yet by his political enemies. A drumbeat of criticism in the second half of 1873 was fed by dramatic reports in the New York City press intent on creating an image of President Grant surrounded by disreputable and self-serving aides and associates, including Shepherd. Shepherd's local critics marshaled their arguments, aided by W. W. Corcoran's active participation. Corcoran, whose wealth and public generosity had drawn to him a host of supporters and admirers in Washington, including members of Congress, now added his money and influence to a full-throated assault on Shepherd and the board. In a coordinated effort, two prominent groups presented

---

[31]Allan Nevins, *Hamilton Fish: The Inner History of the Grant Administration* (New York, 1936), p. 611. The Crédit Mobilier scandal involved collusion and fraud between the firm and the Union Pacific Railroad.

[32]An *Evening Star* investigation into a *New York Sun* article accusing a local "ring" of capturing a contract for the D.C. fire alarm system revealed that the contract was never let, since the legislature appropriated $45,000, and the only bid—for $75,000—was submitted by a New York firm holding the patent (*Evening Star*, Feb. 2, 1874).

[33]Nevins, *Hamilton Fish*, pp. 585, 657–58.

[34]*Evening Star*, Sept. 25, 1873.

petitions to Congress in January 1874 detailing charges against the territorial government and the board for their conduct in carrying out the public improvements program.[35] The more than fifty petitioners besides Corcoran included well-known figures in Washington's business and political establishment such as George Washington Riggs, Columbus Alexander, and John Van Riswick, along with persistent Shepherd opponent Sayles Bowen.

A Second Congressional Investigation

The result was a congressional Joint Select Committee that held its first meeting in February 1874 and took testimony from early March through the end of May, issuing its report on June 6.[36] Having been stung by criticism of the makeup of the 1872 investigating committee—restricted to the House of Representatives and dominated by Republicans—Congress established a Joint Committee representing both houses of Congress, with three senators (two Democrats and one Republican) and five representatives (three Republicans and two Democrats). George Boutwell, a Democratic senator from Massachusetts, was chairman.[37] The charges of the 1874 memorialists did not differ significantly from those of 1872, but the new group was smaller, had the financial resources of Corcoran and Riggs and others behind it, and had learned how to present information in a more effective way than before. There was also a longer period of experience and observation for the critics to examine, including more evidence of financial injury as a result of board activities, territorial government insolvency, the board's desperate funding schemes, and cases of contractor incompetence.

---

[35]Shepherd, perhaps realizing the inevitability of another investigation, sent a letter in December 1873 to the chairman of the House District Committee, officially requesting an investigation of District government and Board of Public Works affairs (*Evening Star*, Dec. 19, 1873).

[36]*Report of the Joint Select Committee of Congress Appointed to Inquire into the Affairs of the Government of the District of Columbia*, 43rd Cong., 1st sess., S. Rep. 453 (Washington, D.C., 1874), part 1, p. vi (hereafter 1874 Investigation). The report consisted of three volumes. There had been a third investigation, held in December 1872, but its mandate was limited to determining the state of the debt of the District of Columbia (H.R. Rep. 7, 42nd Cong., 3rd sess.).

[37]1874 Investigation, part 1, p. 1.

Investigation testimony and documentation eventually filled almost 3,300 pages in three official volumes. Lead attorneys for the petitioners were Richard Merrick, a Democrat and former candidate for the nonvoting D.C. congressional delegate, and Samuel Shellabarger, a former Republican member of Congress from Ohio. Counsels for the territory were William F. Mattingly, Shepherd's personal lawyer and longtime friend; Edwin L. Stanton, son of the former secretary of War and likewise a Shepherd attorney and friend; and Richard Harrington, who was later embroiled in a clumsy attempt to discredit a prominent Shepherd opponent.

The 1874 investigation became a long-running drama in which the best and worst elements of Washington life played out. The petitioners argued that they favored public improvement in Washington but objected to the way in which it was being done. Shellabarger focused his argument on "the bad character of that local government under which they suffer, its forfeiture of all title to the confidence of the country, or right to continue in power" in order "to secure their displacement or such additional legislative protection as shall render them less capable of mischief in the future."[38] Defense counsel Mattingly argued,

> we do not and have never claimed that mistakes have not been made, errors of judgment committed. The District has ample to show for all the money that has been expended. . . . One fact alone should reconcile the citizens of this District to all the indebtedness that has been incurred. . . . the improvements made in the city of Washington, in beautifying and adorning it, have so far excited the admiration of the citizens of the country generally, that the agitation of the removal of the seat of Government, so rapidly gaining ground when these improvements first began, has entirely ceased.[39]

Defense counsel Stanton highlighted Shepherd's personal stamp on the improvements:

> No comment is needed upon the magnitude of the work or its beauty. No fair man can behold it without admiration. No fair man can consider the rapidity and success of its execution without amazement. No doubt it was done rapidly. No doubt it was done, though legally, yet by the use of a strong hand. It could have been accomplished in no other way. If these officers had paused at every step to consult everybody as to what next should be done

---

[38]"Argument of Samuel Shellabarger," 1874 Investigation, part 1, p. 16.
[39]"Argument of William F. Mattingly," 1874 Investigation, part 1, pp. 77–78.

and how it should be done; if they had pondered, hesitated, and faltered, the City of Washington would today possess few of its present attractions.[40]

Defense counsel Harrington elaborated on Shepherd's role as the principal target of the petitioners' attacks. "However much it may be denied, one of the objects of the instigators of this investigation was, the destruction of the character and the reputation of Alexander R. Shepherd. . . . Some grew jealous because a mechanic had brains."[41]

Abundant evidence of board ad hoc procedures was provided to the committee. Treasurer James A. Magruder provided candid insights into how the board managed its accounts: "We paid out the money just as fast as we got it; then we paid whatever we had." Magruder elaborated on how the Board conducted its business:

Q: You paid every certificate that came when you had money?

A: When I had money I paid it, unless there was some particular reason why that particular claim should not be paid at once.

Q: What reason could there be, if he had his certificate? Was not that a final liquidation of it, and a closing-out of that account?

A: Sometimes we thought one man had had enough money for the present, and we would not pay him because we wanted to pay other people.

Q: Then you did exercise a discretion above the fact of their getting there first?

A: Men would come into me with half a dozen certificates, amounting to $30,000 or $40,000, and I would pay half and let them wait for the other half.

Q: Then you did not exactly adopt the rule of first come first serve?

A: O, no, sir; in little affairs I paid off as fast as they came to me, if I had the money. I never let them go out of the office. I always considered that people of small means were rather more entitled to receive their pay than men who had large credit and could do without their money.[42]

While much of the testimony over a three-month period consisted of spirited attack and defense by both sides, the appearance of Adolf Cluss in late May created the greatest sensation and did the most damage to the credibility of Shepherd and the public works improvement program. Cluss

---

[40]"Argument of Edwin L. Stanton," 1874 Investigation, part 1, pp. 86–87.
[41]"Argument of Richard Harrington," 1874 Investigation, part 1, pp. 110–11.
[42]1874 Investigation, part 3, p. 1346.

testified over the course of the last week of the investigation, and his presentation covered almost 180 pages in the published record.[43] Cluss was no ordinary witness. He had been chief engineer of the board and a personal friend of Shepherd who designed Shepherd's K Street mansion and his own house next door. Cluss was the most sought-after architect in post–Civil War Washington, celebrated for many buildings, including the Smithsonian Institution's Arts and Industries Building and schools that set national standards for elegance and efficiency. Cluss was also known as a man of integrity and candor, the kind of witness who could most help, or hurt, the public image of Shepherd and the board.

Cluss painted a picture of an improvements system in chaos, dominated by Shepherd and lacking in rudimentary financial accountability and oversight. Cluss stated the magnitude of the problem early in his testimony:

> (t)he organization of the board is such as to seriously impede the operations of the very best engineers that could be on hand. The vice-president takes the assistant out of the engineer's office and gives him private instructions to take up work and pass bills without the engineer knowing of it. . . . The Government measurements, which I think, according to the reading of the law, are certainly under the engineer in charge of the Board of Public Works, and to be controlled by him, and remeasured by the engineer in charge of public buildings and grounds, were done without my knowing a word of them.

"Government measurements," in this case, referred to challenged measurements for road work next to federal property that were used as the basis for a congressional appropriation/reimbursement to the territory of $1,240,000.[44] Cluss, however, drew an important distinction in his charges: asked if he knew of fraud or corruption in the board, he responded, "I know of gross neglect; I have never said that there was any fraud or corruption." He added, "I blame the system of the Board of Public Works, not the men. I think the system will end in corruption with any sort of men. It will lead to bad results in the end."[45]

Cluss's testimony went over the same ground many times, and his answers were, by and large, consistent, despite efforts by the territorial counsels and

---

[43]Ibid., part 4, pp. 2049–439, passim.
[44]Ibid., part 3, p. 2050.
[45]*Evening Star*, May 23, 1874.

Shepherd, who was present for much of the testimony, to catch him in a contradiction and undermine his credibility. Cluss came across to the committee as a serious, honest person who did not attempt to hide mistakes, including having signed in his official capacity documents of whose contents he was ignorant. An attempt by President Grant to damage Cluss's credibility by dismissing him backfired and generated additional sympathy for Cluss and animosity toward Shepherd, who was assumed to be behind the effort.

Congressional Investigation's Conclusions

The committee's report, taken as a whole, was a damning indictment of the way in which Shepherd and the board carried out the public improvements program in the District of Columbia. Delivered by committee chairman Senator William Allison of Iowa, the key findings were blunt: "The board have expended and contracted to spend, according to the governor's showing in his Answer, $18,872,566, or more than $12,000,000 in excess of the estimate cost of the proposed plan, and largely in excess of the amount of appropriations made by Congress or by the legislative assembly. . . . [G]ood faith required that great burdens as have been imposed should, in some manner, have received in advance legislative sanction." The committee's interpretation of how things came to such as pass is noteworthy:

> Your committee are of the opinion that the present embarrassments of this District, and the serious complications which now environ its finances and affairs, are primarily chargeable to the attempt early made by the authorities placed over it to inaugurate a comprehensive and costly system of improvements to be completed in a brief space of time, which ought to have required for its completion several years. . . . while your committee join in the general expression of gratification at beholding the improved condition of the national capital, the embellishments and adornments everywhere visible, they cannot but condemn the methods by which this sudden and rapid transition was secured.[46]

While critical of the Board of Public Works's practices, the committee did not spare Shepherd personally:

---

[46]1874 Investigation, part I, p. viii.

The vice-president ultimately came to be, practically, the Board of Public Works, and exercised the powers of the board almost as absolutely as though no one else had been associated with him. . . . There were not stated times for board meetings, and but comparatively few board meetings were in fact held, which were, in fact, made up by the secretary from letters and papers that came to the office, and from directions made by the vice-president. Some of these were entries made of business by the vice-president at his private office, and afterwards placed on the public records as having been business transacted by the board. . . . Notwithstanding the powers of the auditor and of the treasurer, the board, during the three years it has been in existence, has done nothing in the way of verifying the accounts of these two officers.[47]

The last paragraph in the committee's report delivered the final blow to the territorial government in the District of Columbia:

Your committee have unanimously arrived at the conclusion that the existing form of government of the District is a failure; that it is too cumbrous and too expensive; that the powers and relations of its several departments are so ill defined that limitations intended by Congress to apply to the whole government are construed to limit but one of its departments; that it is wanting in sufficient safeguard against maladministration and the creation of indebtedness; that the system of taxation it allows opens a door to great inequality and injustice, and is wholly insufficient to secure the prompt collection of taxes; and that no remedy short of its abolition and the substitution of a simpler, more restricted, and economical government will suffice.[48]

The final session of the Legislative Assembly ended in a welter of dust and embarrassment almost two months before congressional cancellation of the territorial government; Shepherd's letter to the legislature of April 27 cited the investigation and a "pending" resolution in the House of Representatives as the reasons for "temporary suspension" of the District legislature. Shepherd's journalist brother Arthur, just elected speaker of the assembly, gaveled the final session to a close, setting off a deplorable display as the members—whose sole legislative act that session had been to approve their own salaries—made off with furniture and furnishings from

---

[47] Ibid., part I, p. xi.
[48] Ibid., part I, p. xxix.

the chamber. One member even thrust a feather duster into his pants, giving the session the sobriquet of "the feather-duster legislature."[49]

A bizarre incident in the waning months of the territorial government came to be known as the "Great Safe Burglary." This ultimately unresolved debacle was to cast a further shadow on the reputation of the Grant administration. In essence, the scandal was the result of a botched attempt by Richard Harrington, one of Shepherd's legal counsels during the 1874 congressional investigation, to entrap Columbus Alexander, a wealthy Washingtonian and a lead memorialist against Shepherd. With the apparent complicity of President Grant's personal secretary, General Orville E. Babcock (who was also commissioner of Public Buildings and Grounds in the District of Columbia), Harrington enlisted corrupt members of the Secret Service in a faked robbery of a safe in the U.S. Attorney's Office and delivery of its supposedly incriminating papers to the home of Columbus Alexander.[50] The operation ended up as a comic opera farce and triggered a side investigation by the Joint Select Committee in May of 1874 that resulted in two grand jury trials, the second of which took place in April 1876, with uneven results, after the Democrats had taken control of the House of Representatives and eagerly sought evidence of illegality by members of the Grant administration. Conflicting testimony eventually resulted in acquittal of all the defendants. Despite allegations that he was involved, there is no evidence to show that Shepherd was aware of the conspiracy at the time.[51]

Appearance of Corruption and Bossism

The end of the territorial government brought to a close Shepherd's dominance in the city of Washington and changed his life. The charge of personal corruption is among the most complex and must be viewed against the standards of Shepherd's time as well as current expectations of public

---

[49]Shepherd to the Legislative Assembly, Apr. 27, 1874, Letters Sent, vol. 3, p. 305, RG 351, NARA. The "feather duster" episode is recounted in "Fiscal Relations between the United States and the District of Columbia," Report of the Joint Select Committee Pursuant to Public Act 268, S. Doc. 247, 64th Cong., 1st sess., vol. 2, p. 1737.

[50]Philip Ogilvie, "The Great Safe Burglary (April 23, 1874)," unpublished manuscript, 1992, pp. 7–8; Henry E. Davis, "The Safe Burglary Case: An Episode and a Factor in the District's Development," *Records of the Columbia Historical Society* 25 (1923):140–81.

[51]Ogilvie, "Great Safe Burglary," pp. 14–18.

servants. Shepherd's active years of public service were in the early phase of the Gilded Age, during which so-called robber barons like John D. Rockefeller (oil), Cornelius Vanderbilt (railroads), Jay Cooke (finance), Andrew Mellon (finance, oil), and Edward Harriman (railroads) created vast fortunes and played fast and loose with the public trust. Shepherd was the object of repeated and often vitriolic attacks on his personal integrity during his years of public service, before the disciplines of urban planning and administration had been established. During his tenure as executive vice president of the Board of Public Works (summer 1871–fall 1873), Shepherd personally oversaw the awarding of thousands of contracts worth millions of dollars. Throughout the period, he maintained an active role in Shepherd and Company, his plumbing and gas fitting firm, the largest in the city, and conducted board work from his company office on Pennsylvania Avenue rather than at the board offices.[52] During the 1874 congressional investigation, there were frequent accounts in testimony about the "steering" of contracts to the Shepherd firm, even if the opposing job bid was lower.[53] However, only 20 percent of total monies spent on the comprehensive improvement plan went to members of "the improver circle."[54]

Despite the barrage of charges of personal corruption, neither the 1872 nor the 1874 congressional investigation turned up credible evidence that Shepherd was personally guilty of illegal activity and of turning public funds to private use, although friends and associates did so. Where evidence arose of culpability near him, Shepherd took swift action to cauterize the wound. Such a case involved William Moore, a longtime friend, fellow Civil War volunteer, and partner in Shepherd's plumbing firm who became involved in an influence-peddling scheme to award a paving contract to the Chicago firm of McClelland and DeGolyer. Even though no evidence surfaced that Moore had taken any action to influence Shepherd after accepting an apparent bribe for that purpose, Shepherd fired Moore and dissolved the plumbing firm, although its work continued.[55] The chairman of the 1874 investigation subsequently wrote a personal letter that became public, in which he told a friend in Washington a propos of Shepherd, "I am sorry that Shepherd was temporarily sacrificed, as he had done so

---

[52] 1874 Investigation, part 3, p. 2325.
[53] Ibid., part 2, pp. 1127–29.
[54] Lessoff, *The Nation and Its City*, p. 79.
[55] 1874 Investigation, part 3, pp. 1414–25; *New York Times*, May 1, 1874.

much for the city. He can afford to wait, however, as no stain is cast upon his honor or integrity by the investigation or report."[56]

Inability to agree on ethical standards for those in public office showed up in discussions during the congressional inquiries of conflict of interest. The District government was riddled with conflicts of interest of the kind for which public officials would go to jail in our time. When investigators pointed out the regularity with which government officials violated an explicit prohibition in the District statutes against government officials profiting from public contracts, friends of the board neither dissembled nor vacillated. Without embarrassment and with confidence that a great many would agree with them, the improvers argued that the prohibition did not really apply to themselves. They emphasized that their activities demonstrated not only business sense but also public spirit. As entrepreneurs, they were instruments of progress. They asked, rhetorically, what could be wrong with making money from the progress they directed?[57]

Freedman's Bank

The efforts of reformers to investigate Shepherd on charges of corruption failed to benefit the economic well-being of Washington's black citizens. One episode in particular demonstrated this failure. Founded in 1865 by congressional charter, the Freedman's Savings and Trust Company (commonly known as the Freedman's Bank) was at once the fiscal repository for the funds of many of the nation's most prudent blacks and a symbol of the nation's commitment to encouraging thrift and economy among its black citizenry. For a time it was also an institution that brought black and white Republicans together. Alexander Shepherd was never an officer or a trustee of the Freedman's Bank, but several of his closest friends and associates, including Henry D. Cooke, Lewis Clephane, W. S. Huntington, and General Howard himself were or had been on the bank's finance committee.[58]

---

[56] *Evening Star,* July 15, 1874.

[57] Lessoff, *The Nation and Its City,* pp. 67–68.

[58] This summary of Freedman's Bank affairs is drawn mainly from the excellent study by Carl R. Osthaus, *Freedmen, Philanthropy, and Fraud: A History of the Freedman's Savings Bank* (Urbana, Ill., 1976), pp. 138–235 and passim.

Until 1870, the bank invested only in conservative instruments like U.S. Treasury notes, but a change in policy authorized the officers to invest up to 50 percent of the deposits in riskier ventures. Perhaps the bank's most disastrous investment was in the Northern Pacific Railroad, owned by Jay Cooke, brother of District governor Henry D. Cooke. The bank's loan committee, including Henry Cooke, advanced money to the railroad from Freedman's Bank at submarket rates, and bank officers also loaned money to each other and to their friends and encouraged others to do so. In 1873 the bank also accepted certificates (in lieu of cash) issued by Shepherd's Board of Public Works at a time when the District was bankrupt from the board's public improvements program. Hit hard by irresponsible loans to white enterprises, the bank collapsed in 1874. Shepherd was never accused of being a party to the collapse or of having benefited from it personally, but for this symbol of black pride to have been, in effect, looted and destroyed by a group of white men—most with close ties to Shepherd—reflects at minimum a lack of concern on his part. The collapse of Freedman's Bank revealed a cruel joke that had been played on Frederick Douglass, the distinguished black champion of rights and dignity for America's black citizens, who had accepted the presidency of Freedman's Bank in 1874, when its managers knew that it had been hollowed out and would soon collapse. Under other circumstances, Douglass's appointment would have been considered a fitting honor. As it was, however, Douglass had clearly been set up by the bank's white managers to take the blame for an outcome they had set in motion themselves.

The public record of Shepherd's activities during the territorial government period suggests that Shepherd's dedication to getting the District properly developed led to methods of doing business—as money dried up and problems increased—that he had rejected in the early stages of the public works program. Shepherd's actions prior to and early in the territorial government pointed to his intention to "do things right," such as creating a single repository of previous laws governing the District of Columbia, collecting historical artifacts (e.g., maps, photos), documenting early improvement activity, and calling for establishment of a city auditor. Shepherd was overtaken by events, however, and adopted the "law of necessity" as his guideline, as he had described it during the 1872 congressional investigation.[59] Perhaps the most generous assessment of Shepherd's policies during the board's heyday would be to describe them as—at a minimum—slipshod and justified only by the need to get the work done one way or another.

One other issue debated to this day is whether Shepherd could properly be called a "boss," in the sense of an urban political chieftain who controlled patronage and made use of public monies to build and maintain a political machine. One student of Shepherd and the territorial government maintained that Shepherd was such a boss, while conceding that Washington was a unique case in that Shepherd held an appointive rather than elective position, the District lacked an existing political structure, and the number of patronage jobs that Shepherd could control was "exceptionally small."[60] The case for Shepherd's status as a boss focused on his ability to obtain the election of those who would give him unwavering support in the territory's Legislative Assembly, a twenty-two-person chamber. It was this body that originated the appropriations (other than direct congressional appropriations for work adjoining federal property) that authorized Shepherd's public works program.[61] Hanging the boss epithet around Shepherd's neck represented success on the part of two otherwise opposed political groups: Democrats desperate to find or create a Republican counterpart to the disgraced Boss Tweed of Tammany Hall in New York City, and Liberal Republicans eager to demonstrate the venality among associates of President Grant, particularly during his second term. New York newspapers led by the *Tribune*, *Sun*, and *Herald* were influential in attempting to make the boss label stick through their steady drumbeat of allegations against Shepherd.

An analysis of urban political bossism in the fifty years after 1870 has traced the forms it took as municipal governance and politics developed. A key element in the ability of anyone to become a boss is the existence of a

[59]House Committee for the District of Columbia, *Affairs in the District of Columbia*, 42nd Cong., 2nd sess., 1872, H. Rep. 72, p. 389.

[60]William M. Maury, "The Territorial Period in Washington, 1871–1874, with Special Emphasis on Alexander Shepherd and the Board of Public Works," PhD diss., George Washington University, 1974, pp. 76–85.

[61]Ibid., p. 76. The territory's Upper House, consisting of eleven members, was appointed by the president and could be counted on to support Shepherd's programs, which were endorsed by President Grant.

political machine, and, in this respect, Washington, D.C., didn't fit the mold because of the tight control exercised over it by its constitutional parent, the U.S. Congress. The terms "boss" and "political machine" originated in the last half of the 1800s and evolved after 1900 into categories of analysis that varied city by city. Shepherd was driven by the determination to develop Washington, and his political activities were in pursuit of this single-minded goal rather than the creation of a continuing political base.[62] Nothing was more vivid in undercutting the argument about Shepherd being a city boss than the swift action of Congress in June 1874 to remove what vestiges remained of the "machine" that Boss Shepherd allegedly ran.

The handwriting had been on the wall by the end of 1873. The last act in the territorial government "play" took place in the early months of 1874 and brought down the curtain on a tumultuous period in the capital's history.

---

[62]James J. Connolly and Alan Lessoff, "Urban Political Bossism in the United States (1870–1920): The Spread of an Idea and the Defense of a Practice," in *Integration, Legitimation, Korruption: Politische Patronage in Früher Neuzeit und Moderne*, ed. Ronald G. Asch et al. (Frankfurt, 2011), pp. 187–212, and exchanges between Lessoff and the author, 2006–11.

Chapter Nine

"A Free Man Once More"

Bankruptcy and Preparations to Move to Mexico,
1874–1880

ALEXANDER SHEPHERD WAS only thirty-nine years old when, in 1874, he was in effect fired from the most important job he had ever held. The years between that event and his departure for Mexico in 1880 were difficult. The letdown—after the fast pace he had maintained through-out his years in business and as a public civil servant—was intensified by his bankruptcy and the bleakness of his professional prospects. It was clear that he would need a new playing field on which to perform, but which one, and where? The answer, when it came, surprised friends and family and, perhaps, even Shepherd himself.

The cancellation of the territorial government and with it Shepherd's dismissal by Congress on June 20, 1874, brought a turbulent era in the life of the capital to an abrupt end. Within a month of Adolf Cluss's sensational testimony before the congressional investigating committee in late May, Congress had passed a bill reinstating the original governing system of three presidentially appointed commissioners. Washington's governance changed overnight. Besides the necessity of installing an interim government for the nation's capital, there were a number of loose ends in the denouement. One final bit of controversy occurred in this long-running political drama. Ever loyal, President Grant nominated Shepherd as a commissioner, but the Senate, unwilling to risk further controversy, vetoed the nomination on the final day of the session by a vote of 36 to 6. Among the majority voting "nay" were several who had worked closely with Shepherd, including

Senators William Boyd Allison of Iowa, Justin Smith Morrill of Maine, and John Sherman of Ohio.[1] One senator told a friend of Shepherd's, "We would like to have confirmed Shepherd, but we felt that to give him any more money would be pouring it into a sieve."[2] It was clear that the experiment in local governance had generated hard feelings that needed time to recede, and the appointment of Shepherd as a District commissioner would have kept those antagonisms alive.

By the fall of 1874 the national mood had changed, and the Republican Party lost control of the House of Representatives to the Democrats, the first time in fourteen years that the Republicans had not controlled both houses of Congress. Reconstruction had weakened dramatically, and a more conservative mood had overtaken the country. Constant criticism of the Grant administration was also a factor in the congressional shift.

For the Shepherd family, life was to go on, superficially much as before. The couple now had five children, four girls and a boy who was born in 1872 at Bleak House.[3] Alexander, the first of the Shepherds' sons to survive infancy, was named after his father and a brother who had died as an infant in 1864. At the end of December 1874, Shepherd's mother, Susan D. Shepherd, died at the age of sixty-six. By this time, the family had been living in the mansion at the corner of Connecticut Avenue and K Street NW for less than a year. However, with the toll the depression of 1873 had taken on his finances, Shepherd decided that the K Street house must be rented out, and the family moved to Bleak House. Shepherd subsequently let the house, furnished, to a bachelor State Department official, prompting the press to lament that the city would not see the "brilliant entertainments" of the past season, since the Shepherds would remain at Bleak House for the winter.[4] Ever the businessman, Shepherd made a number of real estate transactions in the months following the end of the territorial government, including selling the Shepherd Building at Pennsylvania Avenue NW for $90,000

---

[1] *Evening Star* (Washington, D.C.), June 24, 1874; *Senate Executive Journal*, 43rd Cong., 1st sess., June 23, 1874, p. 371.

[2] Wilhelmus Bogart Bryan, *A History of the National Capital from Its Foundation through the Period of the Adoption of the Organic Act*, 2 vols. (New York, 1916), 2:633.

[3] Two more sons would be born at Bleak House: Grant in 1875 and John Conness in 1877.

[4] *Evening Star*, Dec. 9, 1874. Alexander Shepherd was listed in an 1875 city directory as "boarding" at W. W. Corcoran's Arlington Hotel (William H. Boyd, *Boyd's Directory of the District of Columbia* (Washington, D.C., 1875).

and purchasing the Kirkwood House property at the corner of Twelfth Street and Pennsylvania Avenue NW for $94,000. He intended to demolish the hotel and build a new business headquarters, but the plan never materialized.[5]

Putting the best face on being removed as territorial governor, Shepherd spoke his mind in a letter published in July in the *Troy Times*:

> It is a relief to be a free man once more and have time to devote to my private business, which had suffered badly during the past three years. I am worth less today, by $200,000, than I should have been had I given the time and energy to my own business that I spent in improving this city. However, I would not undo it if I could. I have not wronged anybody or any community, have striven to do my duty to God and man and today can look them in the face, conscious of having done right. It required a sacrifice to satisfy the "Independent Press," and it fell to my fate. . . . I shall live it down right here, conscious of having done a great work, honestly, fearlessly, intelligently— and trusting to Time for a vindication.[6]

Always sensitive to attacks on his personal integrity, Shepherd wasted no time in appearing before a grand jury in July 1874 to procure an indictment against Charles A. Dana, owner of the *New York Sun*, for having published "libelous" articles against him the previous year.[7] The court eventually dismissed the suit, but it was not the last time that Shepherd would seek legal recourse against opponents. Early in 1875 he initiated another libel suit, this time against Liberal Republican Whitelaw Reid, editor of the *New York Tribune*, when Reid came to Washington to testify before a congressional committee. Shepherd charged that an article in the *Tribune* two years earlier had libeled him by alleging that he had brought bankruptcy upon the District of Columbia in order to extricate himself from financial difficulties. In a manner calculated to create maximum public embarrassment for Reid, Shepherd had the writ served at W. W. Corcoran's Arlington Hotel as Reid was preparing for a dinner at the home of Democratic House Speaker James G. Blaine. Reid was taken to police court to be arraigned, accompanied by legal counsel and local supporters, including Corcoran, who offered to post bail. This event, or "ambush," as critics alleged, aroused sensitivities

---

[5] *Evening Star*, Sept. 28, 1874.
[6] *Troy Times* (New York), July 8, 1874, courtesy of Mary Wagner Woods.
[7] *New York Times*, July 9, 1874.

in the recently convened Congress, with the House of Representatives now under Democratic control. A grand jury eventually dismissed the suit.[8]

In the immediate aftermath of the territorial government's cancellation, Shepherd played a constructive role in the transition to a new government for the District. He met informally with the new commissioners and helped to provide information to ease the handover. Surprisingly, there was little turmoil in the nation's capital as it adjusted to the radical change in governance, perhaps because of the sense of relief that the death throes of the territorial government were over and politics at least temporarily set aside.

Through it all, Shepherd remained a staunch defender of the territorial government and Board of Public Works. He praised the physical changes in the District of Columbia and emphasized the importance of the District's consolidation into a single entity from its previous components of Washington City, Washington County, and Georgetown. He justified the breakneck pace of his improvements, saying, "If it had not been done in this way, and in this short time, the probability is it would never have been done." Shepherd also argued for a local-federal division of power in the District as necessary to protect both local "property interests" and the substantial federal property ownership. Looking ahead, he underscored the importance of extending the land-based improvements carried out under his leadership to the Potomac River, citing the need to reclaim the "swamp lands" along its banks as well as creating, for the first time, a proper harbor in Georgetown to encourage river commerce.[9]

Now free to turn his focus elsewhere, Shepherd devoted himself to trying to recoup his building operations throughout 1875, continuing to buy and sell real estate and build houses, albeit at a slower pace than before. He expanded into Georgetown, where he built several smaller houses as well as remodeled a pre-1812 residence into two "first-class" houses of eleven rooms each.[10] Less in the public eye, Shepherd returned to his youthful interest in rowing. In the fall of 1875 he donated a racing shell, the *Sue Shepherd*, named after his second daughter, to the Potomac Boat Club. He also expanded sponsorship of amateur rowing by hosting an evening event at his Bleak

---

[8] *Evening Star,* Jan. 19 and May 6, 1875; *New York Times,* Jan. 19, 20, 1875.

[9] *Evening Star,* Aug. 26, 1874

[10] Ibid., Jan. 23 and 25, 1875.

House residence for two local boat clubs, Analostan and Potomac, and the Nassau Boat Club of New York, which was in town for a regatta. Shepherd served as chairman of the arrangements committee and donated a prize. Much later, in 1884, the president of Analostan gave a speech praising Shepherd's contribution to boating in the capital, saying, "We have never had a more generous patron of boating than was Gov. Shepherd." The speech noted that Shepherd had been the largest donor to a new boathouse in 1876 and often welcomed American and foreign crews to Washington.[11] Lyndon Stevens, a devoted friend of Shepherd's who later worked with him in Mexico, was also a boating enthusiast and president of the Analostan Boat Club for a number of years.[12] Besides supporting local rowing, Shepherd also hosted foreign rifle teams for shooting competitions, presiding over receptions at his residence and at the Arlington Hotel for visiting teams.[13]

Declaration of Bankruptcy

Through much of 1876, Shepherd maintained a high-profile social and business life, but, unknown to most Washingtonians, his financial affairs were becoming stressed from losses from the depression of 1873 and the resulting flat real estate market in the District of Columbia. Shepherd found it increasingly difficult to obtain "accommodation," or loans, at the banks, forcing him to resort to alternate sources of financing at higher rates of interest. Finally, in November 1876, Shepherd announced, before a number of personal friends and creditors gathered at his residence, that he was "pecuniarily embarrassed" at the moment even though, as demonstrated by a statement he circulated at the meeting, he had a paper excess of assets over liabilities upward of $600,000.[14] Shepherd maintained that his total indebtedness to local banks did not exceed $75,000, with "all notes being secured by collateral or endorsers."[15]

---

[11]*Washington Post*, Aug. 1, 1884; *Evening Star*, July 13, 1889.

[12]Potomac Boat Club Letter of Invitation, Oct. 28, 1875, box 4, Shepherd Papers, Manuscript Division, Library of Congress, Washington, D.C. (hereafter DLC); *Evening Star*, Oct. 31, Nov. 1, 1875.

[13]*Evening Star*, Sept. 19, 26, 1876; *New York Times*, Sept. 29, Oct. 2, 1876.

[14]*Evening Star*, Nov. 10, 1876.

[15]*Daily Graphic*, Nov. 10, 1876, copied no doubt by Grace Shepherd, Shepherd Papers, DLC; *New York Times*, Nov. 15, 1876.

These admissions, from a man who perhaps more than anyone else represented the bedrock of Washington commerce, came as a profound shock to the assembled group on two different levels. On the one hand, it was distressing to realize that the man who only a few years before had been the fourth wealthiest Washingtonian was now in a position of need. Additionally, it was alarming to consider the impact that Shepherd's financial woes could have on potential investment in Washington commerce and real estate. This prospect was a powerful incentive for the group to rally around Shepherd and to provide him every opportunity to recover quickly from his problems, in the process allowing him to repay some or all of the money that he owed to them.

Within a short time, the five-man committee selected by the group to propose a financial rescue plan for Shepherd addressed the creditors, who met in a room at the Shepherd Centennial Building, a venue no doubt intended to remind the group that Shepherd was not without real property. The plan was straightforward: Shepherd must relinquish all his property, "real, personal, and mixed," with the exception of his share in the plumbing firm of A. R. Shepherd and Company, which was linked by a right of dower to Mrs. Shepherd but would be placed in the hands of trustees. The mansion on K Street was to be sold, and, as a consequence of the bankruptcy, the Bleak House estate was turned over to trustees.[16] Shepherd was to issue five-year bonds, that is, promissory notes, in one-hundred-dollar denominations at 5 percent annual interest. In an exception to customary practice in a personal bankruptcy case, Shepherd was permitted to manage his own financial recovery. Creditors appeared confident that Shepherd would be able to square his accounts, possibly because, it was noted, work on his buildings under construction would continue, thereby providing a revenue stream.[17]

Shepherd's bankruptcy in 1876 has been somewhat overlooked in assessments of his activities in Washington for several reasons, the principal one that he had by then stepped down from the public stage, and the glare of

---

[16]D.C. Land Record, 839/226, W. Sinkler Manning Papers; Separate Deeds in Trust to Lewis Clephane and William F. Mattingly, apparent D.C. land deed, 777-150, Feb. 17, 1875; and George Taylor, Henry A. Willard, and Samuel Cross, apparent D.C. land deed, 839/226, Nov. 15, 1876, all in possession of the author. A handwritten note on a legal document dated July 14, 1910, says, "Riggs Bank held (the) property for years to secure the B.M.C. (Batopilas Mining Co.) debt."

[17]*Evening Star*, Nov. 16, 1876.

publicity had moved on. While the bankruptcy was a local news item for a brief period in late November, the newspapers did not dwell on it, perhaps partly for fear that news stories about the downfall of Washington's most prominent real estate developer could have a chilling effect on the market. For Shepherd, however, the bankruptcy was devastating, not only because it wiped out his remaining assets but also because it removed the basis on which he had made his reputation in the face of condescension from the city's gentry, who had ridiculed his rise to power and influence from modest origins.

In the wake of bankruptcy, Shepherd and his family—now with seven children—were forced to live within significantly reduced means and had to auction a number of oil paintings in 1877 to pay his debts.[18] Nonetheless, he continued to make the occasional grand gesture and to lead high-visibility activities on an ad hoc basis. For example, during a fire at the Patent Office, the press reported that former governor Shepherd provided good service, directing and assisting the action of the firemen, and that his form was conspicuous on the roof.[19] Another opportunity for Shepherd to exercise his penchant for action occurred when he accepted chairmanship of the committee in charge of the inaugural ceremonies for Republican President Rutherford B. Hayes, who had defeated Samuel J. Tilden in the 1876 presidential election.

Shepherd's real estate activity continued to drop steadily, with small-scale transactions and repair work replacing large-scale construction of new houses, and he continued to be beset by his debts.[20] One business deal with W. W. Corcoran stands out as an indicator of Shepherd's financial problems. Shepherd purchased a property from Corcoran in Square 509, at New Jersey Avenue and Q Street NW in August 1877 but failed to pay the balance due of $5,500. Shepherd dodged and twisted for months, receiving at least ten letters from Corcoran and his agent demanding payment; Shepherd reneged on several promises to pay during that time.[21] Corcoran used

---

[18]Ibid., Nov. 9, 1877.

[19]Ibid., Sept. 25, 1877.

[20]See ibid., July 13 and 14, 1877.

[21]A. Hyde to A. R. Shepherd, July 12, 1877, Box 73, p. 209; A. Hyde to A. R. Shepherd, Sept. 4, 1877, Box 73, p. 365; A. Hyde to A. R. Shepherd, Sept. 21, 1877, Box 73, p. 412; A. Hyde to Mary G. Shepherd, Sept. 26, 1877, Box 73, p. 436; A. Hyde to A. R. Shepherd, Oct. 9 1877, Box 73, p. 473; W. W. Corcoran to A. R. Shepherd, Oct. 18, 1877, Box 73, p. 498; Arthur S. Brice to A. R. Shepherd, Oct. 22, 1877, Box 73, p. 513; W. W. Corcoran to A. R.

barbed language to remind Shepherd of the changed relationship between the two men: "I note the failure of the parties who were to have helped you out and your inability to consummate the arrangement until you can effect a sale, having no other way to make the cash payment."[22] This issue appeared to be resolved with a property swap early in the next year. While Corcoran and Shepherd had been adversaries for several years, there is no question that Corcoran was owed a legitimate debt, and Shepherd, in this case, did not act responsibly.

Shepherd continued to champion the cause of forcing Congress to pay its fair share of District expenses. He was a member of the District Committee of One Hundred that presented a petition to the second session of the Forty-Fifth Congress in December 1877, urging formal adoption of the 50 percent payment ratio by Congress for District expenses called for in the law passed by Congress in June 1874 creating a temporary commissioner government for the District of Columbia. The petition cited the history of the District and its current situation, reiterating the arguments that Shepherd had urged so forcefully before and during the territorial government.[23] Inclusion of the fifty-fifty payment formula in the legislation passed in June 1878 that confirmed the institution of commissioner government was an acknowledgment of Shepherd's foresight and determination in fighting for the interests of the District of Columbia. A contemporary observer noted that Shepherd's conception of the city as it ought to be, as well as the rapidity and boldness with which he tried to realize it, influenced the 1878 congressional decision.[24]

The year 1878 started off poorly for Shepherd. He fractured his leg on the ice near his home in early January, severely limiting his movements until mid-March.[25] Moreover, his financial woes continued to pile up. One highly visible and embarrassing problem concerned a suit by George Pepper of

---

Shepherd, Dec. 14, 1877, Box 74, p. 11; W. W. Corcoran to A. R. Shepherd, Dec. 19, 1877, Box 74, p. 28; W. W. Corcoran to A. R. Shepherd, Dec. 24, 1877, Box 74, p. 50, all in Papers of William W. Corcoran, DLC.

[22]W. W. Corcoran to A. R. Shepherd, Jan. 9, 1878, Box 74, p. 100, Papers of William W. Corcoran, DLC.

[23]Bryan, *History of the National Capital*, 2:635–37.

[24]Ibid., 2:641.

[25]Letter to Shepherd from Thomas K. Sharp, Jan. 8, 1878, enclosing undated newspaper account, courtesy W. Sinkler Manning Jr.; letter to Shepherd from O. O. Howard, Mar. 14, 1878, O. O. Howard Papers, Bowdoin College Library, Brunswick, Me.

Philadelphia, who had loaned Shepherd $45,000 against the K Street mansion in early 1874. Because of financial difficulties, Shepherd had not only defaulted on the loan interest payments but also had failed to maintain insurance on the property, and Pepper demanded that Shepherd sell it and pay off the loans. The case became even more complex because, at the time of the loan, the picture gallery at the north end of the building was not yet complete, and the loan technically did not include that portion of the mansion. Neighbor and real estate expert Hallet Kilbourn pointed out that if the picture gallery, part of a separate lot on the north end of the property, were to be severed due to the sale, it would have a "considerable" effect on the value of the property, since the picture gallery had brick walls two stories high. A further complication was an additional loan of $35,000 in August 1875 to Shepherd by a Mrs. Gray against the entire K Street property.[26] Final disposition of the Gray loan is unknown, but it appears that Shepherd, either in haste or under severe stress, or both, had borrowed the money from her under false premises, since the property was already encumbered by the loan from George Pepper. The legal dispute between Shepherd and Pepper was to drag on well into the twentieth century and was only resolved by Shepherd's estate after his death.

Frustrated by economic and other difficulties, Shepherd lashed out at foe and friend alike. He wrote an angry letter to the *Washington Post* in April 1878, responding to allegations by D.C. commissioner Thomas B. Bryan about Shepherd's management of the board. Shepherd's response condemned Bryan's violent attacks on the board, which included the charge of inaccurate board assessments and of what Bryan described as a "corruption fund."[27] Shepherd vigorously rebutted the charges.[28] The depth of Shepherd's personal problems and estrangement was again demonstrated in a lawsuit he filed against Lewis Clephane and William Mattingly, two of his closest friends and most loyal defenders, charging them with having sold him a property with faulty title in which he had invested $50,000 in improvements and now had to sell to pay debts.[29] Even the widow of George Gideon, an early political confidant and supporter, filed suit against

[26]Equity Case File no. 6201, 1878, George S. Pepper v. Alexander R. Shepherd, Record Group 21, National Archives and Records Group, Washington, D.C. (hereafter NARA).

[27]*Washington Post*, Apr. 4, 15, 1878.

[28]*Evening Star*, Apr. 17, 1878.

[29]Equity Case File no. 6529, 1879, RG 21, NARA.

Shepherd for not making good on a promissory note of $3,700 in exchange for a personal loan.[30]

Yellow Fever Campaign

Despite these problems, Shepherd returned briefly to public attention as a result of his leading role in the national response to the yellow fever epidemic that swept the lower Mississippi Valley in the fall of 1878. Starting in early summer, the disease had spread up the Mississippi River from New Orleans, causing the largest damage in Memphis, Tennessee, where an estimated twenty thousand people died before frost killed off the mosquitoes. Early in September, Shepherd participated in a mass meeting hosted by Simon Wolf, a friend and former D.C. registrar, along with a group of distinguished Washingtonians that included Frederick Douglass, George Washington Riggs, *Evening Star* co-owner Samuel H. Kauffmann, *Washington Post* owner Stilson Hutchins, and longtime D.C. police chief A. C. Richards. Shepherd was elected chairman of the National Yellow Fever Relief Committee and would lead a relief expedition to affected areas along the Mississippi River.[31] He offered the committee free use of space in the Shepherd Centennial Building at 914 Pennsylvania Avenue, which was empty and for sale.[32]

The yellow fever relief campaign was a welcome change of pace and scene for Shepherd, giving him the opportunity to be in touch with senior federal officials such as the Secretary of War. Still, he could not escape the shadow of the past: sporadic rumors circulated that he was using relief funds for personal gain. But once again Shepherd was at the center of events, and he loved it. The mission provided a public stage on which he

---

[30]Equity Case File no. 6745, 1879, RG 21, NARA.

[31]The typeset draft from which this information was taken included reporting in Washington, D.C., newspapers and contains texts of numerous exchanges with expedition members as well as public appeals and was assembled by expedition leader Alexander Shepherd. The report was later published as *Report of the Executive Committee of the National Yellow Fever Relief Commission, Organized at Washington, D.C., September 11, 1878* (Washington, D.C., 1879) (hereafter *Executive Committee Report*). The official report of the relief expedition, *Report of the Expedition for the Relief of Yellow-Fever Sufferers on the Lower Mississippi* (Washington, D.C., 1878), was written by expedition member Lieutenant Charles S. Hall and included the ship's logs, lists of delivered supplies, and supporting documentation (hereafter *Official Report*). Both reports are courtesy of W. Sinkler Manning Jr.

[32]*Executive Committee Report*, pp. 2–3.

could demonstrate his ability to carry out a large, important project, but, above all, it kept him active and involved, coming on the heels of the relative inactivity of the two years since he declared bankruptcy. Because no U.S. government ship could be made available for delivering supplies to stricken Mississippi River communities, the group leased the three-hundred-ton stern-wheel steamboat *John M. Chambers*. Shepherd established links with relief committees throughout the country that in turn launched public appeals for support. The relief effort combined private and governmental assistance, with Shepherd's relief committee coordinating national fund-raising and chartering the vessel, and the federal government providing money and goods as well as the services of volunteer, active-duty military officers to command the vessel.[33]

Shepherd and two army officers arrived in St. Louis, Missouri, on October 2 to oversee outfitting and staffing the *John M. Chambers*. Shepherd remained in St. Louis through the end of the month while the relief ship steamed south along the Mississippi River, stopping at points between St. Louis and Vicksburg to deliver supplies. In some cases, however, residents waved the ship away for fear that the crew would become infected with the fever. Army first lieutenant H. H. Benner, skipper of the steamboat, died after allowing a mother whose child had died of the yellow fever to sleep in his bunk aboard the steamboat until other travel arrangements could be made. On the belief that the disease could be spread from person to person, the crew was required to go ashore while the ship was disinfected.[34]

Once the yellow fever project was completed, Shepherd knew that he had made a significant contribution toward an important public need. This was a role he relished, and it became clear to him that he needed a new path for his energy and talents in order to break out of the downward spiral that his bankruptcy and fall from grace had set in motion. Shepherd became focused on how he could recoup his fortune and reassert his family's position in Washington at a level even higher than before. He knew that he would have to make radical changes to achieve this objective, since the well-trodden routes to affluence in the District of Columbia were unlikely to bring satisfactory results.

---

[33]Ibid., pp. 1–4; *Official Report*, p. 5.
[34]*Official Report*, pp. 8–10.

Mexico Beckons

The form these changes took surprised and perhaps shocked many—
Shepherd decided to transplant himself and his family to a remote region
of Mexico, where he planned to redevelop a historic silver-mining operation in the western Sierra Madre Mountains of Chihuahua State. The record does not indicate who persuaded Shepherd to commit to Mexico, but
there are likely candidates. From his years of prominence in Washington
he had become friends with Senator William Stewart of Nevada, who had
made a fortune in the gold and silver fields of California and Nevada before going into politics and being elected to the U.S. Senate from Nevada.
He and his "honest miners' camp" of western capitalists were friends of
Shepherd and were early investors in the DuPont Circle section of Connecticut Avenue in Washington, taking advantage of Shepherd's development thrust northwest from the White House. Shepherd also was close to
General William T. Sherman, whose brother, Senator John Sherman of
Ohio, was the author of a key piece of pro-silver legislation, the Sherman
Silver Purchase Act of 1890.[35] He also knew Senator John Conness of California, who had made his fortune in gold and after whom Shepherd named
his youngest son, John Conness Shepherd. Shepherd's favorite New York
hotel was Gilsey House, one of the city's elegant new hotels after the Civil
War, at Broadway and Twenty-Ninth Street. Built in the Second Empire
Baroque style, it resembled Washington's Willard Hotel and was a favorite
with representatives of western mining interests with whom Shepherd
would have become acquainted. Gilsey House also included among its
guests such figures as Oscar Wilde, Samuel Clemens, and Diamond Jim
Brady.[36]

Other possibly influential associates included Ulysses S. Grant and Lyndon H. Stevens, Shepherd's fellow boating enthusiast and eventual colleague
in Mexico. Grant's interest in Mexico dated from his service as a young army
officer during the Mexican-American War (1846–48). According to a longtime aide, Mexico had made a "lively" impression on Grant, who had opposed the annexation of Mexican territory and was in favor of an invasion

---

[35]"Party Politics in an Era of Upheaval," in *The Enduring Vision: A History of the American
People*, ed. Paul S. Boyer et al., 8th ed., 2 vols. (Boston, 2013), 2:601.

[36]Barbaralee Diamonstein, *New York: An Illustrated Record of the City's Historic Buildings*,
5th ed. (Albany, N.Y., 2011), pp. 227–28.

of Mexico after Appomattox to drive out the occupying French and over-throw the usurping Emperor Maximilian.[37] Grant retained a lifelong interest in Mexican business opportunities and may have put the idea into Shepherd's head (although Grant had a reputation as a poor judge of investments since he, along with other Americans, was an investor in the abortive Mexico Southern Railroad in the late 1870s, which failed and contributed to his own bankruptcy).[38] Stevens, who went to Mexico with Shepherd and stuck with him through good times and bad, held shares in Mexican mines and could have contributed to Shepherd's decision. It is also possible that Shepherd's attention was drawn to Mexico by one or another of the New York financiers who were to provide the capital that permitted purchase of the storied Mexican silver mines. Shepherd was no stranger to New York, and, as a major figure in the nation's capital throughout the 1870s, he was well known, having made it a rule to develop relationships with influential individuals and business sectors. As owner of a thriving plumbing and lighting establishment, he dealt extensively with New York suppliers. As vice president of the Board of Public Works and briefly as governor, Shepherd traveled frequently to New York to inspect paving and other urban technologies and later to seek funding. George Baker Jr., a well-placed banker in New York City, was the son of Washington's comptroller and a regular contact.

Shepherd's decision to move to Mexico seems counterintuitive in key respects. It flew in the face of his lifelong residence in Washington, D.C., and meant accepting financial and managerial responsibility in an industry in which he had no prior experience. It meant exposing his family to dangers and privation in a setting totally unlike the life of ease and indulgence they had known. But this grade-school dropout had long since demonstrated that if there was one thing he loved, it was a challenge on a large scale. With his combative personality, he also loved to prove people wrong, particularly the snobbish Washington social set who had never welcomed him into its parlors. Shepherd had achieved his goal of uniting the disparate parts of Washington into a coherent whole, but that was more than a

---

[37]Adam Badeau, *Grant in Peace: From Appomattox to Mount McGregor* (Scranton, Pa., 1887), p. 348; Allan Nevins, *Hamilton Fish: The Inner History of the Grant Administration* (New York, 1936), pp. 216–17.

[38]John Mason Hart, *Empire and Revolution: The Americans in Mexico since the Civil War* (Berkeley, Calif., 2002), pp. 120–21.

half-decade ago, and the only public roles still open to him in Washington were ceremonial, such as welcoming visiting shooting and crew teams. Inescapable also were the facts that he was bankrupt, the K Street mansion was gone, and his beloved Bleak House was controlled by others.

The Mexico where Shepherd was to spend the rest of his life was in an early phase of economic expansion and foreign, mainly American, investment that was encouraged by President Porfirio Díaz. Díaz, who dominated Mexican life from 1876 until deposed in 1911, enthusiastically embraced American entrepreneurs and capital. Shepherd, one of the most favored of American investors, became a source of resentment toward Díaz, who came to be seen by many Mexicans as the protector of wealth and privilege. His often violent repression of dissent fell most heavily on the poor and dispossessed.

Shepherd embarked on his Mexican venture after being persuaded of a bright future for the American mining industry and for silver in particular. And although Mexico had every reason to distrust American actions because of the Mexican-American War of 1846–48, Diaz encouraged foreign investment, particularly from the United States. The Porfiriato, the name given to the Díaz era, was a product of Mexico's troubled times and its unhappy experiences with the United States and with France, which had invaded and occupied Mexico between 1861 and 1867. These challenges left Mexico committed to resisting foreign domination by establishing a strong central government with a strong leader. Díaz, a war hero and revolutionary, appeared to offer that prospect.

The timing of Shepherd's focus on Mexico could not have been better. In 1876 the newly elected Díaz had inherited a situation that would have discouraged a lesser man: an empty treasury, huge debts, trouble with the United States, and a vast, underemployed bureaucracy with salaries in arrears. Díaz and his advisors saw that foreign investment would be the least costly path—in political and social terms—to the economic development without which Mexico could never move ahead. Díaz understood that foreign investors would require evidence of stability, firmness, and political order, and therefore the rule of law was his first priority.[39] By

---

[39]Michael Meyer, William L. Sherman, and Susan Deeds, *The Course of Mexican History*, 7th ed. (Oxford, 2003), p. 414; Paul Garner, *Porfirio Díaz: Profiles in Power* (Edinburgh, 2001), pp. 146–47.

1880, U.S.-Mexican relations were on an upward trajectory after years of contentious interaction. Following a $4 million payment by Mexico for U.S. financial claims and agreement by Díaz to bolster Mexican troops to prevent cross-border raids, the Hayes administration had granted diplomatic recognition to the Díaz regime in 1877. Contributing to the improved relationship was dramatic evidence of progress in achieving economic reforms, reducing cross-border smuggling, and shrinking the bloated Mexican bureaucracy—all steps that strengthened the Mexican economy.[40] The sense of government control was also aided by defeat in 1880 of the Apache Indian chief Victorio, who had led vicious raids in northern Mexico.[41] In 1880 Díaz had completed his four-year term and assured the Mexican people that he would keep his commitment not to run again. He was not to honor that promise.

By spring of 1879 Shepherd was focusing on silver mines in isolated Batopilas, in Chihuahua State, that had reportedly generated millions of dollars in profits since being opened in the seventeenth century. The mines were owned by a consortium led by former Wells Fargo official John Robinson.[42] An Ohio native, Robinson was well known to the management of the Wells Fargo Express Company, having planned and established company stations in the Midwest. Upon returning from his own exploratory trip to Mexico in 1861, Robinson and a group of senior New York corporate leaders, including Wells Fargo's top management, purchased the mines, and Robinson managed them until their sale to Shepherd in 1879. Shepherd, eager to take a bold new step with the promise of rebuilding his fortune, perhaps failed to consider some of the reasons why Robinson was ready to sell. During Robinson's tenure at the mine, four members of his immediate family died, and Robinson himself was subject to wide swings of elation and despair based on the level of silver production. The burden of living and working as an outsider among a largely poor and uneducated populace also took a toll.[43] More than likely, he had had enough of Mexico and was glad to shake its dust from his boots.

[40]Meyer, Sherman, and Deeds, *Course of Mexican History*, pp. 416–17.

[41]Mark Wasserman, *Capitalists, Caciques, and Revolution: The Native Elite and Foreign Enterprise in Chihuahua, Mexico, 1854–1911* (Chapel Hill, N.C., 1984), pp. 73–75.

[42]John Mason Hart, *Silver of the Sierra Madre: John Robinson, Boss Shepherd, and the People of the Canyons* (Tucson, Ariz., 2008), pp. 12–13.

[43]Ibid., p. 94.

The Exploratory Trip

Shepherd's exploratory party set sail for Mexico by way of Panama June 30, 1879. Aboard the steamer *Acapulco* were people whose judgment Shepherd trusted, at least at the time. In addition to Stevens, the group included Edward McCook of Colorado, a cavalry general in the Civil War who was later appointed governor of the Colorado Territory by President Grant and had served as spokesman for white miners in a mining dispute with the Ute Indian tribe. The sole mining expert was J. C. F. Randolph, a British mining engineer whose perhaps overoptimistic assessment of the Batopilas mines confirmed Shepherd's determination to move ahead.[44]

Shepherd's letters to his wife in the course of the trip (June 30 to late September) provide insights into his thinking, none more vividly than one from Batopilas in August in which he wrote, "An isolation of five years would be exile and banishment, but I believe it would insure a fortune. I presume we could manage to exist here during that period; the trail and the journey are so rough that one getting in would be in no haste to get out."[45] Shepherd told a *Washington Post* reporter, "I am out of politics and shall stay out. I have a large family, and I want to make them comfortable. I have done enough for my party—more than it has ever done for me—and hereafter I shall work for my own kith and kin."[46] From the limited documentation available, it appears that, even before leaving from New York for Mexico on June 30, Shepherd had made up his mind to purchase the mines; a press account of the departure noted that conditional papers were, in fact, signed "two weeks ago," around mid-June, while Shepherd was still at Gilsey House in New York.[47]

After a ten-day journey from New York, the expedition made landfall at Aspinwall, Panama, named for the builder of the Panama Railroad that carried East Coast prospectors to California for the 1849 Gold Rush. The voyage was pleasant; the party took meals at the captain's table, and Shepherd organized a Fourth of July celebration and worship services. Shepherd's account

[44]McCook information from Colorado State Archives online records, https://www.colorado.gov/pacific/archives/edward-moody-mccook (accessed 2/12/2016)

[45]ARS to Mrs. Shepherd, Batopilas, Mexico, Aug. 23, 1879, box 5, Shepherd Papers, DLC (all letters from this trip were later copied by typewriter by an unidentified family member, most likely ARS daughter Grace S. Merchant).

[46]*Washington Post*, July 1, 1879.

[47]*New York Times*, June 15, 1879; *Washington Post*, July 1, 1879.

(*left*) Matthew G. Emery, last Washington City mayor before territorial government. (Courtesy of Kiplinger Library, Historical Society of Washington)

(*right*) George Washington Riggs, a leading Washington banker and Shepherd opponent. (Courtesy of Prints and Photographs Division, Library of Congress)

President Ulysses S. Grant. (Courtesy of Prints and Photographs Division, Library of Congress)

German-born architect Adolf Cluss, who designed Shepherd's K Street mansion. (Courtesy of Kiplinger Library, Historical Society of Washington)

Shepherd mansion at 1705 K Street NW. (Courtesy of James Goode Capital Losses Collection, Kiplinger Library, Historical Society of Washington)

Harper's Weekly print depicts a reception at 1705 K Street NW after the end of territorial government. (Courtesy of Kiplinger Library, Historical Society of Washington)

House perched on cliff after road-grading operations conducted by Shepherd. (Courtesy of Kiplinger Library, Historical Society of Washington)

Dr. William Tindall's house after road-grading operations, ca. 1873. (Courtesy of Washingtoniana Division, Martin Luther King Jr. Library, Washington, D.C.)

Evidence of road-grading damage to "Duddington" estate (I), ca. 1873. (Courtesy of National Archives and Records Administration, Record Group 123)

Evidence of road-grading damage to "Duddington" estate (II), ca. 1873. (Courtesy of National Archives and Records Administration, Record Group 123)

Shepherd children (May, Susan, Grace, Isabel, Alexander, Grant, John Conness) as young adults. (Courtesy of Kiplinger Library, Historical Society of Washington)

Map of Batopilas and its relationship to the United States, prepared by Jamshid Kooros. (Courtesy of Jamshid Kooros)

of Aspinwall (later renamed Colon) is revealing: critical of its run-down condition, he told his wife that had the railroad put the $80,000 spent on a church into filling up the swamps and making the town a decent place, the money would have been well spent. Shepherd's comments on a statue near the railroad are characteristic of his social and racial views: "[The statue] represents Columbus, a colossal figure, upright, one hand raised pointing to Heaven; at his side a magnificent crouching figure of an Indian Princess gazing, awestricken, into the face of the discoverer. I have never seen a statue that more delighted me; it is a thousand times more worthy than the one on the Capitol's East front."[48] There is little doubt that Shepherd saw himself as a "discoverer" who would not only amass great wealth from the silver mines but also bring American civilization to the benighted Mexicans.

After crossing the Isthmus of Panama to Panama City, the party boarded a small steamer and headed up the west coast to Mazatlan, Mexico, with rough weather causing the captain to say he had never seen a wilder storm in his twenty-two years at sea. Nevertheless, Shepherd wrote that the rest on the trip so far was "perfect and continuous," adding, "I feel as young as I did 30 years ago."[49] At Mazatlan, the party learned that securing stagecoach transport for the five-hundred-mile trip to Batopilas in the middle of the rainy season would be prohibitively expensive. Accordingly, they chartered a small schooner and headed north along the Mexican coast to the town of Agiabampo, a point much closer to Batopilas. This leg of the trip also brought rough weather and a bout of seasickness for Shepherd.[50] Agiabampo was a small town lacking hotel accommodations, so the members of the party—Shepherd, Stevens, and Randolph—were put up at the home of a hard-drinking Frenchman married to a local woman. Shepherd noted that the food was mainly "grease and onions" and that they shared dining space with a large pig and three mangy dogs waiting for scraps. Nonetheless, the townspeople were helpful and provided mules for the party to continue its journey to Batopilas.[51]

The mule-back ride from Agiabampo to Batopilas took fourteen days and was a grueling introduction to the rest of Shepherd's life. Within the first few days, Randolph, the engineer, collapsed from sunstroke and fell

---

[48]ARS to Mrs. Shepherd, July 9, 1879, Shepherd Papers, DLC.
[49]ARS to Mrs. Shepherd, July 20, 1879, Shepherd Papers, DLC.
[50]ARS to Mrs. Shepherd, July 31, 1879, Shepherd Papers, DLC.
[51]Ibid.

from his mule. Stevens, attempting to help, became entangled in his stirrups and was thrown and badly bruised. Shepherd and Stevens plied Randolph with brandy, which revived him until they could reach a ranch, where they rested. After a half-day of stimulants, water shock, and massage, Randolph was again fit to ride. For his part, Shepherd felt revitalized, writing home: "If anyone had told me I could undergo what I have during the last two weeks I should have pronounced him crazy. Riding over mountains on the worst trail mortal ever trod and so steep and rocky that only a cat or a mountain mule could hang on; swimming two rivers with current of 8 miles an hour; sleeping on the ground and getting soaked through . . . and yet never so well in my life. I have lost 12 pounds and expect when I get through to be quite a respectable size."[52]

The party reached Batopilas on August 6. The town lies at the bottom of a river canyon cut deep into the mountains, five thousand feet below the mountain summit. Batopilas had been a center of Mexican silver-mining operations since at least the seventeenth century under the Spanish, although there is little activity today. The layout of Batopilas and of Hacienda San Miguel, which became the base of Shepherd's operation, is not substantially different nowadays, although the hacienda is in ruins, with only the walls of the production and residential enclave still standing.

Shepherd's early pronouncements on the potential of the mines support the view that he had already made up his mind to complete the purchase and that the on-site investigation was to an extent pro forma: "Our examination of the property is progressing as rapidly as possible; our engineer, Randolph, is delighted with the mine and pronounces it wonderful. The management is poor and half the product of the mine has been wasted; the machinery used is entirely inadequate. . . . The thing has paid so well with slight effort that the owners have been content to get out merely that which showed on the surface . . . but the whole affair needs reorganization and new blood."[53]

Shepherd's only note of caution in an otherwise upbeat assessment was to add, "I cannot tell how our venture will turn out; it looks well and promising, everything as represented, and better, if anything."[54] A week later he told his wife,

---

[52]ARS to Mrs. Shepherd, Aug. 9, 1879, Shepherd Papers, DLC.
[53]ARS to Mrs. Shepherd, Aug. 16, 1879, Shepherd Papers, DLC.
[54]Ibid.

The mines and property accord with representations made, and I think we shall make a good venture of it. The prospects for a fortune are better here than elsewhere, but it is remote, inaccessible, and lacking all the elements of our civilization. . . . There is nothing like society or neighbors—an utterly different thing from any you ever saw or dreamed of. The wealth and endurance of the mines is magnificent. . . . All that I could desire save news from home, has been given me on this trip; if the journey home is successful and the thing properly managed in New York, money must come of it and as that is our great need just now, I hope it may come.[55]

Every letter was filled with emotional assurances of care and concern for the children, yet Shepherd's last letter before leaving Batopilas on October 28 expressed a wish at odds with the inevitability of the problems the family would face in the living conditions at Batopilas: "I would be satisfied with anything [at the mines] if you and the babies were beyond the reach of harm and need . . . the last thing at night I ask God's care and blessing on you and our babies; the first thought each morning is for you and them with a prayer for your protection and blessing."[56] Shepherd's concern for the children at the rhetorical level is hard to square with his willingness to transport them thousands of miles through difficult terrain to an unfamiliar and challenging environment.

Sealing the Deal

Shepherd returned to Washington and Bleak House September 26— "travel-stained and sore, and with a luxuriant crop of side whiskers of an exclusive foreign growth"—to a crop of legal troubles that must have strengthened his resolve to move to Mexico. The controversy over overlapping deeds of trust to his high-profile K Street mansion as collateral for personal loans continued in court. Creditor George Pepper's intention to sell the property was temporarily blocked, but the situation provided a public reminder of Shepherd's precarious financial position. Shepherd countered with a complaint that the proposed sale price was a "knock down" far below its estimated value.[57] He put four brick houses in Georgetown up for

---

[55]ARS to Mrs. Shepherd, Aug. 23, 1879, Shepherd Papers, DLC.
[56]Ibid.
[57]*Washington Post*, Sept. 27, 1879; Equity Case File nos. 6954 and 7052, RG 21, NARA.

public auction, and another creditor sued Samuel Cross, one of Shepherd's trustees, for return of her investment in a piece of ground to which she alleged Shepherd did not have proper title.[58]

After several trips to New York to complete negotiations for purchase of the mines, Shepherd incorporated the Consolidated Batopilas Mining Company (CBMC) in New York State on December 1, 1879. The purchase price for the Batopilas mines was $600,000.[59] Officers of the new company were George W. Quintard, president; John R. Robinson, resident vice president; Shepherd, vice president and general manager; Charles T. Barney, secretary; and James D. Smith, treasurer. The inner circle consisted of prosperous financial and commercial figures. Major stockholders included the president of U.S. Express Co.; a vice president of the Atchison, Topeka and Santa Fe Railroad; the president of the Southern Steamship Line (Quintard); and leaders of the iron, sugar, and lead industries, as well as New York investment and banking houses.[60] Shepherd, eager to boost investment, said that the venture was but the start of a series of activities that would become "the sensation of the age." The *Washington Post* enthused that "if there is silver or gold in Chihuahua, it must be bedded very deeply in order to escape his indomitable zeal and perseverance."[61]

The spring of 1880 went by in a blur for Shepherd and his wife and large family. The seven children now ranged in age from seventeen (Mary, also known as May) down to three (John Conness); in-between were Susan (fifteen), Grace (eleven), Isabel (nine), Alexander Jr. (eight), and Grant (five). The family remained at Bleak House while Shepherd moved between two Washington locations—the Washington Club and the Willard Hotel—and Gilsey House in New York to complete equipment purchases and financial arrangements for Mexico. In February an advertisement for Bleak House appeared in a Washington paper: "For Rent: The country residence of ex-Gov. Shepherd, on 7th Street Road [now Georgia Avenue], five miles from the city and one mile from Silver Spring Station [Metropolitan Branch, B&O R.R.], will be rented to a good tenant for a term of years. Gas and water, a bowling alley and gymnasium on the place. The farm contains 210 acres, fine barn, and

---

[58] *Evening Star*, Aug. 1, 1879.
[59] Hart, *Silver of the Sierra Madre*, p. 95.
[60] *Washington Post*, Dec. 2, 1879.
[61] Ibid.

overseer's house. Will rent on shares to a responsible party."[62] By 1881 pasturage was also being advertised for rent at Bleak House farm.

Lyndon Stevens left for Mexico in mid-March to supervise the shipment and installation of mine equipment. The Analostan Boat Club, of which Stevens was president, gave him a farewell dinner, no doubt also attended by Shepherd.[63] Senior U.S. Army officers and the secretary of war wrote letters of introduction for the Shepherds to military bases along the route of march in Texas, asking them to provide the Shepherds "courtesy and facilities," which proved to be of great value in alleviating the hardships of the trail. William Tecumseh Sherman, commanding general of the army, directed all members of the army in Texas to give the Shepherds "the most courteous attention," adding that "any favors extended to this party will be approved and appreciated as personal to myself."[64] The Mexican embassy in Washington also sent letters of introduction to the governors of Chihuahua and neighboring Mexican states.

By the end of April the Shepherds were ready to leave Washington. A farewell dinner at the Willard Hotel April 29, the night before departure, brought out leading local businessmen, military officers, press representatives, and political figures to pay tribute to the man who had done so much for the city. Justice Samuel F. Miller of the U.S. Supreme Court presided over the glittering affair. One noted guest was Frederick Douglass, now U.S. marshal for the District of Columbia, who in the past had been critical of Shepherd but had come to support board initiatives. In his remarks, Douglass said that when he arrived in Washington, Shepherd had been "the object of calumny," but after examination of his character and actions, Douglass had concluded that Shepherd was "an honest man" who had treated blacks in a fair way when he was in a position to help them. In response to the tributes, Shepherd left the audience with this observation: "I simply have to say that what I have done has been as I thought an honest man should do, who wanted to make this Capital worthy of the nation it

---

[62]*Evening Star*, Feb. 5, 1880. Bleak House was presumably rented before the Shepherds left for Mexico, but the first press reference to their use of the house after moving to Mexico was in 1885, a reception after the double wedding of two daughters in Washington.

[63]*Evening Star*, Mar. 17, 1880; *Washington Post*, Mar. 17, 1880.

[64]Letters of Secretary of War Ramsey, Apr. 24, 1880, and General W. T. Sherman, Apr. 23, 1880, courtesy of ARS granddaughter Mary Wagner Woods.

represents, and as noble and as fine a city as there is in the world." His final words were, "I am going to be gone for some years."[65]

The party's departure by train May 1 from the Baltimore & Ohio Railroad station at Sixth Street and New Jersey Avenue NW was eased by a reserved railroad car that simplified logistics for the mass of people, belongings, and animals. The party included the immediate Shepherd family; several recently hired mine employees, including a physician; John Bradley, a brother-in-law of Mrs. Shepherd; the longtime family cook, Dora; a nurse; and two large mastiffs and two small dogs. Among those in the crowd saying goodbye were two of Shepherd's younger brothers, Tom and Arthur. The latter would later join Alexander in Batopilas, marry a local woman, and reside there until his death in 1914.[66] Alexander Shepherd's adventure to recover the family's fortunes was about to commence.

As he left on the quest to recover his wealth, perhaps Shepherd recalled the words of Edgar Allan Poe's 1849 "Eldorado," about a "gallant knight" who "in sunshine and shadow" had sought the riches of that fabled city of gold. If Shepherd had known the poem, he would have embraced its exhortation to action in the final stanzas and been unconcerned with its equation of Eldorado with death:

> And, as his strength
> Failed him at length,
> He met a pilgrim shadow—
> "Shadow," said he,
> "Where can it be—
> This land of Eldorado?"
>
> "Over the Mountains
> Of the Moon,
> Down the Valley of the Shadow,
> Ride boldly ride."
> The shade replied—
> "If you seek for Eldorado!"[67]

---

[65] *Evening Star*, May 1, 1880; *Washington Post*, May 2, 1880.

[66] Mrs. Shepherd's 1880 trip diary, written in Batopilas in 1882 and typed by daughter Grace in 1928, courtesy of ARS granddaughter Mary Wagner Woods; "Reports of Deaths of American Citizens Abroad, 1835–1974," box 3772, entry 205, RG 59, NARA.

[67] The poem was first published in the April 21, 1849, issue of *Flag of Our Union* (Boston).

Chapter Ten

"A Life of Labor and Extreme Simplicity"

Seeking El Dorado in Batopilas, 1880–1882

CHIHUAHUA STATE, IN the north of Mexico, bordering the states of
Texas and New Mexico, occupied a special place in Mexican history
and U.S.-Mexico relations. In the nineteenth century the Santa Fe Trail
(St. Louis to Santa Fe, N.M.) and the Camino Real (Santa Fe to Chihuahua
City) became major commercial arteries between the two countries, and by
the early 1880s the recently completed Mexican Central Railroad from
Juarez to Chihuahua City greatly increased the appeal of Chihuahua State
to American investors.[1] The residents of Chihuahua City, the state capital,
had become accustomed to frequent interaction with the United States
through travel, employment, and immigration. But while much of the state
is desert, the Sierra Madre Mountains, interspersed with deep, isolated canyons like Copper Canyon, of which Batopilas Canyon is a branch, dominate the western portion of the state and form its north-south backbone. This
difficult area also contains most of the state's mineral resources.

Chihuahua was the home of the Terrazas-Creel family, the most powerful regional elite in Mexico in the late nineteenth and early twentieth
centuries.[2] The Terrazas-Creel empire was founded by Don Luis Terrazas
(1829–1923) and was both expanded and strengthened by his favorite

---

[1]Mark Wasserman, *Capitalists, Caciques, and Revolution: The Native Elite and Foreign
Enterprise in Chihuahua, Mexico, 1854–1911* (Chapel Hill, 1984), pp. 10–11.
[2]Ibid., p. 4.

son-in-law, Enrique Creel, son of U.S. Consul in Chihuahua City Reuben W. Creel. Terrazas had been governor-general of Chihuahua before the French invasion in 1861 and fought bravely against the French with General Juarez. Terrazas's twelve children married well and enhanced the family's holdings.[3] By ca. 1900, Terrazas oversaw vast holdings comprising some seven million acres with more than fifty haciendas and many smaller ranches; it was "virtually impossible" to calculate either the fortune or the power of the Terrazas-Creel combine, which included land, cattle, banking, manufacturing, and mining.[4]

Enrique Creel succeeded his father-in-law upon Terrazas's 1903 retirement. Creel had become an internationally respected banker and an astute businessman who later served as Mexican ambassador to the United States.[5] His father had connections to power and influence in the United States. By the time Creel took over the vast Terrazas empire, he had also become a trusted friend of Shepherd and a director of his mining company.[6] The importance of Shepherd's association with Creel cannot be overestimated.

Mexico, and Chihuahua in particular, exercised great attraction for foreign investors in the late nineteenth century because of its rich mines and cheap labor, and its potential for the application of modern technology. Foreign investment benefited investors and the Mexican economy alike. Chihuahua's proximity to the United States was a particular attraction to American investors and adventurers like Shepherd. Chihuahua received more nonrailroad foreign investment than any other Mexican region before the 1910 revolution.[7] Mineral and agricultural exports from Chihuahua fueled Mexican president Porfirio Díaz's Porfiriato regime after 1880. Díaz encouraged mining, which became the principal source of state and national revenue, despite its being largely in the hands of foreigners, mainly American entrepreneurs like Shepherd.[8] Under Shepherd's direction, the

---

[3]Michael Meyer, William L. Sherman, and Susan Deeds, *The Course of Mexican History*, 7th ed. (Oxford, 2003), p. 414; Paul Garner, *Porfirio Díaz: Profiles in Power* (Edinburgh, 2001), pp. 440–41.

[4]Wasserman, *Capitalists, Caciques, and Revolution*, p. 5.

[5]Ibid., pp. 27, 30.

[6]Ibid., p. 87.

[7]Ibid., p. 5.

[8]Ibid., p. 71.

Batopilas mines became one of the three most important mining centers in Chihuahua.[9]

The Journey

The transition from Washington to Batopilas revealed important aspects of Shepherd's personality and values, especially the ways in which he viewed relationships. Family was clearly significant to him. Shepherd's letters over the years to his wife Mary and to the children, when some or all were absent, were redolent with emotion; during the exploratory trip to Mexico in 1879, when he went without mail from home, his letters were almost an audible sob. Yet his commitment to family must be tempered by the fact that, when it came to the decision to relocate to Mexico, Shepherd made a business decision. He moved his family to a distant and dangerous locale, far from the city and country of his children's birth, because of his ambition to build a new fortune and to return in triumph to Washington. The impact on his wife and seven children was significant.

Mary Shepherd was a loyal and uncomplaining wife through forty years of married life, during which she bore ten children, only seven of whom (four daughters and three sons) lived to adulthood. Severe-looking in personal photos, she appears to have been a somewhat remote mother to her children, one of whom poignantly described remembering her mother only once asking for a kiss. The same daughter recorded that soon after the demise of the territorial government, she thought she saw her mother cry—for the first time.[10] Throughout, Mary Shepherd remained a staunch supporter of her husband, sharing fully in their social life in Washington and furnishing their homes to the maximum extent allowed by their means at the time. While the resilience of Shepherd in making the eventual move from Washington to Mexico was consistent with his ambition, the change for Mary Shepherd must have been far more arduous. For a woman accustomed to comfort and elegance in Washington, being responsible for the care of seven children in the remote and treacherous environment of Batopilas was challenging and

---

[9]Ibid., p. 85.
[10]Typed records by Grace Shepherd Merchant, box 5, Shepherd Papers, Manuscript Division, Library of Congress, Washington, D.C. (hereafter DLC).

demanding. Nevertheless, Mary Shepherd appeared to absorb the dramatic swings of family fortune without batting an eye and, once settled in Mexico, would enthuse over a new coat of whitewash to the family living quarters despite having presided over a grand mansion on K Street in Washington. Mary Shepherd's unquestioned dedication to her husband was a dramatic example of the loyalty that he generated throughout his life.

The family's trip from Washington to Mexico began by train. The first leg would take them to the end of the rail line at San Antonio, Texas, with a change at St. Louis, Missouri, arriving six days after departure. The second leg of the journey took the travelers, in covered wagons, from San Antonio to the U.S.-Mexico border at the Rio Grande River. Shepherd engaged wagons, drivers, and animals for the overland journey as well as "ambulances" (more comfortable wagons) for the family, and he shared the responsibility of managing the men and animals with a professional wagon master. The expedition departed San Antonio May 11, not to reach the U.S.-Mexico border until a month later.

Both Shepherds kept diaries of the trip from Washington to Batopilas. Mary Shepherd often wrote about the children and their problems: five-year-old Grant would not drink condensed milk, while eight-year-old Alexander Jr. and three-year-old John Conness would drink anything, including beer. The Shepherd children, fifteen-year-old Sue in particular, were often sick, and Mrs. Shepherd had an attack of inflammation that caused deep concern. Alexander's diary was often angry in tone, citing problems the party encountered; Junction City, for example, was "a godforsaken hole," but his indignation reached a peak when he discovered that two baskets of his treasured Madeira wine had been stolen.[11] Despite Shepherd's organizing skills, the wagon trip suffered from the problems inherent in a long journey through hard country via a primitive form of transportation. The party was so large and strung out that sections often became separated, although the family wagons stayed together as a unit. Within a day, a mule had strangled to death on its harness, and a wagon had run over a man's leg. Another problem that plagued Shepherd for most of the

---

[11]A. R. Shepherd 1880 Trip Diary, June 7, 1880, courtesy ARS granddaughter Mary Wagner Woods (hereafter ARS Trip Diary). All entries describing the trip to Batopilas are taken from one or both of the Shepherds' trip diaries.

time in Mexico surfaced early: poor cooks and cooking. One cook after another proved incompetent, all too often leaving Dora, the family cook, responsible for preparing meals for the entire party.

U.S. Army posts in Texas were of special assistance to the Shepherd party. The posts were small and usually had only a satellite community of family members, settlers, and local residents. Although the Shepherd party constituted a logistical challenge, the officers and townspeople were happy to have visitors, including—perhaps especially—the teenaged Shepherd daughters, and made every effort to accommodate the travelers. Shepherd's wagon train was able to attach itself for a portion of the trip to the official party of an army paymaster who was making a scheduled run to other army posts.

On June 10, 1880, one month after leaving San Antonio, the party reached Presidio del Norte, the last town before the U.S.-Mexico border, wearied from the heat, limited water, and sickness along the way.[12] Because the town was an official border crossing point, the local U.S. consul, a man named Kelly, and another American expatriate made every effort to help the travelers, including sending them a bathtub filled with muddy river water. Thanks to the good offices of the American consul, the Shepherd party's boxes and trunks passed without inspection, although the wagons and ambulances were required to pay a Mexican entry duty, delaying movement for a half-day.

The Shepherd party enjoyed Kelly's hospitality for two days before setting out for Chihuahua City on the third leg of their journey. Their spirits revived once they were finally in Mexico, and the U.S. consul in Chihuahua City, Mr. Scott, sent word that he would come to meet them. Tomas MacManus, an American-Mexican businessman in Chihuahua City with whom Shepherd was to do business over the next two decades, invited the party to his ranch, "Bachimba," outside Chihuahua City. The ranch was everything that the trip had not been: shaded and well watered, with fruit trees and milk, fresh beef, and bread—a welcome respite for the family.

---

[12]ARS Trip Diary, June 10, 1880; Mary Grice Shepherd 1880 Trip Diary, courtesy of ARS granddaughter Mary Wagner Woods (hereafter MGS Trip Diary). Her diary entries are not dated, and only occasional arrival/departure dates are recorded.

Chihuahua City and the Last Leg

The party reached Chihuahua City on June 19, pleasantly surprised to see that the provincial capital had trees and a cathedral, that indicator of civilization and urban status. Lyndon Stevens, who went ahead, rented a comfortable house for the family on the main plaza, with two stories and glass windows ("a novelty"), along with a plastered ceiling. Four sets of furniture purchased in San Antonio for Batopilas were in place, and the beds were made, although Mrs. Shepherd noted in her diary that the furnishings did not include such upper-class Mexican standards as mirrors and marble-topped tables. Perhaps surprisingly, the family's modest library was looked upon "with awe" by the local residents, since reading material, including newspapers, was rare in this town of sixteen thousand residents. Mr. and Mrs. Scott from the consulate, the businessman-banker MacManus, and the small contingent of North Americans in the city made an effort to ease the Shepherds' adjustment to a new and unknown culture.

Shepherd, however, was anxious to complete the trip to Batopilas. The urban sounds of Chihuahua City, including the "infernal clamor and clanging of cathedral bells," gave him no pleasure, and, after making final arrangements, he left his family in the city and set out for Batopilas with a small party on July 3, purchasing provisions and supplies at the few stores along the way. The route for the final, 185-mile leg of the journey, which was known to Shepherd from the exploratory trip the year before, would take him and his companions through mountain passes and along precipitous mule trails that led five thousand feet down into the gorge of the Batopilas River. Traveling in the middle of the rainy season, as the party did, made the trails even more dangerous, and in the high-water river crossings mules were lost and supplies soaked. These conditions were unpleasant for the travelers, causing illness and complicating the trip. Shepherd was unwell much of the time; in addition to the expected discomforts of this type of travel, a mule fell on his leg, possibly causing inflammation that would plague him for years. Shepherd also suffered from dysentery and other illnesses that would deplete his energy as long as he remained in Mexico. Stevens wrote to a Washington friend that Shepherd "lost two to three weeks" on the last leg of the journey as a result of illness caused by the excessive heat in the canyon.[13] One bright spot in the trip was meeting a *conducta*—the mule train from Batopilas—carrying silver ingots that Shepherd estimated as worth $80,000. The small party finally arrived at the hacienda in Batopilas in the early evening of July 19, 1880, ready to start work.[14]

Meanwhile, Shepherd's family, resting in Chihuahua City, regained their strength and vitality after the exhausting trip from San Antonio. Both Shepherds combined a deep commitment to their children with a no-nonsense approach to discipline and a philosophy that difficulties were to be endured without complaint, a standard approach to child rearing during that time. Despite their young ages, the children absorbed this outlook and made good travelers, even during difficult portions of the trip. Once in Mexico, the family spent their time studying Spanish, writing letters, being hosted by the leading families, and taking part in local celebrations. In the midst of celebrations for Mexican National Day on September 16, "Uncle John" Bradley arrived with a letter from Shepherd directing the family to pack for Batopilas. Happy to have their marching orders, they took part in the National Day festivities in an even gayer mood. Nonetheless, preparation for the final leg of the journey required a great deal of work—the bureaus, chairs, washstands, and bedsteads purchased in San Antonio had to be dismantled, and their belongings had to be packed into bundles suitable for the mule-back journey.

Departure day, October 8, dawned bright and clear, meaning that the rainy season was over at last. The family began the mule trip into the depths of the Batopilas Canyon in high spirits, but the trip, which took thirteen days, was far more arduous than expected, and far more challenging than the wagon train to Chihuahua City. Each child shared a mule with an adult for safety on the treacherous mountain paths, and the temperature rose steadily as the party descended into the valley. When, at last, the family reached the river and their new home, Hacienda San Miguel, came into view, they must have been relieved and reassured. Shepherd—bearded and hard at work—was startled to see the family several days before they were expected. Most of his time and effort had gone into installing machinery and equipment

---

[13] *Washington Post,* Aug. 17, 1880.
[14] ARS Trip Diary, July 19, 1880.

rather than seeing to furniture and decoration; by all accounts the hacienda was not ready for the family's arrival. After about a month, however, with the furniture finally put together and boxes unpacked, the Shepherd clan began a new life that was to continue in much the same manner until Shepherd's death twenty-two years later.[15]

Batopilas Realities

It is difficult to overstate the dramatic, almost shocking, differences between the life that the Shepherds had left in Washington and their life in the walled enclave of Hacienda San Miguel. The hacienda was a self-contained, 4½-acre mining complex that included the Shepherd residence as well as the industrial plant that processed the silver ore from the San Miguel Mine, which for several years was the most productive of the company's mines. Wedged between the mountains and the Batopilas River, the hacienda was cut off from the town across the river for days at a time when the river became a destructive torrent that repeatedly damaged equipment and machinery as well as buildings. The mountain behind the hacienda rose steeply, blocking expansion of the complex while menacing the buildings with storm runoff from the arroyos (streambeds) cutting into the hillside.

The Shepherds' residence within the hacienda was a modest, one-story adobe building looking out on a small garden, orange trees, the horse and mule corral, and further on to the river and the town. The house remained largely unchanged from the time of John Robinson, the former owner-manager, and had no doubt been built within the previous one hundred years. Life in Mexico, in a simple house across the river from the small town of Batopilas, presented a harsh reality to the Shepherd family that no sugar-coating could mask, and that harshness affected every member of the family.

When they arrived in Mexico, the seven Shepherd children ranged in age from three to eighteen. Their father was strict but loving, and there is little doubt that his discipline helped them adjust with little complaint to the arduous life in Batopilas. Nonetheless, considering that almost nothing that the family experienced in Batopilas was familiar, one wonders

---

[15]Grace Shepherd Diary, 1880 trip diary (retyped), n.d., Shepherd Papers, DLC.

about the extent to which Shepherd considered anyone other than himself in his decisions. This situation also illustrates the incredible loyalty and dedication of Mary Grice Shepherd. With credit to both parents, the Shepherd children survived the transition to Mexico and established life-long bonds to the mines. The four Shepherd daughters married expatriate employees of the mining company, and the sons devoted at least part of their working lives to the grinding business of mining in other areas after leaving Batopilas.

The weather in Batopilas was as dramatic and extreme as the mountains, divided between a rainy season lasting from May until October and a dry season from October to May, with temperatures above one hundred degrees Fahrenheit. The rains, which also caused the wild surges in the Batopilas River and its usually dry feeder arroyos, created a brief growing season, when much of Shepherd's work force would disappear to plant and tend meager crops of corn and beans. But the hot October–to–May dry season was the cause of most of the family's health problems, especially for the father and his four daughters. The girls were frequently ill and unable to put on weight, and the only solution was for them to return periodically to the United States and live with relatives or at Bleak House when it was unrented. Mrs. Shepherd usually joined them and once rented a house in the Dupont Circle area for the better part of a school year.

The town of Batopilas, across the river from the hacienda, was a sleepy place whose population waxed and waned with the fortunes of the local silver mines. When the Shepherds arrived in 1880 the population was about two thousand, but it doubled at the height of Shepherd's operations before receding to its earlier level when mining operations shrank. Despite its isolation deep in the Western Sierra Madre, Batopilas displayed an unusual degree of sophistication fostered by the wealth generated by the silver mines. Both the town and Hacienda San Miguel across the river are wedged into the bottom of a narrow canyon through which the Batopilas River runs. Today the town, three streets wide in the center, straggles along the river bank for the better part of a mile. The town center, little changed from Shepherd's time, features a pleasant square with an ornamental iron bandstand and benches. On one side are the municipal offices and other public buildings, with private homes, restaurants, and shops filling the three other sides. The cathedral is located a short distance along the main street. Slightly to the south lies another, smaller square. The

population is predominantly Mexican, although a few inhabitants are Tarahumara Indians, identifiable by their brightly colored costumes.[16]

Making it Work

The mining complex that Shepherd purchased from John Robinson in 1879
had not changed much in the twenty years that Robinson was owner and
general manager. Robinson made extensive use of so-called *gambusino* labor,
a term referring to miners who worked as semi-independent contractors
under an agreement in which the miner was entitled to keep the proceeds
of at least one load of silver ore he extracted from the mine during the day.
Often it would be the final load of the day, perhaps calculated by the miner
to be one of the most productive. In the *gambusino* system, the pace of work
was set by the miners, who were to a large extent working for themselves.[17]
Robinson's mine operation was a simple system that employed only three
stamps, heavy presses that crushed the silver ore before it was treated chem-
ically and the silver removed. Most of the ore was broken up by men using
sledgehammers before it was moved to *arrastras*, circular structures in which
the ore was treated with salt and mercury before transfer to washing tanks
in which the mercury-silver amalgam was isolated from the rest of the ore.
The final step was to heat the amalgam so that reusable mercury separated
from the silver, which was removed and fashioned into bars for export.
Among the few adaptations made by Robinson was using heavier sledgehammers and giant shears for cutting the sheets of native silver that were a
feature of the Batopilas mines.[18]

One incident during Shepherd's upgrade of mining operations was reminiscent of some of the problems that occurred during his Washington tenure. Lyndon Stevens, Shepherd's friend in Washington and right-hand man
in Batopilas, traveled frequently from Batopilas to the United States on mining business. On one trip, he bought new stamps that were supposedly of
greater capacity than those left over from Robinson's tenure. Stevens somewhat ruefully later reported that he had to return to San Francisco to

---

[16]This description is based on an April 2011 visit by the author and Robert Gullo.

[17]John Mason Hart, *Silver of the Sierra Madre: John Robinson, Boss Shepherd, and the People of the Canyons* (Tucson, Ariz., 2008), p. 46.

[18]Ibid., pp. 57–58.

replace the stamps with those of greater capacity because "we were misinformed as to the size of the stamps required."[19]

The physical plant at the core of Hacienda San Miguel antedated the arrival of Shepherd, but he significantly expanded and strengthened all of the structures. Of greatest concern were the river wall and the retaining wall at the rear of the hacienda, since violent floods were the greatest threat to the operation. Over the course of the first two years, Shepherd lengthened, heightened, and strengthened the river wall, but initial efforts were not enough. A violent storm in May 1881 "literally washed us out [he wrote] . . . the roofs of all my [building] wing and office leaked like sieves and we were wading around in a comfortless condition."[20] Luckily, this storm did not cause much structural damage but served notice that weather conditions were violent and unpredictable. A late July storm that year caused even greater damage, making the river impassable for ten days. Water initially covered the concentrator (processing) floor to a depth of two feet. Part of the retaining wall on the mountain side of the hacienda collapsed, and the commercial batteries stopped working when water overflowed its normal channel and inundated the animal corral, concentrators, and machinery in the small mill, bringing production to a halt. Later in August, Shepherd described this as "the heaviest rain and the most terrible storm I have ever seen," although it did not cause as much damage to equipment as he had feared.[21] The worst, however, was still to come. In August 1882, a massive storm and flood brought destruction and misery on a scale previously unknown. Shepherd described watching "a heavy cone-shaped volume of water pour right out of the heavens." In almost no time the river and contributing arroyos were sending down "great rocks, and trees, remains of houses, and several human forms;" rocks weighing over a ton tumbled down the river bed. The flood blocked the water race, ruined processing machinery and equipment, destroyed the recently strengthened riverfront and mountainside walls, and inundated residences.[22]

---

[19]*Washington Post*, Nov. 23, 1880.

[20]Alexander Shepherd Diary, December 31, 1880–December 31, 1881, courtesy of ARS great-grandson W. Sinkler Manning (hereafter ARS Diary).

[21]ARS Diary, July 25–Aug. 26, 1881.

[22]Mary Grice Shepherd Diary, Aug. 1, 1882, courtesy of Mary Wagner Woods (hereafter MGS Diary).

Illness proved to be one of the most severe personal challenges faced by Shepherd during his early years in Mexico. In Washington he had been prone to injury (e.g., breaking his ankle in January 1878), but Mexico took a heavy toll because of the heat and the physical demands associated with animals, heavy equipment, and defending against violent weather. Despite Shepherd's being only forty-five years old on arrival in Mexico, he described in his 1881 diary his suffering from many kinds of illnesses, most of which put him to bed or diminished his ability to function at full strength. The list included malaria, neuralgia (face and head), cholera, rheumatism (knees), headache, sore throat, colds, attacks of dizziness, lack of vision, leg problems (requiring elastic stockings), back pain, lumbago, "blue days" (implying depression), eczema, prickly heat, and a tarantula bite that briefly threatened leg amputation. More than one in five of Shepherd's 1881 diary entries were complaints of a medical problem.[23] While some of his medical problems were self-diagnosed, he did have access to the company's medical doctor, who could diagnose more accurately and prescribe remedies.

The physical remoteness of Batopilas was one of the greatest problems faced by Shepherd throughout his years in Mexico. Reaching Batopilas, once dubbed the most inaccessible village in North America, was not for the faint of heart. When the Shepherds arrived, the railroad had not yet reached Chihuahua City. From Chihuahua it was a stagecoach ride of several days to reach Carichic, the last town before one was forced to ride by mule-back the rest of the 185 miles to Batopilas, a trip taking on average seven days, and which was grueling and often dangerous. Standard practice was to let the mules pick their way over the narrow track rather than attempt to guide them, since the animals had an unerring instinct for the best route. With the women and children, however, a *mozo* (young man) walked alongside or rode behind them to give support at the most dangerous places on the trail. The trail descended five thousand feet, from seven thousand feet to two thousand feet above sea level at the bottom of the river canyon at Batopilas. Everything that could not be grown or manufactured in Batopilas had to be brought in on mule back, with heavy equipment broken down into sections before it was loaded onto the mules. Railroads were extended closer to Batopilas over the decades, first to Chihuahua City and then to Creel, but there was no way for the iron horse to breach the

---

[23]ARS Diary, Jan. 4–Dec. 15, 1881.

mountain bastion of the Sierra Madre Occidental that shielded Batopilas from the outside world. The narrow dirt road from Creel to Batopilas was not built until recent times, and the last twenty-seven miles were yet to be paved by spring 2011.[24]

Local Society

Even though Batopilas was a small town far from Mexico's urban centers, and even though Shepherd by default became the *Patron Grande* because of his dominant economic role in the community, there was an established social and influence structure with and through which he had to work. The most important figures in Batopilas were the power brokers of the state of Chihuahua. They controlled its vast resources, which consisted mainly of land and mineral and agricultural production, and they maintained close associations with the local elites. One such local family was the Valenzuelas, from whom Shepherd encountered early "stiff resistance" over mine boundary disputes. By one account, the local jefe (political chief) briefly imprisoned Shepherd, who was soon released.[25]

Unlike some other American entrepreneurs who developed investments in Mexico during the Porfiriato, Shepherd did not form alliances through marriage with leading local families or develop Mexican social networks. Just as he had resisted social and political equality for African Americans in Washington, he applied a strict social barrier between the American expatriate community and local Mexican society. Business connections, however, were a different matter, and he developed a close relationship with Enrique Creel, Luis Terrazas's son-in-law, was comfortable conducting business with Mexicans, and became a respected acquaintance of President Díaz. But the massive wall and the river between the American enclave at Hacienda Miguel and the town of Batopilas served as a metaphor for the Americans' voluntary social segregation. Shepherd was more comfortable working and relaxing at the hacienda than getting to know his Mexican

---

[24]Internet travel guides indicate extensive recent road improvements, see http://www
.tripadvisor.com/Attraction_Review-g151927-d152038-Reviews-Batopilas_Canyon
-Copper_Canyon_Northern_Mexico.html (October 5, 2015 entry) and http://www
.mexonline.com/chihuahua/coppercanyon-batopilas.htm

[25]Wasserman, *Capitalists, Caciques, and Revolution*, p. 87.

neighbors; he noted in his diary that a fall 1881 visit to the town was his first in four months.[26] Shepherd occasionally confided his personal views about Mexicans to his diary: "This is a nation of born idlers—no ambition, no elevation" and "another instance of the worthlessness of these people."[27] Tellingly, none of Shepherd's fourteen top employees was Mexican.[28]

By 1882 much of the machinery upgrade was in place in a new mill. This had entailed "extraordinary expenses" and required dynamiting a portion of the mountain wall to create space. The principal addition was three five-stamp units, at 750 pounds per stamp, each of which had had to be transported three hundred miles by mule and reassembled at the hacienda, shutting down production for many weeks. Shepherd introduced a new technique for extracting silver from ore. The old lixiviation system (amalgamating the silver with mercury and separating it with heat) captured only an estimated 60 percent of the silver. The new lixiviation system increased the silver capture by some 20 percent through chloridizing, roasting the ore, and processing it in chemical-leaching tanks.[29]

Shepherd put repeated effort and expense into lengthening and strengthening the hacienda's two major defenses against flooding, the rear wall and the river wall. By 1882 the river wall was eight-hundred-feet long, nine-feet thick at the base, and averaged seventeen-feet high. The rear wall was significantly strengthened and linked to a new guard lodge and tower at the main entrance. Other plant improvements included lengthening and strengthening the *acequia* (water race), with a vertical fall of ten feet, that now ran nearly a mile on the far side of the river and generated power to the electric mill, steam mill, and hacienda buildings. The improvements required erection of heavy stone arches and abutment walls over the three main arroyos that crossed the *acequia* to keep it from flooding.[30] Lyndon Stevens reminded a correspondent what it took to get this far: "All these [improvements], with a hundred other accomplishments necessary to make the system complete, had been done in about a year in a country where labor is

[26]ARS Diary, Oct. 21, 1881.

[27]ARS Diary, Jan. 13 and May 24, 1881.

[28]Wasserman, *Capitalists, Caciques, and Revolution*, p. 126.

[29]*Annual Report to the Stockholders of the Consolidated Batopilas Silver Mining Company, 1882*, p. 2 (New York: John Polhemus, 1882), RB 266819, The Huntington Library, San Marino, California (hereafter CBSMC 1882); L. H. Stevens to a Washington friend, *Evening Star* (Washington, D.C.), June 1, 1882.

[30]CBSMC 1882, pp. 21, 31–34.

scarce, and skilled labor none; where nothing can be bought, and every screw and nail must be thought of months ahead . . . every piece of timber and bushel of lime [and] brick of adobe foreseen. And yet, when its time came, every article was there, and when the mill started it was complete and in perfect working order."[31] Optimistic pronouncements like this were perhaps sincere but were also intended to assure distant U.S. mine stockholders that all was proceeding smoothly and according to plan.

Labor Issues

Shepherd's conception of the future of the Batopilas mines required a large and competent work force, and labor proved to be a planning weakness. The pace of work under Shepherd's predecessor had been much slower, with fewer men needed to mine readily accessible ore. Because the town of Batopilas was small and the scope of Shepherd's mining operation exceeded Robinson's, Shepherd was required to rely on labor contractors who filled his work force with Mexicans and Indians from other regions and with the Tarahumara, a local tribe whose workers proved to be indefatigable but also undependable and unpredictable, in Shepherd's estimation, due to their cultural and social differences with the local Mexicans. Guadalupe Ramirez, a local businessman, one of Shepherd's principal labor contractors, was frequently asked to find "some laborers also Indians" for the mines.[32]

Labor shortages were amply reflected in the annual reports of the corporation. It was not until the end of October 1881 that Shepherd could write in his diary, "For the first time since I arrived I have more men than I can put to work and do not need employ all who want it."[33] By 1882 Shepherd was employing five hundred men, and by 1883, he was employing twelve hundred men, sometimes more, at the mines and at the hacienda.[34]

By the second year of operation, Shepherd had identified the scarcity of workers for the pace of underground exploration work as a major problem: "As miners were wanted, the peons became miners, and there being enough work on the surface, new laborers could not be found who would go through

---

[31]In *Evening Star,* June 1, 1882.
[32]ARS Diary, Feb. 15, 1881.
[33]Ibid., Oct. 24, 1881.
[34]*Evening Star,* Aug. 4, 1883.

the long course of training necessary to make an efficient underground laborer."[35] Shepherd discovered belatedly that local workingmen's habits were at odds with his vision of a modern, efficient mining operation. Drunkenness was a constant problem, particularly among the Indians. Another issue in a Catholic country was the frequency of saints' days, which the local workers celebrated between ninety and one hundred times per year. The combination of alcohol abuse and numerous days off resulted in low productivity.[36]

To meet the challenge of insufficient labor, Shepherd experimented with foreign workers, who he thought would be superior to the locals. In the summer of 1881, Shepherd instructed Stevens to pick up sixty mainly German immigrants in New York and send them on to the mines, but they proved to be a disaster. Shepherd recorded his anger at the new arrivals in his diary: not only were they ill-dressed and unready for work, but they also had a "fearful" stench and immediately began agitating for higher pay and better living conditions. The cook refused to prepare their meals, and Shepherd was forced to disperse them to several locations, some at the mine and some at the hacienda. Within a month it was clear that the experiment was not going to work, and Shepherd responded by closing their barracks and removing the eating utensils. Half the remaining group quit on the spot, and by the fall Shepherd had paid off most of the rest, with a small contingent remaining at a monthly wage of $25.00 plus room and board or $1.50 a day without board.[37]

Workers' compensation was a constant source of difficulty, both in terms of the level of wages and the method of payment. Based on an 1889 U.S. consular report, one historian of the region has observed, "Although ruthless with bandits, Shepherd treated his foreign and native workers fairly, according to the standards of the times, as long as they remained industrious and honest."[38] Indians were paid the least. In early 1881 Shepherd had negotiated with labor contractor Guadalupe Ramirez to pay Indian workers "$US 4 bits [US$0.50] a day and feed them."[39] Ordinary miners received two or

---

[35]CBSMC 1882, p. 9.

[36]Hart, *Silver of the Sierra Madre*, p. 55.

[37]Unmarked press account, July 25, 1881, Shepherd Papers, box 7, DLC; ARS Diary, July 7–30, Sept. 3–5, and Oct. 9, 1881.

[38]David M. Pletcher, *Rails, Mines, and Progress: Seven American Promoters in Mexico, 1867–1911* (1958; rep. ed., Port Washington, N.Y., 1972), p. 202.

[39]ARS Diary, Apr. 1, 1881. At prevailing exchange rates, this equaled roughly 1.25 Mexican pesos a day plus food.

three pesos a day. In Shepherd's time, general wages in the Batopilas area, influenced by his corporate policy, rose from under a peso a day to two or three.[40] Although Shepherd preferred to engage Americans as workers, he found that few were able to adjust to the harsh climate, the hard work, and the social isolation. Some became involved with local women, which made Shepherd uncomfortable, while others succumbed to alcohol.

How to pay the workers proved to be even more of a challenge than how much to pay them, resulting in Shepherd's experimenting with several systems over the years. The only options were to pay the miners in silver money or to find another alternative, and thus every payday he found himself having to obtain payroll funds by importing paper money and silver coins (vulnerable to theft) and scouring the local market. Despite Batopilas being a silver-mining center, minted Mexican silver dollars were difficult to obtain in volume, bulky to import, and vulnerable to theft in transit. For a short time Shepherd cast small silver bars worth thirty, fifty, and one hundred pesos but soon abandoned the effort. Mexican national currency was difficult to obtain, and while Chihuahua State did print paper money, state currency was not readily accepted because of the lack of confidence in locally produced paper money.[41] One report claimed that Shepherd had personally brought into Mexico a large amount of paper money printed in New York and had put it to use in a company store at the hacienda, but the account was written years later, and its reliability is questionable.[42] Most firsthand accounts relate that after initially struggling to pay his workers in silver or available state currencies, Shepherd realized by the fall of 1881 that such an arrangement was not sustainable.

By October 1881 Shepherd recorded in his diary a plan to pay the workers one-half in goods and one-half in currency. However, a delegation of local merchants, realizing that the plan would reduce their sales, called on Shepherd, who accepted their proposal to pay the workers in part in scrip, instead of goods, and part in currency. The merchants agreed to accept payment for their goods with the scrip (*boletas/billetas*), which they could redeem, albeit discounted, at the hacienda. Within a few days, hacienda

---

[40]Pletcher, *Rails, Mines, and Progress*, p. 203.

[41]Ibid., p. 206.

[42]James Morris Morgan, *Recollections of a Rebel Reefer* (New York, 1917), p. 388. Morgan's autobiography was not published until many years after the events in question, and he appears not to have stayed long in Batopilas.

printing presses had created the scrip, and a contract had been drafted, translated into Spanish, and approved by the merchants, and the first scrip payroll accepted by the miners without incident.[43] Despite the attempted "fix" for the currency problem, Shepherd expressed concern within a month that he still could not obtain adequate amounts of acceptable currency and so was forced to resort to Chihuahua-issued currency.[44] Shepherd made several attempts at using company scrip produced by a New York firm in at least 1889 and 1893.[45]

The company's payment scheme continued for about a year until the merchants discovered that they could assess a 6 percent "tax" on notes worth one Mexican dollar and above. When the workers protested, Shepherd took swift action, sending the merchants a letter listing the company payroll and other corporate expenditures benefiting Batopilas and threatening to run the mines with only American workers unless the merchants backed off. The crisis quickly ebbed, and Shepherd held a "courteous" meeting with the miners, assuring them that he was willing to pay in silver as soon as the state government authorized a coinage.[46] In any event, the local businessmen remained unhappy with a system that required them to exchange the scrip at the hacienda, where they lost money due to a discount imposed by Shepherd.

A key element in Shepherd's payroll strategy was the company store, which permitted him to short-cut the currency shortage problem and to address a major social problem among the workers: binge drinking. After getting paid on Saturday afternoon, workers would frequently squander their salaries on liquor, wasting the money needed by their families for clothes and groceries in the coming week. By setting aside half of each miner's pay as redeemable in goods but not liquor, Shepherd's system assured that the workers' families would not suffer. A U.S. consular report in 1883 approvingly noted the system employed by Shepherd and some other American expatriate miners in Mexico: "[The] system properly administered is by far the better one for the families of the operators as some of them are quite inclined to gamble away their entire week's earnings before Monday morning."[47]

---

[43]ARS Diary, Oct. 25–29, 1881.

[44]ARS Diary, Nov. 5, 12, 1881.

[45]Exemplars in Historical Society of Washington Shepherd files.

[46]MGS Diary, Sept. 18–20, 1882.

[47]Letter from U.S. Consul, Chihuahua, Louis Scott, to John David, Asst. Secretary of State, "Despatches from United States Consuls in Chihuahua, 1830–1906," M289, roll 2, vols. 3–4, RG 59, NARA (hereafter U.S. Consul).

By 1882 Shepherd had sold the original company store and built a new, impressive one in town that provided ready access to the miners and their families. It consisted of several buildings and compared favorably with those of the local merchants, having ample space for storerooms and showrooms, with a spacious inner court covered with a permanent roof.[48] The store, later known as *tienda de raya*, moved several times during Shepherd's tenure in Batopilas, but it was eventually placed at the town end of the steel bridge he built across the Batopilas River, where it stands today.

Another distraction for Shepherd in the early years of the silver-mining operation was a running dispute with the powerful Valenzuela family over title to the Roncesvalles mine, which was claimed by Shepherd and included in his original purchase from John Robinson. Shepherd and Valenzuela had overlapping claims to some of the same mine properties, which is not difficult to understand in a region where physical access was often difficult. (Relations were not helped when Shepherd showed up late for a Valenzuela family wedding and missed the ceremony.[49]) The Valenzuela lawyer, Jesus Ulloa, gave a fiery speech at the 1882 Batopilas Mexican Independence Day festivities in Batopilas, attacking the company and Americans in general. Shepherd, present but unable to understand the oration in Spanish, obtained a translation and promptly withdrew in protest. The local organizing committee apologized to Shepherd and cancelled Ulloa's invitation to the banquet the following day. On pain of arrest by the state government, Ulloa also apologized, but the incident left a bad taste in everyone's mouth. Shepherd finally settled the Valenzuela lawsuit in fall 1882 by purchasing the Valenzuela claim to the Roncesvalles mine.[50]

The Satevo Distraction

S. J. Pareja, a local amateur sociologist who published a book that included candid observations about Shepherd's first two years in Mexico, reported a curious incident in the summer of 1882 that highlighted the anomalies of a dominant foreign presence in an impoverished, poorly

---

[48]CBSMC 1882, p. 36.
[49]ARS Diary, Jan. 30, 1881.
[50]MGS Diary, Sept. 16, Nov. 1882; Pletcher, *Rails, Mines, and Progress*, p. 205.

governed, and isolated Mexican town. The incident was triggered by reports from Batopilas, denounced by Pareja as "not only incorrect, but exaggerated and fabricated," about a miners' strike ostensibly fueled by anger over Shepherd's use of scrip, and the consequent political turmoil that resulted in the detailing of a small force of federal troops from Chihuahua City. Pareja confirmed that there was a "peaceful demonstration" in front of the Batopilas Municipal Presidency by workers upset with the company scrip but noted that it was accompanied by "a small organ or barrel organ." The workers disbanded, "and all returned to working quietly and peacefully in their jobs"—even before presentation of their grievance.[51]

The commander of the federal force, Colonel Bosquet, with no turmoil to suppress and "in order to reciprocate the cordial and generous hospitality" given him by the people of Batopilas (and probably also to provide amusement for his troops), arranged at personal expense to treat the general population to a day at a picturesque church in the village at Satevo, a few miles downstream from Batopilas. The townspeople made their way to Satevo by horse- and mule-back, wagon, and on foot; a local photographer captured the outing on film. The soldiers provided the entertainment, staging a mock battle with maneuvers and weapons fired for effect. At the end of the afternoon, the tired and satisfied townspeople returned to the town. Pareja summed up the event by noting, "Batopilas will always remember, with pleasure, that because of false and exaggerated reports, promulgated by deluded, pessimistic persons, they had the opportunity to gather together with a great number of their neighbors and enjoy a day of relaxing and pleasant recreation."[52]

The Rumor Mill and Daily Life

During Shepherd's twenty-two years in Mexico, U.S. press accounts routinely described his life as one of untold wealth and privilege generated by the mines. Among the many such accounts, all false, were reports that at his death his estate was worth $6,000,000; that he converted the mining

---

[51]S. J. Pareja, *Resena Historica*, typescript, pp. 106–8, in possession of author.
[52]Ibid.

camp into "one of the beauty spots in the country;"[53] that his wealth was estimated at "not less than $12,000,000;" that "he created a free public library of several thousand volumes of choice books;"[54] and that within the walls of the hacienda were "the hotel where 1,400 of his workmen lived, his pleasure house, etc."[55] An even more fanciful account said "several of the rooms in the castle are silverplated, floors, walls and ceilings."[56] The reality of Shepherd's family life in Mexico was, in fact, dramatically different from the fanciful stories appearing in the U.S. press. However, because few people attempted the arduous trip to Batopilas or, for that matter, had even been to Mexico, it is unsurprising that these beliefs were common and enduring. In addition, Shepherd's extravagant lifestyle in Washington no doubt fed people's assumptions about how he would live in Mexico. Although the family's lifestyle, such as it was, contrasted dramatically with the poverty around them, the image of luxury bore no relation to reality.

Regardless of the grinding daily life in the mines, Shepherd always made sure to maintain the formal personal style he had adopted in Washington. His daughter Grace Merchant recalled,

> During all the Mexican years Father's only local tailoring was Mother-made coats of pongee or thin white serge for hottest weather, after he grew wistful about the ill-fitting thin jackets made by the Batopilas tailor for the young men.
>
> Father never came to the table with his family without a coat, no matter how hot the weather. Of course no other man ever did either, with that standard! When too tired, too hot, too desperately in need of being undisturbed and undisturbing, he would wait until meal over, dining room empty, [to] sit at his end of the long table, in shirt sleeves, with the *mozo* [young man] to serve him, alone.[57]

No one captured the Batopilas reality better than Shepherd's friend and business partner Lyndon Stevens, who spent years in Batopilas sharing the same challenges and privations as Shepherd: "Life in Batopilas is a life of labor and extreme simplicity. The [Shepherd] dwelling house is a one-story adobe building, one room deep, and substantially the same as Governor

---

[53] *New York Times*, Sept. 14, 1902.

[54] Ibid., Oct. 25, 1898.

[55] Ibid., Sept. 13, 1902.

[56] Cited in Pletcher, *Rails, Mines, and Progress*, p. 207.

[57] Grace Shepherd Merchant, Reminiscence, post-1909, Shepherd Papers, DLC.

Shepherd found it in 1880; the furniture is simple, and the table, while as good as that barren region will afford, is meager. There is, perhaps, no stockholder of our company residing in the United States whose home is not better furnished and more amply provided."[58] As an early visitor to Batopilas put it, "Batopilas is good for mining but not for residence. . . . Living here is a major sacrifice in comforts and privileges. . . . [The region] contains nothing but water, rocks, silver ore, and Gov. Shepherd."[59] The daily routine consisted of hard work, siestas, and simple, homemade amusements. The men worked six days a week, and the managers met with Shepherd on Sundays to review matters and plan ahead. Evenings when there was no equipment failure or weather-related crisis were spent playing cards, with the women reading and sewing. Every Sunday evening Shepherd conducted a simple religious service based on the Episcopal prayer book, with hymn-singing, for the family and his American workers.[60]

One major improvement in the quality of life for the Shepherd family was the arrival on November 18, 1881, of a piano ordered from the United States—no doubt contributing to the impression that the Shepherds had everything they wanted in Batopilas. According to one eyewitness account, the piano was seven months in transit and was hand-carried in sections because the pieces were too heavy for mules. Twenty-nine men took turns carrying the piano for twenty-six days and for 250 miles over the mountains. Mary Shepherd practiced the piano but never felt she made much progress; others used the piano to liven up family gatherings and religious services.[61]

Mrs. Shepherd worried constantly about the effect of the harsh environment on her four teenaged daughters and three small boys. Fresh vegetables, fruits, and milk were hard to come by locally; butter was unavailable except when brought in from Chihuahua City. Chicken was plentiful, but the local beef was stringy and tough because the fat was saved for making candles. Local flour was "abominable," and the bread "almost uneatable." The Shepherds imported canned and preserved foods, without which "we should not have been able to live here so long."[62] The three boys thrived on

---

[58] *Batopilas Mining Company, Annual Report, 1902,* (n.p., n.d.), p. 5, Shepherd Papers, DLC.

[59] F. A. Lowe, quoted in *Evening Star,* Apr. 20, 1882, and *Washington Post,* Apr. 20, 1882.

[60] Pletcher, *Rails, Mines, and Progress,* p. 208.

[61] ARS Diary, Nov. 18, 1881; *Evening Star,* Apr. 20, 1882; MGS letter to daughter Grace, Aug. 30, 1882, Shepherd Papers, DLC.

[62] MGS Diary, Aug. 11, 1882.

the adventure and excitement of the mining operation, but the girls had fewer options, although the isolation and lack of playmates did make the children self-reliant and drew the family together. All three boys eventually spent portions of their lives as miners, and the children returned to Batopilas as long as their parents were there. The girls benefited from Shepherd's policy of importing expatriates as engineers and physicians; each daughter would marry an expatriate American or Scot working at the mines.[63]

A series of illnesses affected several of the Shepherd children in the summer and fall of 1881 and created a dilemma for the parents: if Mrs. Shepherd was to accompany some of them to the States for their health, any children remaining in Batopilas would have only their hard-working father as principal caregiver. By spring 1882 the company physician had recommended that at least three of the girls be sent north for a change of air and diet. By June of that year, May, Sue, and Grace had gone to the States, leaving Isabel, Alexander Jr., Grant, and John Conness at the hacienda. By the fall, Mrs. Shepherd decided to join the three girls in New York and to remain there for the winter, alternating among New York, New Jersey, and Washington. As it turned out, the family was to remain separated until Mrs. Shepherd and the children returned to Mexico in October 1883.[64]

The special demands of life in an isolated riverbank village deep in the Mexican mountains were now clear, and the family settled into a "routine" that resembled no previous family routine but was to become all too familiar over the twenty-two years that Alexander Shepherd spent wresting silver out of the rock.

---

[63]May married engineer Edward Quintard; Susan married engineer Walter Brodie, a Scot; Grace married Frank Merchant, a physician and first cousin; and Isabel married Robert F. Wagner, a physician.

[64]MGS Diary, Nov. 1882–Nov. 1883; *Evening Star*, Oct. 3, 1883.

Chapter Eleven

"Anxieties, Expenses, Delays, and Losses"

Journey's End, 1882–1902

B Y T H E E N D of 1882 the Shepherd enterprise in Batopilas had been in operation for more than two years, and much of the industrial infrastructure was in place. The company consisted of several mining properties in the immediate vicinity of Hacienda San Miguel, with most of the early focus on the San Miguel mine just upstream from the hacienda. Shepherd understood the importance of demonstrating early success, not only to validate his involvement but also to assure his investors and directors of the wisdom of their commitments.

Central to Shepherd's strategic planning was working capital, and his early hopes were dashed when early investors made available only $150,000 for improvements to add to the $100,000 in personal funds provided by himself and Stevens.[1] The 1882 annual report informed investors that the hoped-for dividend on preferred stock would be postponed, listing as causes inefficient smelting methods, the small amount of high-grade ore produced, investment in new machinery, and severe storm damage.[2] The company's 1883 annual report led with a litany of woes, citing an "excessive drought" for six months in 1883 that destroyed animal pasturage, effectively shutting down daily operations dependent on importation of fuel

---

[1] *Annual Report to the Stockholders of the Consolidated Batopilas Silver Mining Company, 1882*, p. 3 (hereafter CBSMC 1882).
[2] Ibid., p. 2.

and freight.[3] Constant plant improvements and expansion were major categories of expenditure. No dividend was reported in 1883.

Not all of the corporate annual reports have survived, but those that have are instructive. First and foremost, they were Shepherd's personal account of the Batopilas experience; although he relied on engineers and accountants for much of the detail, he orchestrated the content to present the most attractive picture possible. Aside from reports from the few years when his miners struck "bonanzas" that permitted debts to be paid off and dividends given to shareholders, these reports provide excruciating detail of the challenges Shepherd faced in trying to turn the mines into the El Dorado that he believed they would become. The reports became a litany of complaints about the perverseness of nature and the difficulties of building a modern industrial complex in one of North America's most remote areas as well as a justification for the large expenditures the task required. Just as he had in Washington, Shepherd had a vision for the future that was grand and expensive, and he was determined to let nothing stop him in achieving it.

The annual reports presented opportunities for shifting profits and losses among accounts, and Shepherd appears to have made creative use of them; entries in his 1881 diary describe him and/or accountants preparing them for shipment to New York.[4] Shepherd's longtime accountant, E. W. A. Jorgenson, worked out of the New York office but spent substantial periods of time in Batopilas, and the family made use of him long after Shepherd's death, until the tangled affairs of the corporation were brought to a close. In fall 1881 Shepherd decided to send accountant George Ford to New York City to present the board with "an intelligent statement" about working capital and the cost of improvements.[5] As in Washington, Shepherd possessed almost dictatorial powers in Mexico. In Washington he had been criticized for his cronyism in selecting contractors, his shoddy record keeping, and basing too many decisions on the "law of necessity." Although no credible evidence of personal corruption was ever confirmed in his Washington dealings, critics of Shepherd's operation in Mexico could raise questions about his personal integrity in distinguishing between what was the company's and

---

[3] *Annual Report to the Stockholders of the Consolidated Batopilas Silver Mining Company, 1883*, p. 3 (hereafter CBSMC 1883).

[4] Alexander Shepherd 1881 Diary, Oct. 15, Oct. 24, Dec. 11, courtesy of W. Sinkler Manning Jr.

[5] Ibid., Oct. 15.

what was his. There is no doubt that what he told his American financiers, and how he told it, provided wide latitude for corruption, should he have been so inclined.

Perhaps no categorical answer as to whether Shepherd was actually corrupt is possible, but several factors deserve consideration. The first is that Shepherd considered Mexico a golden opportunity to regain his personal fortune, prove himself right (always important), shame his detractors, and return to Washington in financial triumph. A number of his comments, echoed by a dedicated wife, about his intention to remain in Mexico for a limited period should be taken at face value, particularly since he made just two trips out of Mexico in the twenty-two years he lived there. Relatives, friends, and the press regularly reported that Shepherd was expected in Washington and New York on business, but he never showed up. The reason he always gave for not making the expected visit was that responsibilities at the mines required his presence. He even missed the double wedding of daughters Sue and May in Washington in October 1885.[6] Until a three-month trip to Europe in 1895–96 with Mrs. Shepherd and two of their daughters that took him to the East Coast, the only visit he made to Washington, in fall 1887, occurred primarily because it was part of recuperation from a near-fatal mine accident the previous spring.[7]

Another consideration in evaluating Shepherd's fiscal integrity in Mexico was the disparity between his willingness to spend money on industrial improvement and his skimpy expenditures on upgrading the family living quarters. Considering Shepherd's conspicuous consumption in constructing two grand residences in Washington, D.C., his parsimony concerning the family home in Batopilas is noteworthy. In 1882 a total of only $843 was spent on improvements to the Shepherd residence, a pittance compared to what was spent on industrial upgrades.[8] When Mrs. Shepherd and several of the children returned from almost a year away in the fall of 1884, they were thrilled to see that "the hacienda had been enlarged and improved; a school room built for the children—all rooms, all parts of [the] hacienda as neat and sweet as paint and whitewash could make it. . . . A great luxury was a bathroom—nicely fitted with steam pipes. This has already been a

---

[6]*Washington Post*, Oct. 23, 1885.
[7]David M. Pletcher, *Rails, Mines, and Progress: Seven American Promoters in Mexico, 1867–1911* (1958; rep. ed., Port Washington, N.Y., 1972), p. 210.
[8]CBSMC 1882, p. 34.

great comfort to all of us."[9] Mrs. Shepherd's enthusiasm over a coat of paint and a new bathroom implies a low threshold for pleasure in daily life at the hacienda, which would have been out of character for the Shepherds in Washington. When it came to spending money on the industrial plant or on family needs in Mexico, Shepherd always chose the former.

As later noted by Stevens, Shepherd put all his personal funds into helping capitalize the company, counting on rising stock value to make him rich. According to his son and namesake, Shepherd died intestate, and what was left after sorting out the affairs of his estate in later years did not amount to much more than the balance of the purchase money for Bleak House, which had been used as collateral for loans for many years.[10] The bottom line for Shepherd was that if the company prospered, he would prosper, and he bet literally everything on that proposition. Against such a grand vision, it is not persuasive that Shepherd would try to skim money illegally from the silver-mining operation. Such activities would only reduce the funds available to pay company debts and provide dividends for the stockholders to whom he was accountable. Shepherd's conduct in Mexico, where he had great personal freedom, was reminiscent of Washington, where no evidence was ever produced to show personal corruption.

Other evidence in the record supports the view that Shepherd played it straight in Mexico and was often in desperate financial straits. In one instance, he responded to a church contribution request from his friend and mentor Oliver O. Howard with the comment that he was so strapped for cash that he could not even keep up his life insurance premiums.[11] Always one to pay his bills when he could, Shepherd is mentioned in scattered press accounts years after his death for his estate being sued for nonpayment by the estates of his 1876 creditors, to whom he had given IOU's in

---

[9]Nov. 4, 1883, Mary Grice Shepherd Diary (hereafter MGS Diary), courtesy Mary Wagner Woods.

[10]Alexander Shepherd Jr. deposition in a property suit (n.d.) against his father. As corroboration, Shepherd's will has never been located, in Mexico or the United States. A Shepherd family safety deposit box yielded voluminous materials relating to disposition of Shepherd's and the company's affairs, most resolved with repayment of loans among family and close friends like L. H. Stevens and transfer of (worthless) stock. See "Statement of Shepherd Estate Accounts, from December 31st, 1907 to January 1st, 1920," signed by Francis D. Merchant, Grace Shepherd Merchant, and Mary G. Shepherd, courtesy of W. Sinkler Manning Jr.

[11]Shepherd to Oliver O. Howard, Jan. 10, 1891, O. O. Howard Papers, Bowdoin College, Brunswick, Me.

one-hundred-dollar increments. Always sensitive about protecting his good name, Shepherd would not have allowed this situation to develop had he had a choice.

Díaz Helps Out

The strong and consistent political support provided by President Porfirio Díaz was one positive development for Shepherd and his ambitions for the Batopilas mines. Díaz's first term ended in 1880, but he returned in 1884 to serve as president continuously throughout Shepherd's twenty-two-year sojourn in Mexico. The Díaz regime, favoring foreign investors, took several concrete actions that strengthened the mining sector and Shepherd's own prospects. One was an 1884 mining code that reversed traditional Hispanic jurisprudence reserving subsoil ownership for the nation; additionally, the surface proprietor was formally granted ownership of all bituminous and other mineral fuels. Later, new mining laws either lowered or eliminated taxes on certain minerals.[12]

A key ingredient in Shepherd's long-range plans was increasing production through large-scale industrial processes. In order to strike the right balance between supply and demand of silver ore, Shepherd needed undisputed control over a larger area believed to contain valuable ores than the property he had acquired from John Robinson. Shepherd was determined, if possible, to avoid issues such as the controversy with the Valenzuela family over control of the Roncesvalles mine in 1882. On April 12, 1886, the Diaz administration made a remarkable award to Shepherd that confirmed the admiration Diaz held for Shepherd and his belief that Shepherd's mining operation in Batopilas should be encouraged as a model for foreign mineral exploitation in Mexico. The concession granted Shepherd the right to exploit all abandoned mines in an area of about sixty square miles, exempted them from import duties on machinery and federal taxes except the stamp tax, and granted an annual rebate on other import duties.[13] Another critical element in the concession was permission to dam the Batopilas River, which

---

[12]Michael Meyer, William L. Sherman, and Susan Deeds, *The Course of Mexican History*, 7th ed. (Oxford, 2003), p. 427.
[13]Pletcher, *Rails, Mines, and Progress*, p. 194.

was essential to generating sufficient electrical power to run the mining operation since every accessible tree had been consumed, making timber scarce and expensive.[14]

The most dramatic improvement in which Shepherd put his faith, and a great deal of money, was the Porfirio Díaz Tunnel, a project cited in the 1886 Mexican concession and appropriately named for the Mexican president. Shepherd began to develop the tunnel, located across the river from the hacienda and next to the San Antonio mine, in 1885, intending to gain direct access to a number of likely or proven silver-bearing veins and to make it possible to bring the ore out via a railway system built the length of the tunnel. The tunnel, not completed until 1899, had as its principal target the Roncesvalles vein, which had been at the heart of the Valenzuela controversy, but the tunnel also crossed many new deposits that were explored with side tunnels. By the time of Shepherd's death in 1902, the workings in the Díaz Tunnel and the Todos Santos silver vein were responsible for more than 90 percent of all ore the company smelted.[15]

A major objective of the concession document was to provide Shepherd a title of property "which may give proper confidence and attract such parties that invest large capital which may be required for the opening of the great Porfirio Díaz Tunnel, a work which is one of the largest of its kind in the present time."[16] In exchange, Shepherd agreed that (1) the mines would become legally Mexican, (2) he would employ at least fifty workers six months a year, (3) he would make a $25,000 security deposit, and (4) he would permit up to five Mexican mining students to gain practical experience in the Batopilas mines.[17] Transferring legal jurisdiction of the mines demonstrated Shepherd's long-term commitment to Mexico. This remarkable document, no doubt drafted by Shepherd and his Mexican lawyer, Carlos Pacheco, was tailor-made for the Shepherd operation and also sent a message to other American entrepreneurs that investment in Mexico would be welcomed.

As it turned out, Shepherd's early years saw some of the mines' best production, providing encouragement to his American directors and investors.

---

[14]Ibid.

[15]Ibid., p. 197.

[16]Concession Text, article 1; full text in *Report: The Batopilas Smelting and Refining Co., Ltd.*, written by Gillmore Goodland for a British firm to which Shepherd's successors hoped to lease the properties, London, Nov. 1, 1909, p. 62 (hereafter Goodland Report). The report was published for the new firm's directors; courtesy of W. Sinkler Manning Jr.

[17]Ibid., pp. 64–65.

Two of the best years were 1884 and 1885, with production (in pesos) worth M$1,055,864 and M$1,004,090, respectively. Except for the year 1893, these levels were not repeated until the decade from 1900 until the onset of the Mexican revolution, when six of out nine years saw production between M$1 million and M$1.5million.[18] By that time, however, the Mexican political situation was deteriorating so rapidly that the long-sought financial success could not be sustained.

Family Matters

Life for the Shepherd family in Batopilas eased to some extent in the 1880s as they improved their physical surroundings, but "home" remained the L-shaped, one-story adobe building that had changed little externally since their arrival. A portico along both sides of the "L" and trees provided shade from the sun. In later years the family planted a vegetable garden, one of the few in the area, which provided a semblance of balance in their diet. Arrival of the piano added music,[19] and, in 1886, Shepherd purchased a small ice-making machine from Chihuahua. The family relied on imported, canned foodstuffs, particularly meats and vegetables, along with wine and whiskey, to add a civilized note to the local cuisine of *carne seca* (dried meat) and tortillas. The children adjusted readily to Mexican food, but the parents never became used to it. Shepherd loathed the goat's milk served with coffee and often said, "Please give me some more of the goat," to underscore his distaste.

Understandably, the Shepherd family (*La Familia*) was of interest to the town residents. Daughter Grace, in her early teens, described a chaperoned shopping trip to town on horseback and scenes in the shops: "In the patio of the merchant-prince's house in the rear of the store, flowers had been gathered and a bouquet for each shopping-guest arranged, to be presented by the merchant-princes when the ceremony approached the final rites . . . we rode on through the town, greeting friends and acquaintances in windows and doors, for everyone knew by this time that *La Familia* was at the

---

[18]Ibid., p. 53.
[19]Shepherd 1881 diary, Nov. 18, 1881.

stores, and no one missed voluntarily a glimpse of the senoritas on their prancing horses."[20]

Almost from the start, Mrs. Shepherd had accompanied some or all of the children to the States for summers in New York, New Jersey, and Washington but began having them spend the school year in the States as well, in 1882 and again in 1886.[21] Along the way, the parents experimented with importing tutors to Batopilas, including a Miss Griswold, who lasted two years teaching the youngest two girls and the boys, but this arrangement proved unsatisfactory. Reflecting on the experience, Grant Shepherd later implied that the time spent with Miss Griswold on "preliminary book-learning" might have been better spent on practical topics such as skills needed for a successful mining venture.[22]

Not surprisingly, the boys thrived in the rough-and-tumble life at the mines, which had also made them unsuitable for a standard school regime. After the family spent the summer of 1885 in the States, Alexander Jr., then thirteen, remained behind and was enrolled at Lawrenceville School in New Jersey.[23] Grant and Conness enrolled for the 1887–88 school year at the (Sidwell) Friends School in Washington, D.C., which Grant hated, and they lived with their mother in a rented house near DuPont Circle.[24] The two younger boys joined Alexander Jr. at Lawrenceville, but by the fall of 1889 all three had been expelled for getting drunk and carousing in town when they were not supposed to leave the school grounds. After receiving a sanctimonious letter from the school headmaster about the expulsions, the boys' father sent a sarcastic response, rejecting expressions of concern for the boys' welfare and noting that "the loss of time and money which their stay in your establishment has entailed upon them and me is the largest expenditure for the smallest result which it has ever been my misfortune to experience."[25]

---

[20]Grace Shepherd typescript, "Shopping in Batopilas," box 11, Shepherd Papers, Manuscript Division, Library of Congress, Washington, D.C. (hereafter DLC).

[21]MGS Diary, Nov. 4, 1882; Nov. 18, 1886.

[22]Grant Shepherd, *The Silver Magnet: Fifty Years in a Mexican Silver Mine* (New York, 1938), p. 76.

[23]MGS Diary, September 1885.

[24]Shepherd, *The Silver Magnet*, pp. 77–78; personal communication to the author from the Sidwell Friends School archivist, July 20, 2011.

[25]ARS to James S. MacKenzie, Oct. 7, 1889, Lawrenceville School Archives, Lawrenceville, N.J.

None of the Shepherd boys would graduate from college, although all three enrolled at the University of the South at Sewanee, Tennessee, where Alexander Jr. spent three years and was captain of its first football team.[26] Grant and Conness later took special courses in mining at Columbia University and the University of Pennsylvania.[27] Back in Batopilas, the boys reveled in their roles as sons of the *Patron Grande* and enjoyed outings in town, where they socialized, drank, danced, and got into occasional trouble with the authorities.[28]

The pattern of life for the Shepherd family in Batopilas became familiar and stabilized. Alexander Shepherd Jr. managed the mine after his father's death in 1902 until the family was driven out by the revolution around 1912. His daughter described a lifestyle during her father's era that resembled her grandfather's era so closely as to create uncertainty in the listener's mind as to which generation was being discussed.[29] For the Shepherd family, Batopilas was a social bubble around which the very real problems of wresting silver out of the mines went on nonstop. As the years stretched out, however, the uncertainties of mining under difficult circumstances accumulated, and the toll began to show on Alexander Shepherd.

Expectations Dim; A Close Call

Shepherd's hopes of building an even greater fortune in Mexico than he had in Washington dimmed as the years went by. Profits that could have gone to shareholders, including himself, were delayed because Shepherd insisted on plowing profits back into the expansion of the silver-mining operation in order to gain economies of scale. As the years passed, Shepherd suffered from accidents and ill health that sapped his energy, and he began to delegate responsibility at the mines to his sons and sons-in-law, a silent acknowledgment that even he could not make the mountains give up the silver that he had so confidently predicted he could obtain.

The bonanza of 1884 produced a record M$1.05 million and provided a glimpse of the potential that Shepherd had been preaching since the

[26]University Library Archives, University of the South, Sewanee, Tenn.

[27]Shepherd, *The Silver Magnet*, p. 86.

[28]Ibid., pp. 147–48.

[29]Comments by Mrs. Ludson Worsham to the author, La Jolla, Calif., Aug. 1987.

beginning, but, after 1885, production dropped sharply for the next eight years, and questions arose as to whether or not the lure of the Shepherd name and reputation had been oversold.[30] The year 1887 proved to be critical for both Shepherd and the mines, and none of the news during that year was good. The first serious event was a near-fatal accident Shepherd had in May while he was riding on horseback through a new mountain tunnel that was part of a three-mile aqueduct to provide waterpower for the electric generators. His horse reared and drove Shepherd's head against the tunnel wall, peeling away much of his scalp.[31] He described his head as having been "swollen double" for some days due to the onset of erysipelas, a skin infection that almost killed him. Although he kept up a brave front, Shepherd admitted to a Washington friend that he had been very near death, or "the bank of the river," as he put it, but had been spared.[32] His wife, in the United States with several of the children, left immediately for Mexico. Despite reassuring reports within the month that Shepherd was recovering and back on the job, company physician Charles Lee was concerned that his patient was not progressing in the Batopilas heat and prescribed a trip to the United States for an extended convalescence.[33]

A small party consisting of Alexander and Mary Shepherd and attendants left Batopilas in mid-June, and Shepherd insisted on riding all the way to the stagecoach connection by mule, even going so far as to send back to the hacienda a special travel chair made by one of his American employees.[34] En route, the party stayed for several days at the family's mountain retreat to escape the heat of the valley, and Mrs. Shepherd reported that Shepherd devoured the small library at the rate of three or four books a day. Once aboard the train heading for the East Coast, Shepherd gave an upbeat interview to a reporter in which he pointed out that, except for one trip to Chihuahua City in December 1882 to settle the Valenzuela affair, this was the first time he had left Batopilas since arriving in 1880. Speaking of

---

[30]Alexander Shepherd Jr., "A Summary of the Native Batopilas Silver Mines: Their Past Record of Production and Outlook for Future Yield," unpublished report (Arizona State University Library, 1935), p. 3, courtesy of W. Sinkler Manning Jr.

[31]ARS to son Alexander Jr. at Lawrenceville, May 17, 1887; *Evening Star* (Washington, D.C.), May 26, 1887; Shepherd, *The Silver Magnet*, pp. 238–39.

[32]ARS to A. H. Evans, June 25, 1887, Shepherd Papers, DLC; *Evening Star,* July 8, 1887.

[33]ARS to May Shepherd, May 31, 1887 (typescript), box 11, Shepherd Papers, DLC.

[34]MGS letter to a daughter, June 21, 1887 (typescript), box 11, Shepherd Papers, DLC.

the mining operation, Shepherd characteristically overstated. "I have not been connected yet with anything that was a failure," he said, citing how his plans for rebuilding Washington were initially seen as excessive, yet "there are very few now but who will say I did just the right thing. So it is with Batopilas, and time will show the truth of what I say."[35]

After arriving in Washington, where the family took over Bleak House for a brief visit, the Shepherds decamped to the New Jersey lakes so that Shepherd could continue recuperating before returning to Washington.[36] Shepherd's Washington friends reached out to him to offer hospitality and public tributes, but Shepherd, weak and unaccustomed to the demands of Washington life, tried to fend them off. Shepherd had done everything possible to avoid coming back to the States before he was ready, but the mine injury had left him no choice other than to return or die of infection in Batopilas. Anticipating the situation in Washington upon his arrival, Shepherd turned for help to William F. Mattingly, his longtime confidant and his counsel during the congressional hearings some fifteen years earlier. Mattingly once again served as Shepherd's gatekeeper. In a revealing letter written to Shepherd during his train trip east, Mattingly wrote, "I fully comprehended the situation before the receipt of your letter and have in substance already informed several parties that you were neither in a financial or physical condition to do anything and when you came up must not be annoyed by any such matter."[37] However, once Shepherd had committed to a Washington visit, public pressure would demand a proper tribute led by the business community, who understood better than most how much Shepherd had meant to Washington's prosperity.

Visitors to Bleak House in the early days of Shepherd's return reported encountering a man they would not have recognized: he was thinner and wearing a black silk skullcap over an almost hairless scalp, across which ran "an ugly purple scar."[38] Nevertheless, Shepherd gave several press interviews and appeared to gain strength as time went on. With an eye on his New York investors, Shepherd spoke expansively of the mines, drawing a

---

[35] *St. Louis Globe-Democrat*, July 14, 1887, copy in box 9, Shepherd Papers, DLC.

[36] MGS Diary, late summer, 1887; *Evening Star*, Aug. 9 and 16, 1887.

[37] William Mattingly to ARS, July 12, 1887, courtesy of W. Sinkler Manning Jr.

[38] *Evening Star*, July 18, 1887. Mary Shepherd described a photo of Shepherd taken en route east as fit only "for a medical museum." MGS to Grace, July 9, 1887 (typescript), box 11, Shepherd Papers, DLC.

parallel between the vision and hard work required to transform Washington and the same requirements needed to make a success of silver mining in Mexico.[39]

Washington Turns Out; New York Disappoints

Plans for a gala welcoming ceremony in Washington moved ahead once Shepherd acceded to public demands. At a mass meeting in late September in the armory of the National Rifles, Shepherd's Civil War outfit, Mattingly offered a resolution to hold a "popular demonstration" to include a parade and review, inviting participation by local civil and military groups; the response was dramatic.[40] The formal invitation to Shepherd noted how "the continuation of the system you so boldly inaugurated became an imperative necessity," and the official welcoming letter was accompanied by the signatures of almost eleven thousand Washingtonians, filling 180 pages.[41] October 6 was set as the date for the main program, with the Shepherds to receive well-wishers at the Willard Hotel the next evening. Ever loyal to his Civil War unit, Shepherd also agreed to participate in a National Rifles reception the night after that.[42] An old Shepherd colleague, Colonel William Moore, chair of the military committee, declared that despite a ban on official participation in an unofficial event, all twenty-four organized companies of the Washington Light Infantry intended to take part; his view was endorsed by General Albert Ordway, commander of the D.C. militia.[43] There was widespread support for the parade, but there were groups that still had bad memories from Shepherd's Washington years. A northeast D.C. citizens committee grumbled that Shepherd had systematically bypassed their area in favor of improving northwest D.C.,[44] and labor unions declined to support the gala because of unhappiness over the sponsors' anti-union practices and perhaps memories of Shepherd's own anti-union views.[45]

---

[39]*Washington Post,* July 17 and 18, 1887; *Evening Star,* July 18, 1887.

[40]*Washington Critic,* Sept. 20, 1887.

[41]Copy courtesy of W. Sinkler Manning Jr.; original in Washingtoniana Room, Martin Luther King Jr. Library, Washington, D.C.

[42]Edward T. Matthews to ARS, Sept. 30, 1887, courtesy of W. Sinkler Manning Jr.

[43]*Evening Star,* Sept. 27 and Oct. 1, 1887.

[44]*Washington Post,* Aug. 30, 1887.

[45]*Evening Star,* Sept. 29 and 30, 1887.

On October 6 the Shepherd family was picked up at Bleak House by Mattingly, *Evening Star* owner Crosby S. Noyes, and the Reverend Myron M. Parker of New York Avenue Presbyterian Church and escorted by carriage down Seventh Street Road to the Willard Hotel before taking their places on a reviewing stand on the Treasury Building lawn across the street. The streets were lined with crowds, who were given a show by marching soldiers, civic organizations, bands, and high-wheeled bicycle clubs. There were also three authorized fireworks stations shooting rockets (one young woman was hit by a wayward roman candle), bombs, and cartwheels.[46] The Capitol dome was illuminated by calcium lights and reflectors. Shepherd's remarks to the crowd were generous in that he shared credit for the city's transformation with others, especially the late president Grant, who had died in 1884. After commending the city on its progress, Shepherd left his listeners with hard-earned advice: "Don't quarrel among yourselves. . . . Stand shoulder to shoulder and fight for the good of the District. . . . If you quarrel among yourselves, you can achieve no grand results."[47]

Behind the scenes, Shepherd was scrambling to maintain stockholder confidence in the Batopilas operation. From the beginning, he had sent trusted employees back to the States with letters and oral messages presenting an upbeat account of the mines. Besides having joined Lyndon Stevens in advancing the company almost $100,000 in cash, Shepherd had committed everything he owned to the mining venture. This audacious, even desperate, strategy meant that if the mines succeeded, he would again be wealthy, his vision rewarded, and his investors enriched. Nonetheless, Shepherd's serious injury and illness deepened public realization that he was the one person upon whom everything depended, thus increasing skepticism in the rumor mill. The press picked up on the negative speculation while Shepherd was commuting that summer between New York and Washington for corporate business. The *New York Times* observed, "It has been stated that Shepherd's errand to the United States was to boom the Mexican mining enterprises with which he has been connected. . . . The point has been reached, it is said, where it is absolutely necessary that these enterprises should be assisted with something like a million dollars or else collapse."[48]

------

[46]Ibid., Oct. 7, 1887; reprinted in *Washington Post*, Dec. 6, 1927.

[47]*Washington Chronicle*, Oct. 9, 1887.

[48]*New York Times*, Sept. 29, 1887, quoted in Katherine Howe, "The Batopilas Flask," *Winterthur Portfolio* 23 (Spring 1988):71–72.

Even Shepherd's old news outlet, the *Evening Star*, pressed the point when a reporter confronted him bluntly, "It has been said that you stopped in New York to drum up more money to carry on failing mining operations in Mexico." Shepherd responded only with a plug for his plans to consolidate the firm's corporate structure in New York.[49]

Despite the impressive display of support he received in Washington, Shepherd could not avoid the challenge that would meet him in New York on October 12: the stockholders meeting where he would present a proposal for consolidation of the mining operation into a single new corporation, the Batopilas Mining Company (BMC), and issuance of bonds to finance an aggressive expansion program. Shepherd reminded the stockholders that the Mexican mines had generated $1 million in dividends under his management.[50] The corporate consolidation and stock swaps were duly approved, but shrunken investor confidence in Shepherd's El Dorado resulted in only a fraction of the anticipated $1 million in bond sales that he had hoped for. After paying old corporate debts, Shepherd was forced to return to Mexico with only $200,000 in new money. The weak bond performance in New York must have created a sense of déjà vu for Shepherd. When he had started the mining operation seven years previously, he had projected returns estimates that far exceeded actual output, forcing him to rely on mine output for expansion funds. History was now repeating itself, since the $200,000 was insufficient for the scale of expansion Shepherd had counted on. He returned to Batopilas in spring 1888 after having completed his convalescence and business affairs on the East Coast, but a case of malaria, apparently contracted on the trip, kept him in a weakened condition for much of the following year.[51]

In a retrospective written years later, Lyndon Stevens pointed out,

> To carry on the work he was soon forced to rely on what the mines could produce and what he and a few others could loan the Company or borrow for it on their personal guaranty. This prolonged the work for years, made every part of it cost far more than it would had it been crowded through with ample money, gave additional burdens in interest and otherwise, and led to

[49]*Evening Star*, Oct. 6, 1887.
[50]Goodland Report, Nov. 1, 1909, p. 19.
[51]Pletcher, *Rails, Mines, and Progress*, p. 210.

all the anxieties, expenses, delays, and losses to arise from lack of money for a large enterprise in an isolated mountain region in a foreign land.[52]

Insoluble Problems

Shepherd's ability to prosper in Mexico was influenced also by national and international issues over which he had no control. In the years after the Civil War, currency questions played an important role in American politics and the economy. President Lincoln had authorized printing "greenbacks," paper currency without gold or silver backing, to pay for Union debts in the Civil War, but once these were retired, debate continued for years over how to assure currency integrity. Gold and silver discoveries in the West confirmed that the country was blessed with an abundance of these minerals. Even though alliances shifted, gold was favored by many Republicans, the banks, and major industrial forces because it kept the money supply modest and required debtors to repay in "sound money." Silver, on the other hand, was favored by many Democrats, farmers, and others dependent on loans and mortgages since silver-backed currency would expand the money supply, create inflation, and thereby reduce the net cost of repaying debts.

Not long before Shepherd committed himself to Mexico and silver mining, Congress passed the Bland-Allison Act of 1878, a response to the lagging economy since the depression that followed the Panic of 1873. The bill specified that the Treasury must purchase a set amount of silver each year and convert it into silver coinage. The law, never popular with industrialists and bankers, was later repealed, but by then Shepherd was launched on the mining venture. The Sherman Silver Purchase Act of 1890 reenergized the hopes of the silver-mining industry in the United States and Mexico because it directed the Treasury to purchase a larger amount of silver and also convert it into silver coinage. This act remonetized silver by again making it legal tender but without damaging the nation's commitment to gold. For Shepherd's purposes, the brief period between passage of the silver purchase act and the Panic of 1893 was not sufficient for the mines to benefit from higher

---

[52]The Batopilas Mining Company (hereafter BMC), Annual Report, 1902 (n.p., n.d.), p. 4, Shepherd Papers, DLC.

prices for silver. The years of silver production before 1894 were lower than normal, meaning less silver to sell at the higher prices then prevailing.

Chihuahua's financial base rested on agricultural and mineral exports, both vulnerable to circumstances in the U.S. markets they served. After Shepherd returned in 1888 with far less capital from the New York corporate reorganization than he had wanted, profits from the Batopilas mines continued to struggle. The mining operation suffered a major new blow when the Panic of 1893 struck the American economy and depressed economic activity throughout most of the 1890s. Like the depression of 1873, which drained Shepherd's resources in Washington, the Panic of 1893 was triggered by excessive railroad construction, starting with the Philadelphia and Reading Railroad, whose investors dumped one million shares of its stock on one day in February 1893. Other significant industrial enterprises failed, and, before the year was out, more than fifteen thousand American businesses had failed. With the contraction of business activity in the United States, advocates of returning to tight money and the gold standard for currency gained ascendancy, and silver advocates were portrayed as leading the country down the path to unlimited credit and debased currency. The 1894 midterm elections brought Republican gains in Congress that indicated a national preference for the gold standard.

The issue came to a head in the 1896 presidential campaign between Republican candidate William McKinley, former governor of Ohio, and populist Democratic candidate William Jennings Bryan. The Republicans backed the gold standard while the Democrats supported a 16:1 ratio for purchasing silver for coinage, which would have given a major boost to the silver industry. Bryan, endorsed by farmer and labor groups, gave what turned out to be one of the country's best-known speeches at the Democratic convention in July, when he famously declared, "You shall not press down upon the brow of labor this crown of thorns, you shall not crucify mankind on a cross of gold."[53] The election swept McKinley to victory on a platform of the gold standard and protective tariffs for U.S. businesses. Passage in 1900 of the Currency Act with McKinley's backing committed the United

[53]Paolo Coletta, *William Jennings Bryan*, 3 vols. (Lincoln, Neb., 1964–69), 1:141; Paul S. Boyer et al., *The Enduring Vision: A History of the American People*, 8th ed., 2 vols. (Boston, 2013), 2:613.

States to the gold standard and doomed hopes that Shepherd might have had for a high demand for silver in the United States.

Shepherd's Mexican venture suffered from a steady diet of bad luck and bad timing over the twenty-two years of his stewardship. The mines' greatest production year, 1894, came at the same time as a dramatic downturn of business in the United States led to the evaporation of the American market for silver. The annual reports of the mining operation repeated the usual litany of (a) detailed accounts of development initiatives undertaken, often at great effort and expense, (b) long lists of reasons why the high hopes for the year had not been realized, and (c) assurances by Shepherd that great results could be discerned and would surely prove him right and make the investors rich. Particularly in his later years in Mexico, Shepherd or his wife made comments that he wanted to turn the mines over to his sons and sons-in-law and spend more time in Washington. He still owned Bleak House, so the family had a pleasant and familiar residence to which they could return when it was not rented. But it never happened. The story was told that during one attempt to sell the mines in later years, an engineer tried to determine the amount of "ore in sight," to which Shepherd responded, "We have *no ore* [emphasis in original] in sight. Just as soon as it gets in sight we take it out of sight." Life at the Batopilas mines was a constant saga of ups and downs, including one occasion when Shepherd drew a check for $90,000 against a virtually empty bank account. Fortunately for Shepherd, as the days and hours counted down, with no silver in sight, a bonanza came in to cover the check with plenty to spare.[54]

By the 1890s, and even more so by his death in 1902, Shepherd had completed the infrastructure for a vast, sophisticated silver production operation. The 1901 Annual Report, the last complete year before Shepherd's death in September 1902, summarized the state of operations at that time. Perhaps sensing that his time was running short, Shepherd indulged in a brief history of the mine acquisition and proudly quoted the advisory from his friend General of the Army William T. Sherman to officers in Texas, saying that he would consider assistance to the Shepherds as assistance to himself. Shepherd contrasted the initial holdings of Hacienda San Miguel and the mine of the same name, along with three old stamps and two

---

[54]Mark Lamb, "Stories of the Batopilas Mines, Chihuahua," *The Engineering and Mining Journal* (Apr. 4, 1908):689–91.

arrastras, to a list of the current holdings of the forty-five-acre Haciendas of San Miguel and San Antonio: forty-three miles of mine tunnels, a five-hundred-horse-power electric generator fed by a three-mile aqueduct, five fully equipped relay stations for the silver-bearing mule trains, a permanent metal bridge spanning the seasonably turbulent Batopilas River, plus ranches and other holdings. The report added that the operation included machinery for a wide variety of castings and general machine work. Total silver production in the twenty-one-year period had been worth fourteen million Mexican silver dollars.[55]

Passing the Reins

By the mid-1890s Shepherd was feeling the strain of years of hard work and disappointment. In June 1895 the Shepherds set off from Batopilas on a trip that would take them to several European countries over three months and from which they would not return to Batopilas until early summer 1896. During a brief stay in Washington in mid-July 1895, Shepherd told a local newspaper reporter, "I have aged a good deal—I show it in my face—I haven't been feeling as well lately, as usual, either. I've suffered a good deal from vertigo, but I'm better now."[56] He couldn't resist weighing in on the local political situation, saying, "The difficulty with suffrage here [Washington] is in the slum element." Despite a disclaimer that he did not intend to include blacks in the assessment, Shepherd identified the problem as "a large population who would dominate affairs if there were suffrage." He went on to endorse commissioner government for the District.[57] Shepherd was feted at least twice in Washington, albeit on a much smaller scale than on his previous visit in 1887, once by the National Rifles and again by a citizens group at the Arlington Hotel, where the charge was twenty-five dollars a plate ($600 in 2012 currency).[58]

---

[55]BMC, Annual Report, 1901 (n.p., n.d.), Shepherd Papers, DLC.

[56]*Evening Star*, July 13, 1895.

[57]*Baltimore Sun*, July 15, 1895.

[58]George W. Evans, *To the Memory of Alexander Robey Shepherd, Former Governor of the District of Columbia, a Native Washingtonian, the Master Mind and Rebuilder of the Nation's Capital; Paper Read before the Society of Natives of the District of Columbia, October 20th, 1922* (Washington, D.C., 1922), pp. 21–25; *Washington Post*, July 21, 1895.

After side trips to Sewanee and Chattanooga, Tennessee, the Shepherds spent two weeks in New York before sailing with daughters Grace and Isabel on July 31 on the SS *Germanic* bound for Liverpool.[59] Other than a letter to Robert Wagner, a son-in-law in Batopilas, in which Shepherd stated his strong preference for Scotland over England, there is no record of where the family went in Europe. By August, however, Shepherd confessed to "getting very tired of loafing," and he arrived back in New York on October 26, shuttling to and from Washington on business until April 1896.[60]

The Shepherds arrived back in Chihuahua City at the end of April, where the Chihuahua State governor hosted a banquet at the statehouse in Shepherd's honor.[61] Before returning to Batopilas, Shepherd visited other areas in Mexico with prospective mineral resources as well as Mexico City, where he was received by President Díaz.[62] Once the family was back in Batopilas, local residents and company employees provided a hearty welcome to the returning travelers. Mrs. Shepherd, always looking on the bright side, wrote, "Our rooms are as fresh and sweet as paint, etc., can make them and look as though I had not been out of them for a year."[63]

Shepherd did receive one bit of news in 1897 indicating that his life and career had not gone unappreciated. After a visit to the wife of General Powell Clayton, U.S. minister in Mexico, Shepherd's daughter Susan Brodie reported to her mother,

> When General Clayton was in Washington during his interview with President McKinley, the President spoke of my Daddy and said he wanted to do something to reward him for all those years spent in Mexico, and asked Gen'l. Clayton if he did not think Daddy would be a good man to appoint as Minister [equivalent of Ambassador]. Gen'l. Clayton said, 'fine,' [but] when the President learned that Gen'l. C. was willing and desirous of continuing in office, the subject was dropped, [even though] the impression given to Gen'l. C. was that the President would have appointed Daddy.[64]

---

[59]SS *Germanic* Saloon Passenger Manifest, Departing July 31, 1895, New York to Liverpool, Shepherd Papers, box 16, DLC.

[60]ARS to Robert Wagner, Aug. 22, 1895, courtesy of Mary Wagner Woods.

[61]Robert S. Wagner Diary, May 4, 1896, courtesy of Mary Wagner Woods.

[62]Pletcher, *Rails, Mines, and Progress*, p. 211; President Díaz to Shepherd, June 16, 1896, courtesy of W. Sinkler Manning Jr.

[63]Letter fragment dated July 1 by Mary Shepherd, courtesy of Mary Wagner Woods.

[64]Susan Brodie to Mrs. Shepherd, May 18, 1897, Shepherd Papers, DLC.

According to the same source, Shepherd's Mexican friend, admirer, and business partner Enrique Creel also lobbied unsuccessfully with President McKinley to the same end.[65]

Shepherd made several unsuccessful attempts to sell the mines in the last decade of his life, despite his stubborn commitment to the Batopilas operation. His son Grant briskly summarized the effort: "All this resulted in visits upon three separate occasions by representatives of syndicates who came to investigate and examine the mines with the object of buying the property. The Spanish American War [1898] killed one opportunity to sell; the [Second] Boer War [1899–1902] killed another; and the Madero Revolution [in Mexico 1910–20] settled the affairs of Batopilas."[66] The first serious negotiation was between Shepherd and George Cristall, a Scottish financier who became friends with Shepherd and made several trips to inspect the mines, starting in 1898. Shepherd spoke candidly with Cristall about the situation, saying, "I am not as young as when I came here, and . . . the work begins to tell on me."[67] Enrique Creel, familiar with the Cristall negotiations, urged Shepherd to strike a deal: "I have many times spoken to Mrs. Creel and to Gov. [of Chihuahua] Terrazas about these great sacrifices to [*sic*] your family, and we all agreed that it is time for you and Mrs. Shepherd to come out of Batopilas and spend the rest of your life with as much comfort and easiness of mind as possible."[68] The 1898 BMC Annual Report acknowledged that the Board of Directors intended to take the steps necessary for legal transfer of title of the company's property "if the negotiations prove successful and require such transfer of title."[69]

On the eve of the Mexican Revolution (after Shepherd's death), the best-documented sales attempt for the mines took shape, to prospective British buyers led by Gillmore Goodland, a British financier who made several trips to Batopilas, the last in summer 1909. Goodland organized the Batopilas Mining, Smelting and Refining Company, Ltd. (London) and created a board of directors. Goodland's report to his board in November 1909 appeared to describe the completed purchase of the Batopilas Mining Company, citing fifty thousand British pounds "handed over to you," along with

---

[65]Ibid.

[66]Shepherd, *The Silver Magnet*, pp. 242–43.

[67]BMC, Annual Report, 1898–99, Shepherd Papers, box 12, DLC.

[68]Creel to ARS, Mar. 18, 1898, courtesy of Mary Wagner Woods.

[69]BMC, Annual Report, 1898–99, pp. 10–11, Shepherd Papers, box 12, DLC.

an equal amount raised by the British purchasers.[70] Despite the apparently advanced status of the purchase, it came to naught and is hardly mentioned in the Shepherd family papers. In 1913 Goodland declared personal bankruptcy, giving as main reasons for his insolvency "the stoppage of his work in Mexico by the revolution there," as a result of which his household furniture and effects were seized and sold.[71]

As the nineteenth century drew to a close, there was little good news to report about production from the Batopilas mines. The company's annual report for 1900 was unusually short, with a minimum of justifications and explanations for disappointing results.[72] By inference, Shepherd may have felt that he had said it all too many times in the past, had never been able to deliver on extravagant predictions of success, and was embarrassed to repeat the old excuses for unfulfilled promises. Faced with the persistent problem of too few skilled workers available in the Batopilas area, Shepherd resorted to his predecessor's *gambusino* labor strategy and consolidated work in a handful of locations: the Porfirio Díaz Tunnel and Todos Santos mine, the Roncesvalles mine, and the San Miguel mine.[73] Company debt soared to roughly half a million dollars in Mexico plus almost a million dollars in the United States, exclusive of the bonded debt of almost half a million U.S. dollars that would come due in September 1902.[74] The bonanza year of 1894 receded even further into the past, and the company was forced to borrow more in Mexico at prevailing high rates.

As could be the case in the unpredictable mining business, however, silver production in 1901 proved to be the highest in the history of the company, permitting Shepherd to pay off BMC's Mexican debts. Moreover, 90 percent of Shepherd's creditors in the United States agreed to a three-year extension of outstanding corporate bonds, so that they would mature in 1905.[75] Nevertheless, Shepherd was forced to consolidate further, closing the San Miguel mine, the starting-point for all his efforts, in March 1902, due to the shortage of workers.[76]

---

[70]Goodland Report, pp. 5–7.

[71]"Summary of Bankrupt's Amended Statement of Affairs," High Court of Justice (London), No. 208 of 1914, July 31, 1914, courtesy of W. Sinkler Manning Jr.

[72]BMC, Annual Report, 1900 (n.p., n.d.), pp. 1–8, Shepherd Papers, DLC.

[73]Ibid., pp. 6–8.

[74]BMC, Annual Report, 1898–99 (n.p., n.d.), p. 7, Shepherd Papers, DLC.

[75]BMC, Annual Report, 1901, p. 3.

[76]BMC, Annual Report, 1902, p. 13.

Death Comes Quickly

By coincidence, Shepherd's brother Arthur arrived in Batopilas on September 4, 1902, in order to obtain Alexander's signature for a personal services contract already signed by the provincial governor.[77] In a compelling first-person account in the *Evening Star* later in the month, Arthur reported being struck by his brother's robust, healthy appearance. The newspaper account also related that Alexander mentioned that he weighed 247 pounds, exactly the same as in 1871.[78] By the next day, however, Shepherd remained in his room, feeling ill. By September 8, Shepherd's illness had been diagnosed as appendicitis by his son-in-law Dr. Robert Wagner, the company physician, and apparently was not treatable surgically. Shepherd told Wagner, "Well, Robert, it's a fight. Let's you and I start into the battle determined to win out." Despite this bravado, a worried Dr. Wagner telegraphed Mrs. Shepherd in Washington, who left immediately for Mexico with her daughter Grace and Grace's husband, Dr. Frank Merchant. By September 11, Shepherd was unable to speak, although he still recognized his family "by look." Shepherd died at 7:45 a.m. on September 12 at age sixty-seven, in the house he had lived in for the most part of the previous twenty-two years, within the hacienda he had worked so hard to restore and improve. He was surrounded by sons Alexander Jr. and John Conness, brother Arthur, and sons-in-law Edward Quintard and Robert Wagner, the attending physician, but without his devoted wife or daughters, still en route to Mexico.[79] The primary cause of death was listed as appendicitis, and the immediate cause of death, peritonitis.[80]

---

[77]Details about the contract are not available. Although Arthur was to die in Mexico in 1914 with a Mexican wife and two children, his newspaper account of the meeting cited a nine-year gap since last seeing Alexander.

[78]*Evening Star*, Sept. 25, 1902.

[79]Ibid.

[80]Ibid.

Chapter Twelve

"The Law of Necessity"

Denouement and Final Assessments

DEATH IN ISOLATED, rural Mexico required immediate burial because of the heat, and, according to Mexican law, interment had to take place not later than 10:00 a.m. the following day. The law also required the grave to be lined with and covered by stone. The skilled craftsmen of the hacienda built a casket that could be hermetically sealed, and arrangements were made to bury Shepherd temporarily in the family cemetery that had been built on the steep hillside behind the hacienda. Flowering trees, winding paths, and benches gave the site a pleasant appearance and a peaceful feeling.[1] American and Mexican flags flew at half-mast by the hacienda entrance the day of the funeral. The stores in town were closed, and Batopilas society turned out en masse for the funeral, with crowds covering the hillsides on both sides of the river. Following the reading of the Episcopal burial service by Alexander Jr., the sons and Mexican helpers carried Shepherd, with a large American flag covering the casket, up the hill to his temporary resting place.[2]

Mrs. Shepherd and her other adult children and their spouses arrived in Batopilas shortly after the funeral and sorted out business and family affairs before making plans for returning to Washington. A further incident shocked

---

[1]The family graves were long ago looted and destroyed, no doubt in search of valuables (confirmed by visit of the author and Robert Gullo, 2011).

[2]*Evening Star* (Washington, D.C.), Sept. 25, 1902.

the grieving family—the unexpected death of Edward "Ned" Quintard, the husband of May Shepherd, who died suddenly in Batopilas before the funeral party left for the United States. May was the Shepherds' oldest child, and Ned's father was a well-known American businessman in New York and one of the original investors in Shepherd's mining project. Ned had come to Batopilas and worked as an engineer for the corporation. He was only forty-two years old at the time of his death.[3]

Alexander Shepherd's coffin lay in the hillside cemetery for almost nine months while arrangements were made to transport it back to Washington. Because the coffin would be transported across the Mexican–U.S. border, medical and legal certifications were required, not only from the Mexican authorities but also from the U.S. consulate in Chihuahua City. Doctors Wagner and Merchant certified that Shepherd had not died of an infectious disease and that his coffin had been hermetically sealed in their presence.[4] The family reserved a Pullman car from the Chesapeake and Ohio Railroad Company to transport the funeral party from San Antonio, Texas, to Washington.

When the funeral party reached Chihuahua City on April 30, 1903, the U.S. consul completed an official death certificate and provided authorization for Shepherd's body to be transported across the international border. The report section entitled "Disposition of Effects" listed "valuable mines and mining machinery in possession of widow and adult sons and daughters at Batopilas."[5] When the train arrived in Juarez, across the Rio Grande from El Paso, Texas, members of the Terrazas-Creel family paid their respects to the Shepherd family and filled the car with huge bouquets of flowers.[6] Mary Shepherd wrote and received letters and telegrams en route home, including one from William Mattingly that described plans for the Washington funeral.[7]

---

[3]Mary Grice Shepherd (MGS) to Belle (Isabel), May 2, 1903, courtesy of Mary Wagner Woods.

[4]Medical certification by Drs. Wagner and Merchant, courtesy of W. Sinkler Manning Jr.

[5]Official Death Certificate, U.S. Consular Records, Chihuahua, Mexico, 1903, Record Group 84.3, National Archives and Records Administration, Suitland, Md.

[6]Letter from Grace Shepherd to Isabel Wagner, Apr. 30, 1903, courtesy of Mary Wagner Woods.

[7]Letter from MGS to Belle (Isabel), May 2, 1903, courtesy of Mary Wagner Woods.

Upon arrival in Washington on the morning of May 4, the coffin was taken to New York Avenue Presbyterian Church, where Alexander and Mary had been married forty-one years previously. A throng of local officials, organizations, and citizenry passed by the flower-draped coffin to pay their respects. After the ceremony, the mourners walked or rode to Rock Creek Cemetery, where the coffin was interred in Crosby Noyes's family vault until completion of the Shepherd mausoleum.[8] The handsome granite mausoleum, which was contracted for that summer and completed by the end of the year, was the third and final resting place for Alexander Shepherd. The coffin was transferred from the Noyes vault to the new mausoleum on January 24, 1904, with Mary Shepherd; sons Alexander Jr., Grant, and John Conness; daughter Grace; and Alexander's brother Thomas the only family members present for the simple service.[9]

The Statue

Several years after Shepherd's death, the people of Washington expressed their gratitude for his contribution to the welfare of the city by donating a bronze statue, which was given to the District of Columbia and erected in front of the new District Building at Fourteenth and E Streets NW. The campaign to create a statue of Shepherd commenced as soon as news of his death reached the capital, and Henry McFarland, president of the Board of Commissioners, suggested to his associates that a statue be erected by popular subscription. The committee was headed by Theodore Noyes, *Evening Star* publisher and son of Crosby Noyes. The fundraising campaign was able to raise the full subscription amount before Shepherd's body was returned to Washington in May 1903.

Local sculptor Ulric Stonewall Jackson Dunbar was selected to create the statue of Alexander Shepherd, and the Boston firm that had built his mausoleum was chosen to design the pedestal. Dunbar proved to be an excellent choice. Born in Canada and trained at his brother's art academy, he came to Washington around 1885 and specialized in statues of American and Canadian Indians and Eskimos for Smithsonian Institution dioramas.

---

[8] *Evening Star*, May 4, 1903; *Washington Post*, May 5, 1903.
[9] *New York Times*, Jan. 25, 1904; *Evening Star*, Jan. 25, 1904.

Among his more than twenty-six busts and statues were those of W. W. Corcoran, Vice President Thomas Hendricks, Samuel Gompers, Chief Sitting Bull, and President Warren Harding.[10] Because of the Shepherd statue's importance, its erection was postponed until completion of construction of the District Building across the street.[11] The May 3, 1909, unveiling of the statue attracted a full complement of local and national figures. Mary Shepherd, her seven children, and their families led the list, which included cabinet secretaries, U.S. senators and representatives, judges, and other officials.[12] Theodore Noyes gave a fulsome paean to Alexander Shepherd's contributions, Shepherd ally William Mattingly spoke movingly in the same vein, and Commissioner McFarland carried on about the same themes.

Despite general approbation, the Shepherd statue had at least one significant critic, William Tindall, who served as secretary to Shepherd when Shepherd was executive vice president of the Board of Public Works and later governor of the territory. In a paper delivered to the Columbia Historical Society (now the Historical Society of Washington) in December 1921, Tindall bemoaned the fact that "advanced age and disease had impaired the features of [Shepherd's] countenance, and corpulence the symmetry of his form."[13] Press accounts announcing the award of the commission to Ulric Dunbar reported, "The pose of the statue is characteristic of the original, Governor Shepherd having stood for many photographs for the use of the sculptor during his last visit to Washington, and the likeness is excellent."[14] Years later, Grace Merchant confirmed that the photographs on which the statue was based were taken while the Shepherds were returning from their European trip in 1896, and Shepherd was wearing a morning coat made by a London tailor. His daughter commented that the London coat never fit properly, and Shepherd was overweight and tired out from sixteen years of hard work in the mines.[15]

---

[10]Collateral descendant Charles Dunbar to the author, November 2014.

[11]William Van Zandt Cox, ed., "The Unveiling of a Statue to the Memory of Alexander R. Shepherd in Front of the District Building, Washington, D.C., May 3, 1909" (Washington, D.C. [1909]), pp. 7–8.

[12]Ibid., p. 10.

[13]William Tindall, "Governor Alexander R. Shepherd's Photograph," *Records of the Columbia Historical Society* 24 (1922):192.

[14]*Evening Star*, n.d., 1908.

[15]Grace Shepherd Merchant typed reminiscence post–1909, Shepherd Papers, Manuscript Division, Library of Congress, Washington, D.C.

The saga of the Shepherd statue was by no means over. After having over-looked Pennsylvania Avenue, the Treasury Building, and the Willard Hotel for seventy years, the statue was unceremoniously removed in 1979 during reconfiguration of the area now occupied by Freedom Plaza. The statue was banished to a remote corner of the District's Blue Plains sewage treatment plant, where it lay on its back in the weeds, supported by old car tires. The District Department of Public Works (DPW)—successor to the Board of Public Works—gave the statue a shred of dignity when it was erected in a space in front of the DPW temporary building in farthest southwest Washington, beyond the fire department training center and looking out from behind a chain-link fence at the city's vehicle-impoundment lot.[16] There the statue stood until 2005, when the Association of Oldest Inhabitants of Washington, D.C. (AOI) joined forces with members of the District City Council in obtaining permission to move the statue to its current location in front of the District Building (which had been renamed the John Wilson Building), only a few yards from its original location.[17] In 2013 the D.C. Humanities Council allocated funds to undertake cleaning and preservation of the statue, and an AOI donor provided funds to insure periodic refurbishing until at least 2032.[18]

Another memento of Alexander Shepherd in Washington, D.C., a handsome oil portrait, hangs in the Wilson Building. The 1871 portrait by German artist Henry Ulke shows Shepherd seated at his desk, holding a copy of the *Evening Star*. The painting remained in the Shepherd family until 1921, when Alexander Shepherd Jr. presented it to the city of Washington on his mother's behalf.[19] Despite having been part of a National Gallery exhibit of paintings of "History Makers" in 1950, the painting had disappeared into the basement of the Wilson Building until Council Member Betty Ann Kane rescued it and had it hung in her office at about the same time that the Shepherd statue was removed from its pedestal in front of the building.[20]

---

[16] *City Paper* (Washington, D.C.), Jan. 21, 1994; verified by visits by the author.

[17] *The Downtowner* (Washington, D.C.), Feb. 9, 2005.

[18] Bill Brown, president of Association of Oldest Inhabitants of Washington, D.C., conversation with the author, 2014.

[19] *Evening Star*, Jan. 21, 1921.

[20] Ibid., Apr. 3, 1979.

Contemporary bird's-eye view of Batopilas River valley. (Courtesy of W. Sinkler Manning Jr.)

Contemporary bird's-eye view of Batopilas mining works. (Courtesy of W. Sinkler Manning Jr.)

Front gate of Shepherd hacienda, Batopilas (contemporary view). (Courtesy of W. Sinkler Manning Jr.)

Mining company administration building, Batopilas (contemporary view). (Courtesy of W. Sinkler Manning Jr.)

Silver ingots ready for shipment, Batopilas (contemporary view). (Courtesy of W. Sinkler Manning Jr.)

Shepherd on horseback, Batopilas (ca. 1880s). (Courtesy of W. Sinkler Manning Jr.)

Mexico business partner Lyndon H. Stevens (*left*) and Shepherd. (Courtesy of Mary Wagner Woods)

Batopilas Mining Company stock certificate issued to daughter Susan Shepherd Brodie in 1935. (Courtesy of Mrs. W. Sinkler Manning Jr.)

Shepherd family at home, Batopilas. Back row, *left to right*, Mr. and Mrs. Shepherd, May Quintard, Ned Quintard, Grace Merchant, Frank Merchant, Dorothy Quintard, Robert Wagner, front/ middle, *left to right*, Conness Shepherd, Grant Shepherd, Alex Shepherd Jr., Isabel Wagner. (Courtesy of W. Sinkler Manning Jr.)

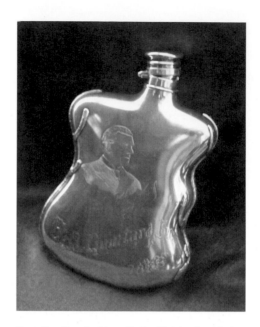

Batopilas silver flask inscribed to Shepherd son-in-law Edward A. "Ned" Quintard. (Courtesy of Sandra S. Garrett)

Shepherd-built bridge over Batopilas River, photographed in 2011. (Courtesy of Robert M. Gullo)

Ruins of the company administration building, Batopilas, photographed by W. Sinkler Manning Jr., ca. 1974. (Courtesy of W. Sinkler Manning Jr.)

(*left*) The 1909 statue of Alexander Shepherd by U. S. J. Dunbar was re-erected in front of the Washington, D.C. City Council Building in 2005. (Courtesy of Association of Oldest Inhabitants of Washington, D.C.)

(*right*) The Shepherd mausoleum in Rock Creek Cemetery, Washington, D.C. (Photograph by the author)

Sorting Out the Pieces

After Shepherd's death in Mexico in 1902, the Bleak House property was sold to a developer in 1910, and the house was torn down in 1916.[21] The southernmost forty-three acres of the property became part of the U.S. Army's Walter Reed Hospital in 1906.[22] Only one likely Bleak House outbuilding still survives, serving as the garage behind a private residence in the Shepherd Park neighborhood built on the Bleak House property. The immediate vicinity of Bleak House also contains an old well that neighbors say belonged to the home.[23] Both the neighborhood and its elementary school carry the Shepherd name.

The Batopilas Mining Company was a victim of the Mexican Revolution, which commenced in Chihuahua State in 1910, in part amid anger targeted at foreign entrepreneurs like Shepherd, who were the beneficiaries of Porfirio Díaz's warm embrace of foreign investors.[24] The chaotic 1910–20 period in Mexico served as the death knell for the Shepherd operation, which struggled on for several years but was abandoned in the face of political instability, theft, and threats. The property was reportedly given to a former employee who had protected it from looters, but the plant fell into ruin once the metal roofs were appropriated by townspeople for their own use.[25] The company's records and files, open to the weather, were burned and scattered; only a few volumes of correspondence and accounting information remain today, some in the small municipal museum in Batopilas and some at a local inn. The items at the inn have been preserved and displayed thanks

---

[21]Ibid., ca. July 1916.

[22]War Department General Orders No. 83, May 2, 1906, J. Franklin Bell, Brigadier General, Chief of Staff, Military Reference Branch, NARA; also published in United States War Department, *General Orders and Circulars, War Department, 1906* (Washington, D.C., 1907).

[23]Bleak House neighbor Robert Melendez to author, 2006, citing former resident, Mr. Zinn, who remembered Bleak House from living in Shepherd Park as a boy. The garage belongs to Richard Hage, also an amateur historian.

[24]According to Shepherd's granddaughter, Mary Shepherd Worsham, Pancho Villa provided charcoal to the company and mistreated his donkeys, triggering the wrath of her father, Alexander Shepherd Jr., then the mine manager. It was apparently Villa's anger at her father that caused him to bring his band to Hacienda San Miguel sometime around 1912, when he burned the plant and forced the family to flee up the mountain for safety.

[25]Ivan Fernandez, Batopilas guide and photographer, to the author, April 2011.

to recovery efforts by two Americans, who lovingly converted a former mansion into the Riverside Lodge, in the process scouring the area for Shepherd memorabilia and artifacts.[26]

The Shepherd mansion and two other bluestone mansions designed by Adolf Cluss that made up "Shepherd's Row" on the north side of K Street NW between Connecticut Avenue and Seventeenth Street were among the most elegant row houses in Washington. Later occupants included prominent members of Congress, cabinet members, and the Russian and Chinese diplomatic legations until after World War I. The immediate area slowly changed to offices in the early twentieth century, and Shepherd's Row was razed in 1952; the Shepherd site became the entrance to a Washington subway station in the 1970s.[27]

Other traces of Shepherd in Washington, D.C., are three streets: (1) Shepherd Parkway SW, which leads to the District's Bureau of Public Works; (2) Shepherd Street NW; and—the most intriguing—Shepherd Road NW, a short, twisting street that was once the road leading to the Shepherd farm near Rock Creek Church. The street is clearly an anomaly in the overall street grid, since it predated the neighborhood development but was left intact.

Alexander Shepherd's personality and achievements outshone his successors. His three younger brothers all worked for or otherwise benefited from his businesses and his political leadership role in Washington. Thomas remained in Washington and worked in mid-level city jobs after Alexander went to Mexico. Arthur became a journalist and editor of the *National Republican* as well as a functionary in the Republican Party in Washington. Arthur supported his brother's efforts and was often singled out as evidence of Alexander Shepherd's manipulation of Washington affairs. After later writing for a Denver newspaper, Arthur joined Alexander in Mexico, where he held a low-level position working with transport animals at Batopilas, married a local woman, fathered two children, and died there in 1914. Wilmer, who also spent time in Batopilas, married Laura Shedd, of a well-known Washington family, and eventually relocated to Chicago, where he became a real estate developer.

---

[26]Skip McWilliams and his sister, Lynn Clancy.

[27]James M. Goode, *Capital Losses: A Cultural History of Washington's Destroyed Buildings*, 2nd ed. (Washington, D.C., 2003), pp. 183–85.

Oldest son Alexander Jr. served as general manager of the Batopilas mines for several years after his father's death and lived for many years in the Washington, D.C., area. Middle son Grant, seriously wounded in the First World War, also worked in mining but moved back to Charles County, Maryland, and devoted his time to researching the War of 1812 exploits of his maternal grandfather and writing an account of life in Batopilas, *The Silver Magnet*. Youngest son John Conness spent the rest of his life as a miner, mainly in the Southwest and in Mexico. Unlike their father, who sired ten children—seven of whom lived to adulthood—Grant and John Conness married but had no children, while Alexander Jr. had a daughter and son. The four Shepherd daughters all married expatriates whom their father had hired to work at the mines as engineers or physicians, and they had several children each. No direct male descendant carries the Shepherd name today.[28]

Alexander Shepherd's life was lived to the full, and his final twenty-two years in Mexico added a significant dimension to the better-known Washington years. Shepherd's personal qualities were even more vividly on display in Mexico, where it was primarily man against nature, rather than man against man in Washington. What can we make of the whole Alexander Shepherd?

Assessments

In Washington Shepherd set out to achieve three related objectives: consolidate the capital's three jurisdictions, build a unified urban infrastructure, and force Congress to accept its responsibility for the city's financial welfare. Shepherd substantially achieved these goals, but Washington paid a high price. In his wake, all residents of Washington lost voting rights for the next one hundred years,[29] and black citizens, having only received the vote in 1867, held it for a scant seven years. Commissioner government, the original form of Washington governance, was reinstituted temporarily in 1874 and made permanent in 1878. The fifty–fifty congressional payment formula for matching the local budget remained a guideline, even though

---

[28]Family status from records and conversations between descendants and author.

[29]Spawning "D.C.: Last Colony" bumper stickers.

diluted and reworked in subsequent years. Much of Shepherd's public works development, done hastily and often by amateur contractors, had to be redone. For example, all city streets paved with wooden blocks—at one point considered a technological breakthrough—had to be torn up and replaced, at great cost. Sewers laid improperly or constructed poorly had to be torn up and rebuilt, often after road surfacing was in place. Homes fronting on streets that were graded often remained high above or below street level.

Shepherd had sought—and accepted—a public works challenge arguably greater than that faced by any American urban planner until that time, since his intention was to create a unified, coordinated city infrastructure where one had not previously existed, other than as lines on the L'Enfant map. As events were to show, there was at the time no science of urban planning, and Shepherd's seat-of-the-pants approach proved costly and inefficient. Armed with good intentions, Shepherd's formal plans and safeguards eroded as problems mounted and money became scarce. By the end of the territorial government, there was little difference between Shepherd's and his predecessors' financial procedures, except that Shepherd's corner cutting and dubious financial arrangements were more evident.

While it is clear that Shepherd wanted to do as little as necessary politically to acknowledge black rights and aspirations, he did publicly endorse Lincoln's and Grant's legal actions on behalf of blacks. In his personal life, however, Shepherd kept his distance. The vexing issue of corruption remains one of the most complex questions surrounding Shepherd and his public works programs. The public record is littered with evidence of corner cutting and his bending, and often breaking, the rules. While there should be no apologies for this conduct, it is significant that, despite aggressive digging and newspaper allegations, neither of two in-depth congressional investigations turned up verifiable evidence of Shepherd's having taken personal advantage of access to public funds to enrich himself in the manner of, as a classic example, "Boss" William Marcy Tweed of New York. In the course of the 1872 congressional investigation into District affairs, Shepherd responded to a question about what law he observed by saying "the law of necessity." As the territorial government's and the board's difficulties accumulated, Shepherd embraced "the law of necessity" to the point where it may have become a blanket rationale for doing whatever he thought necessary at the time to achieve his development objectives. This entailed using the ends to justify the means, which is not acceptable today, but may shed light on the Shepherd worldview.

In Mexico, Shepherd had one overriding objective: to build a modern, large-scale silver-mining operation that would make him very rich and permit him and his family to return in triumph to Washington after a few years. A secondary but important objective was to prove his critics wrong by doing the thing that others might not have thought possible. Critical to his success was the establishment of a modern production facility able to process multiple times the previous volume of ore production. Despite generating significant profits in several years, the Mexico venture must be considered a disappointment when viewed against Shepherd's own criteria. Mexico presented Alexander Shepherd with many challenges. He overcame many of them, but whereas in Washington the obstacles were primarily human and political, in Mexico he confronted a nasty combination of the rock under his feet and the international economy. In the case of the former, there was either silver in the veins he mined, or there wasn't; no amount of extra work or determination could create silver where it did not exist. In the case of the international economy, Shepherd was likewise at the mercy of two linked forces beyond his control: the dollar-peso exchange rate and the price at which he could sell silver in the United States. Shepherd bet everything he owned on success in Mexico, ignoring every consideration not directly related to extracting silver from the mountains. Collateral damage included the impact on his family of being relocated to a remote, often unpleasant Mexican mountain fastness; wearing himself out with an extremely difficult, physical job; and investing all his own resources in the venture in the expectation that success would mean rising stock prices and renewal of his personal fortune. Shepherd gambled on his initial expectations being borne out, and they were not. The family was not without imported pleasures in Mexico, but when the corporation was closed and expenses paid off in the 1920s, there was little more than enough to settle outstanding debts related to Bleak House. If there was a place where Shepherd could have put money into his own pocket without being noticed, it was Mexico, but the evidence, once again, simply is not there.

Two questions hang in the air: could the nation's capital have been built by means other than those employed by Alexander Shepherd, and was it worth the cost? It is my view that the major progress from public works development from 1871 to 1874– a time when the White House and both houses of Congress were in friendly (Republican) hands—could not have been duplicated, or at least in anywhere near so comprehensive a manner, once divided government again came to Washington. The hectic building pace proved necessary to complete the work within an advantageous political time period. It is also my view that the progress achieved by Alexander Shepherd and the Board of Public Works was worth the cost. The District of Columbia occupies a unique place in the world, and its physical development made it possible for the city to take its proper place in the world. The cost in terms of social, human initiatives not taken is still being counted. "Beauty" is still the winner over "Justice" in the nation's capital.

Acknowledgments

Writing a biography takes a village. When the process lasts thirty or more years, the village expands and ages. Some people named in this section have died, some moved on; in a few cases the name of an institution has changed or even disappeared. Helpful institutions and individuals in libraries, historical societies, and archives were numerous, but I wish to acknowledge the following: the Library of Congress Manuscripts and Prints and Photograph Divisions for unfailing courtesy and assistance; the Washingtoniana Room at the Martin Luther King Jr. Library in Washington, D.C. (Roxanne Dean, Mark Greek, Derek Gray, Jerry McCoy); District of Columbia Archives (Clarence Davis, Bill Branch); Charles County architectural historian Richard Rivoire, who documented the Shepherd ancestral residence before it fell to plans for an unbuilt nuclear power plant; National Archives D.C. history expert Bob Ellis for finding obscure photos and documents; the Historical Society of Washington's Kiplinger Library researcher, Laura Barry; urban historian Zachary Schrag, who edited a part of the Shepherd story for the 2010 issue of *Washington History*; Bell Clement, former Historical Society of Washington, D.C. (HSW) executive director, who created opportunities for telling the Shepherd story to HSW audiences; Bowdoin College Library Special Collections specialist Susan Ravdin for unearthing letters between Shepherd and Union Civil War general (and Howard University president) O. O. Howard; Columbia Historical Society (predecessor to HSW) (Larry Baume); Historical Society of Charles County (Mrs. Gregory Dyson), who helped find records of the Townley Robey family, Shepherd's maternal ancestors; Charles County Community College, Southern Maryland Room curator Dr. William Close; the staffs of the Maryland Hall of Records (Annapolis) and the Charles County Courthouse; and Bill Brown, president of the Association of Oldest Inhabitants of Washington, D.C., for providing speaking opportunities and general encouragement as well as having orchestrated the return of the Shepherd statue to downtown Washington.

Several individuals provided assistance with specialized aspects of the project: Diana O'Neil, who created and maintained the book website; niece

235

Kate Murray, a 2015 graduate of Middlebury College, who as an undergraduate artfully translated a key Spanish-language document; Jamshid Kooros, the artist-calligrapher who drew the Mexico maps; and Dr. Jim Butcher, who took time out of a busy research and teaching schedule to create a psychological profile of Alexander Shepherd.

Contacts in Mexico who became friends include Batopilas mayor Leonel Hernandez Vega, who provided guidance and introductions to local sources during a 2011 visit; Martin Alcaraz Gastelum, manager of the Riverside Lodge and a source of essential documents from the Batopilas Mining Company; Rafael Ruelas Gastelum, director of the Batopilas Museum and Cultural Center, which has preserved a number of documents from the Batopilas Mining Company; and Ivan Fernandez, a professional photographer and owner of "3 Amigos," a cultural tourism company, who provided historical context for the Shepherd experience. An American enthusiast, Skip McWilliams, carefully restored Riverside Lodge to an elegant, Shepherd-era standard and, with sister Lynn Clancy, acquired many Shepherd family photographs that grace the walls.

Manuscript readers included Kathryn Jacob of the Radcliffe College Library and author of, inter alia, *Capital Elites*; Kate Masur of Northwestern University, author of *An Example for All the Land*; Matt Gilmore of Washington, D.C., author of several books on local history, who researched factual anomalies and dug out elusive sources; Kenneth R. Bowling of the First Federal Congress Project at George Washington University and author of *The Creation of Washington, D.C.*; Howard Gillette, author of *Between Justice and Beauty*; and last in order but leading all the rest, Alan Lessoff of Illinois State University (Normal) and author of *The Nation and its City*, who served informally as mentor and long-distance guide over the several decades of my work on the biography. I hasten to note that the above individuals provided textual critiques and suggestions, not all of which were incorporated. I absolve them all of any responsibility for the final product.

Personal thanks go to my good friend, former professional colleague, and Mexico fellow-traveler Bob Gullo, who provided informed and thoughtful comments as the project went on—and on; he cheerfully read and critiqued more than one version of the manuscript, as well as providing documentary and oral Spanish translation during a memorable ten-day visit to Batopilas in April 2011; Richard Hage, a former neighbor in the Shepherd Park neighborhood of Washington, D.C., who owns the private garage that may be the last surviving outbuilding of Shepherd's Bleak House; the late Bill Maury, former chief historian of the U.S. Capitol Historical Society and author of the first scholarly study of Shepherd and the Board of Public Works, who encouraged the writer and offered USCHS institutional shelter for the project's first and only research grant; Martha Hill, an indefatigable research assistant early in the book's life, who dug into documentary troves in the Maryland Hall of Records in Annapolis and elsewhere concerning Shepherd's Charles County origins; Nelson Rimensnyder, an early Shepherd enthusiast from his years with the House District Committee; and Joe Browne, a writer on the work of architect Adolf Cluss, who was helpful in providing a better understanding of Cluss's complex role.

A grant from the Loughran and Loughran Foundation provided support in the 1980s for a research assistant when my day job kept me from work on the book. Principal text editor Dr. Donald Kennon, recently retired chief historian of the U.S. Capitol Historical Society and project sponsor with Ohio University Press, has provided unstinting support and practical suggestions about improving the book. Many thanks also to Ohio University Press director Gillian Berchowitz, who has seen the process through.

Shepherd family members have been generous, mailing irreplaceable documents to me sight unseen, based only on my promise to copy and return them. Family members who provided special support include the late Mary Shepherd Worsham, daughter of Alexander Shepherd Jr., who offered me hospitality in La Jolla, California, in 1987 and recounted stories of growing up as a young girl at the mines; the late Mary Wagner Woods, daughter of Isabel Shepherd Wagner, who endured endless telephone debriefings about the family and annotated family photos; Bill Nisbet, a great-great-grandson of Alexander Shepherd, provided documentary and oral accounts; W. Sinkler Manning Jr., a great-grandson of Alexander Shepherd and son of a former governor of South Carolina, who shared family photographs and an account of a 1974 flying trip he and his bush pilot son made to Batopilas; and likewise Alexandra Malek, a great-great-granddaughter of Alexander Shepherd, who has retained artifacts from the Mexico years and shared family stories.

Researching and writing the Shepherd biography took place over several decades, with starts and stops occasioned by my serving overseas with the U.S. government. From 1990 until 2002, the late Dr. Philip Ogilvie, former secretary of the District of Columbia, creator of the D.C. Archives, and president of the Association of Oldest Inhabitants of Washington, D.C., was my coresearcher, waiting patiently until I would finally return home and dig into the project again. Sadly, Phil passed away just after my final foreign tour began. Phil was a polymath who enriched our research efforts. On a more cheerful note, I also wish to recognize Bill Dickinson, a local historian who became an advocate for publication of the biography at a critical point. Finally, I wish to acknowledge the role of my wife Joyce, who was always supportive from the sidelines but truly earned her stripes when she undertook a line-by-line edit of the manuscript in a late stage. A first-class editor, Joyce wrestled the text into a more readable and logical product than the one she received. Her contribution is unique.

John P. Richardson
Arlington, Virginia
July 2015

Note on Primary Sources

Researching the life of Alexander Shepherd meant following a bumpy and winding road. His life can be divided into two parts: the first forty-five years in Washington, D.C., and the final twenty-two years in Batopilas, Mexico. Because of Shepherd's prominence on the Washington scene—as businessman and political activist—there was a great deal of press attention paid to his activities. A part owner of the *Evening Star* from 1867 to 1871, Shepherd received sympathetic coverage from this center-right journal. The *Star*'s reporters employed a shorthand technique that permitted them to record verbatim accounts of their subjects' comments, a boon to readers seeking more than pithy quotations. The uproar generated by Shepherd's public works projects during the territorial government (1871–74) triggered two congressional investigations—in 1872 and 1874—that fully document the period and contain extensive verbatim testimony by Shepherd as well as his many critics. The Board of Public Works published annual volumes for 1872 and 1873, which detailed the board's accomplishments and included documents of historical relevance. The Washingtoniana Division of the Martin Luther King Jr. Memorial Library in Washington, D.C., holds an extensive set of city directories for the years of Shepherd's residence. The Alexander R. Shepherd collection in the Library of Congress Manuscript Division contains some thirteen document boxes, along with scrapbooks and photos, but they are surprisingly thin on documents that detail how he developed his business and political strategies. There are a number of documents from his Mexican silver-mining years. The collection contains numerous letters from Shepherd to his children when they were young and back in the United States for schooling or medical reasons. The absence of business or political letters is evident. It is the view of the writer that two factors may account for the uneven nature of the collection: the first is that the family moved, lock, stock, and barrel, to Mexico in 1880, which required severe constriction of possessions. Even though the Shepherds maintained their suburban Washington residence, Bleak House, where they no doubt stored items of value, the move to Mexico, coupled some thirty years later with an abrupt departure from Batopilas during the Mexican Revolution, no doubt caused the loss of other material. The other possible consideration is that the Shepherd daughters, Grace Shepherd Merchant in particular, were quite solicitous of their father's reputation (Grace sought a known writer to tell his story but found no takers), and it is possible that the materials donated to the Library of Congress had been edited to remove unflattering or revealing material.

Primary sources on the Mexico years (1880–1902 for Shepherd himself) are tantalizingly revealing as well as uneven. Shepherd descendants played a vital role in providing irreplaceable documents for copying and return. A granddaughter, Mary Wagner Woods, provided Shepherd's diary of the 1880 trip to Mexico and Mary Grice Shepherd's trip diary as well as a diary she kept intermittently from 1882 to 1892. A great-grandson, W. Sinkler Manning Jr., provided Shepherd's 1881 diary, which covered the first full year in Mexico and all its frustrations. Fragmentary diaries of Shepherd family members also shed light on the Mexico experience. Shepherd's few surviving personal documents reveal an articulate and insightful writer, which makes the lack of personal documents covering much larger portions of his life all the more disappointing. Shepherd was not introspective, and his writing addresses mainly practical subjects, although the Mexico documents discuss his physical ailments at length. There is little in the way of reflection and self-analysis. According to knowledgeable residents of Batopilas, the former employee who was given custody of the mining operation when the family departed during the Mexican Revolution considered the inherited archives of no value and burned or gave most away. A small Batopilas museum has acquired a few corporate letter books, as has the owner of Riverside Lodge; wide gaps in numbering mean that most are gone. There are stories of local residents who have acquired other Shepherd documents but demand payment for access. Several mining company annual reports are in U.S. library collections and are essential because Shepherd's personal contribution is apparent and reflects the highs and lows of the mining business. Second son Grant Shepherd wrote a personal account of his youthful years in Mexico entitled *The Silver Magnet*, which provides commentary on family activities but little insight into his father, other than standard portrayals of his size, energy, and stern-but-loving persona.

It is the writer's view that Alexander Shepherd "was what he did," which is commendable and apparent, but because of his lack of introspection and

self-awareness—compounded by the nonexistence or disappearance of revealing material—much of the Shepherd story remains one of recounting
his activities. Because of his Washington years in the public eye, and because
of the controversial nature of his results, there is no end of published criticism, but this does not reveal his nature, other than when he struck back at
his opponents, which he did instinctively and with vigor. Shepherd's final
twenty-two years of life in Mexico, punctuated by only two visits to the
United States before his death, were spent out of the public eye, other than
for his own accounts of mine activities and often gushing accounts written
by journalists and other visitors who subjected themselves to the grueling
mule-back trip to the canyon bottom and Batopilas. These often fanciful accounts did little else than to embellish the Shepherd legend, providing fuel
for friend and foe alike.

Index